HELP!!

How To
Find | Hire | Train | & | Maintain

Your Household HELP

MARTA PERRONE

Illustrations by Sharon Watts

Many forms contained in this book are available for download from
www.domestic-connections.com in full size format.

All efforts have been made to ensure the accuracy of the information contained in this book as of the date
published. The author and the publisher expressly disclaim responsibility for any adverse effects arising from
the use or application of the information contained therein.

No part of this book shall be reproduced, stored in a retrieval system, or transmitted by any means,
electronic, mechanical, digital, photocopying, recording, or otherwise, without written permission from the
publisher. No patent liability is assumed with respect to the use of the information contained herein.
Although every precaution has been taken in the preparation of this book, the publisher and author assume
no responsibilities for errors or omissions. Neither is any liability assumed for damages resulting from the use
of information contained herein.

Cover and interior illustration art by Sharon Watts
Cover design and interior layout by Debbie Kirchen
Author photo by Maura P. McCarthy

For information, contact www.domestic-connections.com
or www.domesticpublications.com

International Standard Book Number: 1-930754-84-1
First Edition

Library of Congress Catalog Card Number 2005935732

Durban House Press, Inc.
7502 Greenville Avenue, Suite 500
Dallas, Texas 75231

Printed in India

This book is dedicated to my wonderful children,
Christina and Michael, for all their
love, support and understanding,

and to my clients and their domestics
for giving me a career rich in humanity
and an opportunity to serve the needs of others.

ACKNOWLEDGEMENTS

This book required the expertise of several people who were kind enough to share their time and knowledge with me.

A special thank you to my publisher, John Lewis, President of Durban House Press, Inc. for all your kind support.

Thank you to my mom and dad, Juliana and Jim Kozen, and my brother Frankie for your love and enthusiasm. To Vincent, for all your steadfast support over the years and for inspiring me to enter the domestic field and ultimately write about it. To Jill Degan, Orna Ered, Stephanie Hausfater, Nora Helfer, Alexandra Simpson, Carol Stulberg, Claudia Tschudin, and Wendy Weitzman for all their encouragement and support. To a very special person in life, my big sister, my colleague, my friend, Helen Kulungian, for being my guardian angel.

To Robert E. King of Legally Nanny (www.legallynanny.com), who practices labor and employment law in Orange County, California. His company offers legal, tax and insurance guidance for household employees. His work has been featured in *The Wall Street Journal*, *Kiplinger's Personal Finance* and *California Lawyer* magazine.

To Dan E. Korenberg, who is a senior partner of Korenberg, Abramowitz & Feldun in Sherman Oaks, California. Mr. Korenberg is a member of the American Immigration Lawyer's Association and the Immigration Sections of the Los Angeles County Bar Association. He has taught immigration law and sociology, and he has been practicing immigration and naturalization law for over twenty-one years.

To Richard Pass, RN, BS, who is the program & course director for Save A Little Life. His experience includes many years as a clinical practitioner in critical care areas, including many years in large emergency departments.

To Steve P. Pepe, who is a senior partner in O'Melveny & Meyers LLP's Newport Beach office in California. He represents employers in collective bargaining negotiations, arbitrations and before the National Labor Relations Board, as well as in federal and state court. He is a co-author of various books and a speaker for the ABA Section of Labor and Employment Law.

TABLE OF CONTENTS

TABLE OF CONTENTS

TABLE OF CONTENTS

TABLE OF CONTENTS

INTRODUCTION

My intention for writing this comprehensive guide (first in a series to be published in this area) is to educate those who need my help with many of the issues that have caused domestic employers serious problems. Since 1989, I have interviewed and placed housekeepers, nannies, companions, housemen, couples and overall domestics. With a client list that is extensive, it has become clear to me that there is so much the potential employer does not know about the process of hiring help. Those of you who are new to this experience, and even the old pros who have gone through the process several times over, will benefit from the guidelines of this book. What you might think is normal practice for hiring domestics could be grossly wrong. You might even be violating the law and not know it. This book specifically discusses the details of this entire process from beginning to end.

Many of my clients have chosen to do things the way they feel is best. You, too, may decide to only take bits and pieces from this guide and apply them. No matter how much you actually adopt as your own practice, you will definitely walk away better informed on everything you need to know when hiring domestic employees.

The book begins by outlining what type of person fits your needs as we create a job description for your home and family. There are details about the different domestic titles that will make it easy to see what each domestic can provide you in terms of service. There is a wide range of salaries and schedules that vary depending on the type of employee and whether the position is live-in or live-out as well as part-time or full-time. We will help you clarify and understand your needs without exceeding your budget as we suggest the type of domestic that would be most suitable for you.

Once you know what you need, you will want to know the various resources for finding domestics and when to begin your search. There is much to say about agencies, the one resource mostly utilized, and how to choose a good one. We will cover agency fees, terms and the overall procedures as we point out very carefully the due diligence process when using any of your resources. As you get ready to interview prospective applicants, you will want to know how to handle the interview process. We provide you with an "Employment Application and its Review" as well as "Suggested Questions" for the interview. After you have successfully found the person to fill your position, you now must be aware of all your obligations as an employer. These obligations extend from the Immigration and Naturalization Service to the Internal Revenue Service, Employment Development Department and finally, to the Labor Commission.

Before you offer the dream candidate the job, you will want to perform all the necessary background checks. You want to start on the right foot by knowing that your employee has the proper documentation to work. We will cover the legal procedure to obtain such information.

When you enter into a verbal agreement with an employee, many of the issues discussed during an interview can be easily forgotten. The best way to avoid any confusion about what was initially discussed and agreed upon is to get it all on paper by utilizing an Employer/Employee Agreement. This will prevent any surprises down the road and help to get your employee back on track by reviewing the issues that were previously discussed. Being a conscientious employer and employee is the key to a successful relationship.

Training your domestic is not an easy thing to do. Often the very reason why many domestic positions fail within the first month of hire is because the domestics were not trained properly. Every household is routinely run in a different manner and every employer holds different standards. No matter how experienced the employee, within each family there will always be new approaches. As a general rule, the more time that you spend training an employee, the greater the success rate of employment will be.

Accidents and emergencies can be avoided with proper instruction and knowledge of safety issues. Most tragedies with children happen in a home setting. This part of the book will empower those who are in charge of the children with the necessary knowledge to prevent an accident from happening and to react properly if an emergency should occur. We cannot take it for granted that any of these terrible emergencies will never happen nor assume that those who are caring for your children have the common sense to know what and what not to do in order to avoid any of these emergencies.

Finally, as with all relationships, problems tend to come up that need discussion. Having a review period and knowing how to handle those discussions could help avoid further problems that might result in a termination. It would be an excellent time to go over cleaning and/or child-care guidelines and agreements already in place. If there was something that bothered you, this is a good time to share it so that your disappointments and concerns do not fester. The employee may also have some issues and may be reluctant to discuss them. You might be able to avoid a sudden termination by drawing out and correcting any problems before they turn into a disaster. The problem at hand might be solvable rather quickly by your taking a proactive and professional approach. In preparation, it is good to understand how these terminations take place both from the employee and employer perspective. Ultimately, you may need to start the process over and hire a domestic once again. As a review, you will have a checklist of the dos and don'ts of hiring so that you start the next employee on the right foot and with a positive outlook.

SO, LET'S GET STARTED!

Chapter One

WHERE DO I BEGIN?

WHERE DO I BEGIN?

L et's assume your house is in shambles and the laundry is piling up. You either do not have a clue as to how to get your house in order or simply neither have the time nor desire to do so. Perhaps you work or are scheduled to return to work soon, and you are scrambling to find someone competent with whom you can trust your children. Perhaps you have an infant who is keeping you up day and night and needing so much attention that you can hardly take a simple shower. Perhaps you have been blessed with more than one infant at the same time, and you are now literally going out of your mind. Perhaps your children are toddlers and are running every which way…and they never seem to stop until they sleep. Or, perhaps you have school-age children with busy afternoon activities. Or, worse, you have teenagers who hardly speak to you but have you working as their personal chauffeur as you suddenly find yourself driving a car more than ever before in your entire life. Or, sadly, perhaps one of your parents, or both, are failing and you need to find help before you end up being the one doing everything for them in addition to caring for your own family.

No matter your situation, you are exhausted and feeling somewhat desperate at this moment. The only thing on your mind is when the day is going to end so that you can get some sleep! You need someone to help you ***now!*** While you know you need help, you are not sure *what kind of help* you need, because you have never done this before. Or perhaps you attempted this process of hiring domestic help in the past, but it resulted in a total disaster. So, let's begin this voyage on the right foot, step by step, and let's figure out what exactly it is you need as we discuss ***"your job description."***

Tailoring a Job Description

WHAT ARE MY NEEDS?

Before you search for a person to help you in your home, you must be clear about ***what kind of help you need.*** Consider all these topics as you think carefully when writing your job description.

HERE ARE THE QUESTIONS YOU WILL NEED TO ANSWER:

The Salary Range
What is my budget? How much can I afford to pay weekly to get the best

possible person for my needs? What are the current rates for each type of domestic? Will I be putting this person on payroll?

Type of Domestic Job Title

Do I need a Housekeeper who only helps watch the children when I need to go out, or would it be better to have a Nanny who does light cleaning and focuses more on childcare? Do I need just a Mother's Helper? Do I need a Personal Assistant that can run all my errands and work as a quasi-secretary? Do I need a House Manager who runs my house and staff? Should I hire a separate Cook, or a Housekeeper who also can handle light cooking?

Live-In or Live-Out Position

Do I have a household with private quarters for a live-in to stay? Would I feel comfortable having someone there 24-hours a day, or does my family need privacy at night? Is my work and/or social schedule such that it would necessitate a live-in domestic working extended hours? Or, can I hire a live-out domestic who can work my schedule?

Days of the Week and Hourly Schedule Needed

Do I need Monday to Friday because I work? Would I prefer Tuesday through Saturday so I can get Saturday night babysitting covered? Should I have weekend help? Does the domestic need to work early hours and end the day around 3 or 4 PM, or should the Nanny stay later to cover the "witching hour when all hell breaks loose"? Can I offer a standard 9-5 work schedule, or do I need beyond a 40-hour week? How does overtime work?

Level of Experience Required

How much experience should I require for my particular job? Can I accept someone with a few years of experience because I am a stay-at-home mom? Do I have time to train a person? Or, due to my tough work schedule, do I need someone to take charge, in which case having someone with more experience would be essential? Do I need someone with infant experience or just overall child experience?

Level of English Required

Can I get by with a person who speaks broken English and, for example, fluent Spanish? Will having a person who speaks broken English be a problem for my household? Perhaps a person with other language skills would be an asset to the household and beneficial to my children.

Location of Job

Where is my job located? What is the travel time to reach my house from a domestic's perspective? Is this a consideration when hiring a person who works as a live-in versus a live-out? Is my house within easy access to public transportation and/or in walking distance from it? Am I willing to pick up my domestic from the bus stop or station, or must I require that the employee have transportation?

Driver/Non-Driver with or without a Vehicle

Do I need someone to drive my children or me around town? Perhaps I will never need driving, or perhaps down the road the idea of having a person to help out with the driving would be an asset. Do I need someone with a car, or will a driver's license be sufficient because there is a car available for the domestic's use? If I ask the Nanny to drive and use her car to drive my children, what are my obligations with respect to gas, mileage and insurance liability? What should be my concerns when hiring someone to drive for me?

Full-time or Part-time Domestic?

How much help do I really need? Is my social and work schedule so busy that I need full-time help? Since I am not a working mother, then maybe I can get by with a part-time helper. Or, am I a slave to my job and need a person who can also work as a slave for me? Maybe I just need someone to work mornings or afternoons or evenings? Should I begin with a part-time helper and then increase to full-time?

Before you begin interviewing, you will need to be very clear about all of your needs.

Before you begin interviewing, you will need to be very clear about all of your needs. One of the major factors that will play a big role in your decision will be your budget and what it will cost to get the kind of help you need.

WHERE DO I BEGIN?

JUST HOW MUCH WILL THIS DOMESTIC COST ME?

Most people hope to hire someone who will do the most and be paid the least. This is human nature. Somehow, when it comes to people's outlook on domestic help, many seem to unfortunately view the work as "menial." "A menial task deserves menial pay." However, cleaning your house properly without any damage to your beautiful possessions and household materials *is not menial.* Caring for your child or children is certainly not a simple endeavor. You are kidding yourself if you think that there is a great pool of qualified domestics who would easily accept a job for less than what is fairly paid across the board. This is not to say that there aren't many undocumented aliens, with limited experience and language skills, desperate to work and who would accept a low paying job for obvious reasons. You do not have to look too far to find plenty of those candidates. This is a perfect example of *"you get what you pay for."*

Experienced legal immigrants who have come to this country and are working hard to establish themselves value their work just as any other American citizen. If you happen to be lucky enough to find someone legal who will clean your home and/or watch your children and accept your lower-than-average salary, I can only warn you that your luck will not hold out forever. Eventually, you will need to conform to the going rates and pay appropriately. Otherwise, your domestic will soon become privy to what other employers are paying and leave. Your home will become a revolving door, unless you are willing to pay the going rate.

In short, you need to pay consistent with market rate and the demands of the job. This doesn't mean that you always get what you pay for, but you definitely should never get what you don't pay for. Being incompetent is not confined to domestics; there are useful and useless employees in every field. As with all employees, you may have to hire a few people before you find the right one. Some domestics may have been poorly trained and others are simply lazy and have no initiative, no matter how many years at the job. However, the good news is that there are plenty of hard-working domestics who are experienced and competent and deserve a good salary.

WHAT ARE THE GOING RATES FOR VARIOUS DOMESTICS?

You need to know what current market rates are for the various domestic positions. Below is a list of the general "Domestic Job Titles" and their respective starting salaries for the Los Angeles area. These rates may vary from city to city as from state to state. Generally speaking, however, the rates are similar in most metropolitan areas.

You need to know what the current market rates are for the various domestic positions.

Baby Nurse/Doula	$20 to $35/hour
Nanny/Light Housekeeper	$15 to $20/hour
Babysitter	$10 to $15/hour
Nanny/Housekeeper	$12 to $20/hour
Au Pair	$150 to $250/week
Housekeeper	$12 to $15/hour
Housekeeper/Cook	$15 to $20/hour
Caregiver/Companion	$500/week on up
Certified Nurse Assistant	$20 to $25/hour
Chef	$1,000/week on up
House Manager/Major Domo	$1,250/week on up
Houseman/Butler	$850/week on up
Chauffeur	$750/week on up
Couple	$1,000/week on up
Personal Assistant	$20 to $25/hour

WHAT IS MINIMUM WAGE?

The Fair Labor Standards Act (FLSA) and state wage and hour laws require employers to pay a certain minimum wage and set a limit on the number of hours an employee can work in a week before the employer is obligated to pay a higher, "overtime" rate of pay. You are not allowed to pay an employee less than the current minimum wage. As of 2005 the minimum wage in the state of California is $6.75 per hour. Every state has its own minimum wage requirement, and you will want to know what it is in your particular state. (Certain employees are exempt from the provisions of the FLSA and state wage and hour laws. Domestic employees are not included in this exemption. It is very important that the employer not mischaracterize a non-exempt employee as a salaried exempt employee.)

Domestic employees are not exempt from state wage and hour laws.

Keep in mind that most domestics anywhere who work in a home environment are often looking for wages higher than the state minimum wage. Accordingly, in California, you will find that the lowest wage a domestic worker will demand is $8.00 per hour net of taxes. Even $8.00 an hour will not get you someone who drives and/or speaks English. We will get into this later in greater detail. The average domestic in today's market will ask for $10.00 to $12.00 per hour net or gross. Highly qualified domestics are as high as $15.00 to $20.00 per hour net or gross. You may or may not know what *net vs. gross* means. This is very important when talking about salaries to domestic workers, in particular, since so many of them are still receiving their wages in cash.

GROSS VS. NET VS. CASH

It may seem ridiculous that this should even be mentioned; however, this question is often asked by employers as well as applicants and is usually misunderstood. A "gross earning" is one that shows earnings BEFORE any taxes have been deducted. A "net earning" is one that shows earnings AFTER taxes have been deducted. Note: There are mandatory federal and state payroll taxes- Social Security and Medicare (FICA), Unemployment Tax (UI), Employment Training Tax (ETT), State Disability Insurance (SDI)- that must be taken out from a gross salary; however, PIT (Personal Income Tax) and federal withholding are not one of these when paying a qualifying domestic. The employee must still report and ultimately pay personal income taxes to the State Franchise Tax Board and the Internal Revenue Service, but these do not have to be deducted from each paycheck and can be paid annually if the employee qualifies. (This is further discussed in Chapter 5.)

When you are offering an applicant a specific wage or salary, be sure to explain to the applicant whether that salary is a "gross" or "net" salary. If the applicant has been paying taxes previously, he/she will understand the process. It would be best to do the tax calculations as you are discussing money. Have your accountant help you by providing the exact amounts that are being deducted so you can present this calculation to the applicant. Be clear in your explanation. It is very often a misunderstood issue. Many domestics who are accustomed to receiving cash do not have a clue about the necessary tax deductions. When they begin receiving their paycheck on payroll, they are surprised at the amount of money deducted. As a result, they often quit after receiving the first paycheck as they utter the words "I cannot survive on this amount of money." Others appear to understand the entire payroll situation while nodding their heads "yes," only to find themselves in tears at the end of the year when their taxes become due in a lump sum from money they never saved.

Whatever salary you are offering, the key question is: Does the domestic worker accept their earnings in "net" or "gross" terms? For example: are you offering $500/week net of taxes (take home amount for the employee after all necessary taxes are removed) or are you offering $500/week gross salary (translating to $421.70/week net for a person who is married, claiming one exemption). Keep in mind that, unless you are paying $15 and up per hour, more often than not, the highly experienced domestic worker will NOT be happy with a net or cash salary less than $12/hour. ($14/hour gross translates roughly to $12/hour net.) It is a shame that, due to the fact so many employers are NOT complying with the tax laws and pay under the table, so many of these domestic workers prefer cash and will seek the jobs that pay cash. As a law-abiding citizen, you, in effect, have to pay above the normal amount so that the employee actually nets an amount equivalent to what others are paying in cash. Therefore, you are being penalized for doing the right thing. If everyone paid domestic employees legally, this dilemma would not occur.

For the employer, the bottom line is what it will cost to hire the employee. Conversely, the take home amount is all that matters to most domestic workers. Rarely are domestic workers interested in the benefits of Social Security. As long as they are reporting some form of income to the tax authorities, they are in the system in a minimal way; yet they are still eligible for other benefits, such as unemployment. Now you should be wondering just how many of these people who are paid in cash might also be receiving "unemployment" for given periods of time while employed by, perhaps, you. This could not occur if they were on payroll. The domestic's perspective is that if all earnings were reported, there would be less money available, making it very difficult to survive in this very expensive economy. Consequently, as a result of this, employers who do not care about paying taxes for their help opt to hire legal and illegal employees who are very happy to accept their salaries in cash. Now, you can understand why it is so important to discuss wages *clearly* with your prospective employee.

Demographics play a role: Check with domestic agencies and neighbors in your area to establish what domestics are earning.

Check with domestic agencies and neighbors in your area to establish what domestics are earning.

When checking around, be sure to rely on more than one source for this answer. Wages do change depending on demographics. If you rely on friends and neighbors who tell you what they are paying their current domestic, be sure to weigh all the facts. Is the job description the same as yours? Do the qualifications match what you are seeking? There are many factors to take into consideration when arriving at the correct pay scale for a particular domestic.

Check with reputable agencies that will give you honest answers. Two agencies in the same area may have very different rates for what seems to be the same job description. You then need to investigate the agencies and see what quality of people they are actually providing for that specified rate. They also may give you a lower rate to hook you into the agency. A reputable agency in your area that has been in business for some time will be more apt to give you accurate pay scales for your particular job description.

SALARIES ARE BASED ON MANY FACTORS

As you can see, there is a wide salary range for domestic positions. The salary you offer should depend on the following factors:

WHERE DO I BEGIN?

- Level of English
- Driver with/without Vehicle for Use on the Job
- Work Permit/Resident/US Citizen
- Years of Experience
- Quality of References
- Previous Salary
- Live-In versus Live-Out
- Part-Time versus Full-Time

Level of English

When asking an applicant whether or not he/she can speak English, you will get a variety of answers anywhere from "a little" to "yes, I understand everything" to flat out "no." Unfortunately, self-observation is often understated or grossly over-stated, especially when it comes to speaking a language. The best way to find out someone's language skills is to have a lengthy conversation that requires answers in full sentences and to have the person read and write for you.

There are some cases where the level of English is not as important. For example, a housekeeper whose level of English is minimal but who is very experienced and understands everything pertaining to cleaning a house may be sufficient when you are hiring just a "day cleaner." This means that she/he knows how to clean and what products to use, and she/he will most likely not need too much communication with you. After all, a housekeeper is employed to clean, not to chitchat. Some of the most experienced house cleaners, in fact, speak NO ENGLISH. Therefore, if you are hiring just a "day cleaner," the level of English will not be as important. However, do not think that just because the domestic's English is not great that you are about to get a bargain. Experienced cleaners will charge just about the same, whether their English is fluent or not. Remember, your domestic is not being paid to recite Shakespeare!

On the other hand, perhaps you need a domestic who must communicate well with you and the children. There are many issues that come up with children where good English could be necessary. Good English can play a big role with child development skills. If the English is very good, but not fluent, and you are worried about the Nanny not being able to communicate in an emergency situation, keep in mind that 911 and hospitals have translators who speak almost all languages. In California, for example, practically all public services are bilingual in Spanish and English. The level of English for most domestic positions will be a major determining factor for salary.

All other domestic positions such as House Manager, Personal Assistant, Houseman, Chauffeur, Chef and Certified Nurse Assistant, are highly paid positions that require excellent English skills.

Driver *with or without* Vehicle for Use on the Job

Driver *with* vehicle for use on the job - If the applicant is picking up children and doing errands, this is an added responsibility when qualifying an applicant. Certainly it is preferable if the domestic's car is one in good condition and with working air bags and seat belts. The car must be sufficently insured. Bodily injury coverage of at least $100,000 per person and $300,000 per accident, with $50,000 property damage coverage, are recommended. The minimum limits required by the state of California are $15,000 and $30,000 respectively. Other states will differ. This would not be sufficient when driving children. If the applicant has limited liability insurance and cannot afford to pay for more coverage, you could offer to pay the difference. You should take into consideration the payment of miles and gas for use of an employee's car. A salary for a driver with a vehicle for use on the job should be evaluated as follows:

> Driving Skills and Driving Record
> Amount of Insurance Coverage on Vehicle
> Insurable on your Policy
> Condition of Vehicle for Use on the Job
> Driving Experience in a Previous Job

Driver *without* vehicle for use on the job – An applicant who has a good driver's license but does not have a vehicle may accept less wages because a car and insurance are being provided. Many employers prefer providing the vehicle because they make a safe choice on what type of car is being utilized when driving their children. If you are providing a car, be very sure that the applicant has a clean driving record and that you have driven with this person to know more about his/her driving skills. Check with your insurance company to determine what it would cost you to insure this employee on your policy before considering the salary.

Work Permit/Resident/US Citizen

If an applicant has a current *Work Authorization (Work Permit)*, he/she is legally able to work for you. This work authorization is renewable on an annual basis. If the applicant has been receiving renewed work permits consistently, the likelihood is that this process will continue, but there is no guarantee. Therefore, the only issue with having a Work Permit is whether or not at the time of expiration, the applicant is able to renew the card. Sometimes, Work Permits are NOT re-issued due to changes in the immigration laws at the time, as well as a myriad of other factors that might impede the re-issuance. If this were to happen, you would no longer be able to employ this applicant under the immigration and Internal Revenue laws. Keep in mind that if your applicant only has a work authorization, he/she cannot leave the country until residency is sanctioned.

An applicant who has a *Resident Card* is a permanent legal resident of the United States. This means that the applicant can travel in and out of the country. (Residents may return to their own countries if need be without any problem of re-entry.) An applicant who is a resident and has complied with the federal requirements to enable the application for citizenship would be eligible for the next step, which is U.S. citizenship. There is an advantage in hiring an applicant who is already a resident or a US citizen in that this type of legal status is secure, enabling this candidate to travel anywhere for employment.

Years of Experience

This is not an easy point of evaluation. If someone has over 10 years of experience working in the capacity of the job he/she seeks, then you would assume

If you are providing a car, be very sure that the applicant has a clean driving record

this applicant could demand top dollar in any domestic specialty. With many years of on-the-job experience, you would expect this applicant would be "excellent." However, this is not always the case. Some applicants who have so much experience are very set in their ways. They may want to do the job only their way, and appear adamant about knowing what is best for the child and/or household. The truth of the matter is that they might simply not want to be told anything. When interviewing an applicant who has 10 years or more of experience, one of your key questions would be, "Do you mind taking orders and doing the job the way I want it done?" Of course, the applicant would be crazy to say, "No." However, a more convincing response would be, "You are the boss and make all the decisions for this child and/or household; therefore, whatever way you wish to have things done is the way I will do it." Only through careful observation will you know the honesty of that response. This is where a reference will give you further clarity.

The goal is to try to get someone with the most experience for the job, who has not developed an attitude, who isn't "burned out", and who doesn't insist on doing things "her/his way only."

Another caveat with regard to a person with so much experience is that sometimes an "attitude" may develop. Being a domestic and working for many families over the years is not an easy career. People do not always treat their household help with the same respect and courtesy that they would other types of employees. This employee may be "burned out," with somewhat of a chip on his or her shoulder. This is normal, and intrinsic not only to the domestic field. It may be that this very experienced domestic should have moved on to bigger horizons long ago. He/she may be overqualified, but due to possibly never having developed any other skills, remained stuck in a field no longer of preference. Sometimes, you will find that this very experienced domestic prefers working in a household alone where there isn't a lot of supervision. The goal is to try to get someone with the most experience for the job, who has not developed an attitude, who isn't "burned out," and who doesn't insist on only doing things "her/his way."

Keep in mind that there are those individuals who have worked 2 to 5 years who may be just as qualified as those with more years of experience. They may demand top dollar and deserve it if they have all the other necessary qualifications. These applicants may be very amenable, flexible and easy to manage. This is why qualifying a person by the "number of years of experience" is such a gray area.

However, you should be careful when hiring, for example, a Nanny who has ONLY worked a few months, unless you are hiring a mother's helper. A child care provider who works alongside you may learn from you and gradually be given greater responsibility once you achieve a comfort level to do so. You would begin by paying this domestic a lower salary until the experience is gained. If you are hiring a housekeeper with approximately 1-3 years of experience, you can be more flexible in your assessment of salary. You will know immediately how skilled this person is as a housekeeper by doing a trial day or two. A good cleaner could just be starting out and still be excellent, whereas a child care provider requires skills that must be attained prior to being left alone with your child. To determine a domestic's expertise, whether the experience is one year or 10 years, you must always observe the domestic on a trial basis. At least a few days up to one week would be prudent. If you are getting this person through an agency, request a trial period of at least one week. Most applicants prefer the trial period for themselves so that they can also check out the position before making a commitment.

Quality of References

References are highly important but not always accurate. You will be surprised by some excellent reference checks that turn out to be for poor quality, unproductive employees. For this reason, a trial period is mandatory. A previous employer will sometimes be more candid with you than with an agency; therefore, check the references even if you are using an agency. Many times references will be fake and provided by family members and/or friends. You need to ask numerous questions to match information provided by the employee and previous employer.

If the reference is less than enthusiastic about describing the applicant's qualifications, you must weigh all the factors. Is the reference provider angry because the applicant left without notice or because he/she simply left? Don't be afraid to flat out ask the previous employer, "Are you angry about your employee leaving you?" "If the applicant hadn't left, would you have kept him/her employed?" Slowly but surely you will get an honest answer.

On the other side of the coin, sometimes a previous employer will be dishonest

To determine a domestic's expertise, you must always observe the domestic on a trial basis.

about the applicant's qualifications for fear of jeopardizing future employment or having the "bad" reference get back to the former employee. Once again, you want to ask all the questions you can so that hopefully, in the end, the truth comes out.

Letters of reference are wonderful and very helpful when deciding on an applicant. If the letter is lengthy and detailed, it can indicate the former reference must have been very happy with this employee to take the time to be so descriptive. However, sometimes a former long-time employee will not have a letter of reference. This could be because the former employer did not have the time to write a letter or simply doesn't want to document a reference. (A former employer of an employee, whether long-term or short-term, should write a letter of reference if only to acknowledge on paper that this employee worked specific dates and held certain responsibilities.) Applicants may tell you about a long list of references and then finish by indicating that each and every reference is no longer reachable because all of them have moved. It would seem that a former reference that was very happy with an employee would provide a forwarding number to the applicant. This same reference might even want to stay in touch and write or call with a new number when they got to their new destination. My point here is that there is no excuse for not having a reference of some sort if, in fact, the applicant worked. No verification of having worked might simply indicate that the applicant *does not want you to speak to the reference.* The most professional domestics will come to an interview with a résumé and letters and/or numbers of prior references, most of which are reachable. This makes a strong impression to any prospective employer and is a strong consideration when determining salary.

A former employer of an employee, whether long-term or short-term, should write a letter of reference.

Previous Salary

It is always a good idea that if the current job description is the same as the previous one held by this applicant, so should the salary offered be close to what the applicant was previously earning. All other criteria in the new position must also be the same. If an applicant was previously grossly underpaid or overpaid, then this would not apply. If you are offering the applicant an amount that is considerably less than what was formerly earned, be sure that there is no problem with the decrease in pay. Perhaps this is only a starting salary. If you do not discuss an increase at some point in the near future, then the likelihood is that the employee will not be happy with a decrease in pay indefinitely.

Begin by analyzing the job responsibilities in a previous job versus your job. Does your position require more work and hence a greater salary? A $25 to a $75 difference in pay per week from a previous job may not be a major issue. Anything from $100 and up is a significant difference. Obviously, you never want to start an employee who is sincerely not happy with the salary being offered but is willing to take it out of desperation. The same desperation may move this employee out of your job into another one that is better paying.

Live-in Versus Live-Out

Domestics who live-in are not necessarily less expensive than those who live-out. I emphasize this point because it is often misunderstood and questioned. If you are providing "meals and lodging" this can officially be construed as a deduction from wages as long as you are complying with the Labor Code's definition. Effective January 1, 2001, the Industrial Welfare Commission Order No. 15-2001 regulating "Wages, Hours and Working Conditions in the Household Occupations" states that a "meal" means "an adequate, well-balanced serving of a variety of wholesome, nutritious food" and that "lodging" means "living accommodations available to the employee for *full-time occupancy* which are adequate, decent and sanitary according to usual and customary standards." Also note that "meals and lodging may not be credited against the minimum wage without a voluntary written agreement between the employer and the employee." When credit for meals or lodging is used to meet part of the employer's minimum wage obligation, the amounts are limited. See the chart for this calculation in Chapter 5 under "Important Labor Issues."

Therefore, when making your analysis of what salary you are offering for a live-in, consider the first question, "Do you have the proper accommodations for the live-in?" Do you have a separate room, or would she have to sleep on a pull-out sofa in the den? Does the live-in have a room that is a standard-size room with a closet and a window, or would the employee have to sleep in a makeshift room that was formerly part of the garage or laundry area with substandard conditions?

Domestics who live-in are not necessarily less expensive than those who live-out.

Equally important, is the employee able to live there 7 days per week without having to seek housing elsewhere on days off? Are you providing healthy well-balanced meals, or do you usually keep the refrigerator empty unless you are eating at home?

Let us assume you are providing all meals and excellent full-time quarters, or better yet, the ideal situation of a guesthouse. This would definitely be an attractive part of your job offer and warrant a deduction in salary. However, anything less might make a live-in situation less attractive and not warrant a deduction in salary.

Providing all meals and excellent full-time quarters would definitely be an attractive part of your job offer.

This misnomer of live-in help being cheaper than live-out help comes from a time when immigration opened its doors freely and was allowing slews of people into the country. Most of these immigrants would be non-English speaking and undocumented or undergoing the process of documentation. Many would desperately seek employment as domestics where they could find a place to work and live simultaneously. Employers for many years accepted these people into their homes because they could get cheap labor. Some people find it easy to justify overworking and underpaying an undocumented worker. This is still occurring with domestic help today, but not at the same rate as in earlier years. The public is now more aware of the law and potential liabilities associated with hiring illegal help. More significantly, there are less people looking for live-in positions. Most of the people who years ago started out working as live-ins for low salaries are now fully acclimated to our society. The immigration doors, for now, are closed as of April 30, 2001. Those immigrants already here for many years now speak fairly good English and have their own families here. They are now legal, own and operate vehicles and many own their own homes. They do not want to return to those days working as live-ins, where in many cases they were overworked, underpaid and away from their families.

What we have today is a continued high demand and a much lower supply of live-in help. If anything, live-in help should be paid more due to the low supply. It is my observation that most employers are NOT complying with the applicable Labor Code with respect to the number of hours and breaks that a live-in must be provided. For example, per the Labor Code, "A live-in employee shall have at least 12 consecutive hours free of duty during each 24 hour work day. The employee shall also have at least 3 hours free during the 12-hour span of work. Such off-duty hours need not be consecutive, and the schedule for free time shall be set by mutual agreement of employer and employee. An employee who is required to work during scheduled off duty hours or during the 12 consecutive off duty hours shall be compensated at the rate of 1 1/2 times the employee's regular rate of pay for all such hours worked." Most employers who are hiring live-in help are working their employee a 12-hour or longer shift, not providing all the breaks, and not paying overtime.

Part-time versus Full-time

If you need someone to work part-time in the mornings or in the afternoons, it is sometimes *more* difficult to find this person than if you were offering a full-time position. Especially hard would be if you needed hours that were in the middle of the day, such as 10:00AM to 2:00PM. A schedule such as this would not make it easy for this domestic to find other work to complement the salary. If you absolutely must have a person during the middle of the day, you may find yourself offering more per hour to keep this person financially happy with your job. Sometimes you have to pay more per hour for a part-time job to make it worth the gas and time to get to your house for only 4 hours of pay. Let's say, for example, that you want to start a person out on a part-time basis until you return to work, at which point you plan to provide this same person with a full-time job. The applicant may not be able to survive on a part-time job for very long. Therefore, you would want to make it attractive by offering more per hour to keep this employee happy until you can offer a full-time salary that meets this person's financial requirements.

A person seeking full-time work but who is willing to take part-time while looking for another position may never find that other part-time job and end up choosing to leave your job for a full-time position.

The best way to approach hiring a permanent part-time person is to be sure that "part-time" is all this person needs. A person seeking full-time work but who is willing to take part-time while looking for another position may *never* find that other part-time job and end up choosing to leave your job for a full-time position. A full-time position is what most people want to work. An employee may be less concerned about the hourly wage and more concerned about the overall salary for the full-time job. Whereas with a part-time job, the hourly wage is very important and sometimes is paid higher to maintain the loyalty of the employee.

WHAT ARE THE VARIOUS DOMESTIC TITLES AND RESPONSIBILITIES?

Baby Nurse

A Baby Nurse is someone who assists a new mother with the complete care of her baby, including bathing, feeding, changing, and putting the baby on a set schedule for sleeping. The Baby Nurse will bring the baby to the new mother at night for breast-feeding and return the baby to bed so that the mother gets the optimum amount of sleep. Baby Nurses are often certified by having passed the British Certification of the Nursery Nursing Examination Board (NNEB), and others are Certified Nurse Assistants (CNA). The cost to hire a Baby Nurse can be very expensive; however, for first-time mothers, it is almost a must, even if only for the first 2 weeks of your child's life. A Baby Nurse will work either a 24-hour shift or a 12-hour nighttime schedule, arriving late in the evening and leaving early morning.

Doula

As provided by Missie Philips, an experienced Doula for more than 20 years in Los Angeles:

A postpartum doula is a teacher and a source of information.

"The name *doula* is derived from a Greek word meaning *server*. A postpartum doula's role is fluid: family to family, day to day, even hour to hour. Her role is constantly changing. She is a teacher and a source of information. She will provide reliable, evidence-based information on infant care while integrating a baby into the family. She offers practical support regarding proper diet and baby organization. The postpartum doula also has a thorough knowledge of services, products and professionals available in her community and offers quality, reliable referrals when they are needed. At all times, the doula provides reassurance, support and the belief that these parents can and will be successful in nurturing their family."

Usually a Doula will come to your home for a few hours per day up to a full day. Unlike a Baby Nurse, a Doula does not normally live-in.

Professional Nanny

A Professional Nanny in traditional terms is someone who is trained and certified by an accredited institution that teaches child-development skills and how to care for children of all ages. She is usually an educated individual who can speak and write the native language of employment fluently. She must be CPR trained and possess on-the-job experience working as a Nanny with children of all ages.

A Nanny of this caliber will most likely NOT do any serious housekeeping. She is responsible for anything that relates to the child's room, toys and laundry. Her primary responsibility is to feed, change, bathe, dress, read to, and play with the baby. She also takes the baby on walks, to any classes, play dates, or doctor appointments. She is at the child's side at all times. If she is a live-in Nanny caring for an infant, she may agree to wake up at night to help with the night feedings. If you ask her to do this, be sure that you understand that if she is up all night with the baby, she is going to be too tired to work early the next day. You want her in top form when she is caring for your child. Therefore, you will need to offset the evening hours by making an adjustment with the day time hours. (This is why it would be a good idea to hire a Baby Nurse first to get your baby on a schedule as soon as possible.)

These days, it may be difficult to find a Nanny who has attended a "Nanny School" and received credentials qualifying her as a Professional Certified Nanny. What you will find more commonly is a person who has on-the-job experience working many years as a Nanny with some child development education from a local college. Those who may not be educated as a Nanny could still be professional, nurturing and very experienced. This will, at times, speak volumes over any institutional training. The best of both worlds, of course, is to have someone with both the education and job experience. However, it simply is not as common. Other classifications for a Nanny are as follows: Nanny/Light

Housekeeper or Nanny/Housekeeper.

Nanny/Light Housekeeper

This is a person whose primary function is caring for children with some household duties falling under the category of "light housekeeping." As mentioned above, institutional training may be limited, but she/he should be trained in CPR and have on-the-job experience with children of all ages.

Wages will vary depending on factors such as driving, level of English skills and how many children are present and their ages. While this Nanny may have experience working with children of all ages, there may be a preference for only working with babies, toddlers or school-age children. The previous job experience should indicate her specialty and expertise. Sometimes a Nanny will have worked with many babies and now prefer to work with toddlers or older children. You will need to investigate this carefully to be sure that the Nanny will work well with your children. Keep in mind that working with babies and toddlers will demand more effort and skills and should be compensated accordingly.

Light housekeeping includes the following: making the beds, taking care of the children's laundry (adult laundry is optional), keeping the toys and children's rooms clean and organized, dusting, providing meals to the children, and keeping the kitchen clean after meals for the children. She may agree to do more and she may insist on doing less. Cleaning bathrooms and floors are usually NOT included; vacuuming and dusting is optional. Generally speaking, the above-mentioned duties are the most common. Be absolutely sure that you both are in agreement with what you expect as "light housekeeping" and with what your Nanny is willing to do.

If you have an infant that is under 10 months of age, there is more time to handle light housekeeping chores. Once your baby begins to walk, and especially if there is another baby or toddler present, the Nanny will not have a lot of time to do as many light housekeeping chores. Consider the age of your children and the number of children under the Nanny's care to decide on the amount of housekeeping one is able to accomplish.

Nanny/Housekeeper

This is a person who has agreed to function both as a Nanny caring for the children and as a Housekeeper doing any housekeeping chore required. This full charge employee is the kind of person most employers want to hire. However, not all employers have the kind of household that should hire one person to do all functions.

First, think about the square footage of your home and how much attention your house requires to clean it in the manner that you like. Think about the number of times you need to vacuum, clean the floors, do the laundry, keep the bathrooms clean, etc. Do you have a separate housekeeper who comes once or twice a week to do the heavy cleaning? Think about your family and the number and ages of your children. Think about how much attention each child requires and how much time is needed each day to care for each child. Consider whether both parents are working or whether a mother is a stay-at-home mom who participates in the care of the children or the household chores. Consider the hours you expect your employee to work and whether within that workday, there would be sufficient time to accomplish everything. Consider that you may need to split up the household functions to a few items each day OR have one day be solely devoted to cleaning.

Once you have carefully thought about the above, then you should be able to determine whether you can reasonably ask a domestic to do both functions. Remember to be very specific about what you expect done in your home as it relates to your children and your house. Make sure that when hiring a Nanny/Housekeeper that she is used to doing both functions in a previous job. If she is only used to doing light housekeeping, she might be less comfortable doing full-charge cleaning along with childcare.

Try not to expect any human being to do anything that you, under similar circumstances, would not be capable of handling. Review what is most important to you and make that very clear to your employee. A Nanny/Housekeeper should

Try not to expect any human being to do anything that you, under similar circumstances, would not be capable of handling.

always know that when you are not home and there are young children present, the focus must be only on the children.

Au Pair

"The words *au pair* mean *equal with*. An au pair should not be considered as a maid or servant or even an employee. An au pair should be treated as an equal in your family. It is a sort of cultural exchange opportunity that has childcare attached to it," says Paula Lotz of Au Pair Homestay USA. Basically, an Au Pair is a young woman anywhere from 18 to 26 years of age who is from an international country coming to another country to work as a live-in Nanny. She usually has some formal training given by the program that places her, as well as some work experience. She is committed to a position for a minimum of one year. She is paid a small weekly stipend and must be provided with an educational allowance to enable her to attend post-secondary educational courses during the program year.

These candidates have been carefully screened and well trained. As in all cases when choosing an employee to work in your home and care for your children, personality will play a large role in your selection of an Au Pair.

Au Pair candidates have been carefully screened and well trained.

The companies representing Au Pairs will complete a thorough background screening on each Au Pair. They provide a police record check, current health check-up, confirmation of schooling, and a standardized personality analysis called a "Cross Cultural Adaptability Inventory" (CCAI) that is specifically designed for assessing personalities in different cultures and languages. They also have local representatives who work as a liaison for the Au Pair and Host family.

The only caveat to hiring an Au Pair is that their commitment is usually for only one year. Normally, they do not work in one place for more than the original commitment. Although they work as live-ins, they want the freedom to go out at night and have a separate life from their work. Other Nannies who work as live-ins do not leave at night and usually make themselves available for babysitting as needed. Although this is NOT always the case, having an Au Pair can sometimes be like having another teenager around. On the other hand, by setting the proper parameters and rules, having an Au Pair can be a wonderful experience for you and your family.

Housekeeper

A housekeeper is either a *day cleaner* or a *full-charge housekeeper* who is capable of doing all cleaning duties. This person is paid either by the day, hour, week, or a flat price per house.

Day cleaners are housekeepers who work as live-outs and go into a home and clean it 1-3 times per week for 4-8 hours and get paid either by the hour or the job. They may be very fast workers and able to do general cleaning rather efficiently. They usually don't like spending too long in one house so that they can clean two houses in one day. Depending on the size of your home, they can usually clean a 3,500-square-foot or smaller home within 4 hours. This includes general cleaning in the bedrooms, bathrooms, living room, family room, study or library, and kitchen. Unless they are working a longer day, often they will not do laundry, ironing, or cooking. If your house is large and you require laundry as part of the daily housekeeping function, then you must make sure they are working a full day to allow enough time to do it. Day Cleaners generally want to be paid hourly at $10-15/hr. *Remember: A Day Cleaner does general housekeeping and rarely does projects around the house, unless you offer longer hours per day and extra pay.*

A *Full-Charge Housekeeper* can work 3 or more days per week, and will accomplish almost everything in the house. At 5 days per week, there should be enough time to get to projects such as silver polishing, organizing the pantry and other cabinets, cleaning the patio, laundry, ironing and even some cooking. At less than 5 days per week, it will be difficult to accomplish everything. Go over the Cleaning Guidelines and choose what you want cleaned on a daily and weekly and monthly basis. See if all the duties you want accomplished can be done in 1-2 days or 3-5 days. Weigh everything with respect to the duties you need completed, and be sure that you are reasonable in your requests for the number of hours and days you have this domestic scheduled to work.

Be sure that you are reasonable in your requests for the number of hours and days you have this domestic scheduled to work.

Babysitter

This is a person who is paid on an hourly basis to baby-sit only. A Babysitter will NOT do any cleaning other than maybe the dishes after a meal and picking up the toys. She should have references for babysitting other children of your child's age. A Babysitter should be CPR certified. Keep in mind, this is not a Nanny. This is someone who will simply watch a child to make sure the child is secure, safe and happy while the parents are out of the house. Other than that, do not expect a lot from a Babysitter, who may ultimately watch TV, do homework or chitchat on the phone. Very often, Babysitters are young students who are looking to make extra money while attending school. Be sure to set parameters with them since they might not have a lot of job experience. As in all domestic positions, what one family will let their Babysitter do may be something you would never dream of allowing. Due to the fact that a Babysitter may be young and have less experience, be sure to go over the emergency procedures and leave all necessary numbers to contact you. In addition, always leave the telephone numbers of where you will be for the evening. Babysitters get paid approximately $10 to $15 per hour.

Companion

This is a person who takes care of an elderly couple or an elderly individual who needs someone to *perhaps* make all meals, hand-feed, help dress and bathe, but who does not require any professional nursing. A Companion should speak enough English to communicate with the elderly person. Older people like to talk and often feel lonely without someone who can communicate with them. A Companion may or may not drive or have a car. However, it is often preferable that she/he does drive since an elderly person will ultimately reach a point where it will be necessary to be driven to places like the doctor's office, the market, and other errands. If the Companion has a current driver's license, but does not have a car, that may be OK if the employer has a vehicle for use on the job. The employer should add the Companion on the insurance policy as "Additional Named Insured."

Most Companions will do *some* housekeeping chores and cooking for their employer. This includes general light cleaning, laundry and basic cooking. However, many Companions will NOT do heavy cleaning. Cooking will not typically entail gourmet meals, but a basic, nutritious breakfast, lunch and dinner. If a Companion is hired to live-out, then he/she may arrive early enough to eat a late breakfast and stay late enough to serve an early dinner. However, most employers who have adequate living quarters would be better off with a live-in Companion to be available in case the elderly employer needs special attention at night. Once again, whether or not a Companion works as a live-in or live-out depends on the age and medical condition of the elderly employer.

One of the key issues when hiring a Companion for yourself or your loved one is to be sure that the chemistry between the employer and employee is good. Elderly people can be depressed, in pain, and miserable. They are often not the easiest people to get along with. They need the right kind of person to handle these emotions. The Companion should be compassionate, nurturing, patient and understanding, with good experience working with elderly people.

Full Charge Caregiver

This Caregiver will do both caring for an elderly person as well as full-charge cleaning, marketing, cooking and driving. This most likely means that the elderly person is NOT incapacitated and does not require constant care. If the elderly person does need constant vigilance, then there may not be any time to do the housekeeping. Again, you must determine the size of the house and the amount of housework necessary to keep the house in order as well as the amount of attention needed to tend to the care of the elderly person. This job is difficult if the elderly person requires any medical attention. Be sure to evaluate the elderly person's condition before delegating the domestic duties.

Certified Nurse Assistant, Home Health Aide, LVN/LPN

These titles belong to those who have been trained and licensed to care for people of all ages who are ill, perhaps incapacitated, and need special medical assistance. Due to their education and ability to perform more duties than a non-certified Companion/Caregiver, they are usually paid higher salaries. They are graduates of their field and hold certifications. They very often drive and have their own transportation, speak fluent English and will live-in or live-out. They are experienced and licensed to give medication, check blood pressure, administer oxygen and shots, and check vital signs. An LVN, in particular, is more capable

Elderly people can be depressed and are often not the easiest people to get along with. They need the right kind of person to handle these emotions.

than a Certified Nurse Assistant but not as qualified as a Registered Nurse. If the patient requires some serious care either at home or in a convalescent or retirement center, they should hire one of these licensed health care providers. The choice would depend on the severity of the patient's condition. This of course should be discussed with the patient's doctor to know exactly what kind of personnel is most suitable for the patient.

A Caregiver who is an LVN, Certified Nurse Assistant, or Home Health Aide will be devoted solely to the patient and in most cases not be responsible for any housekeeping chores or cooking. In other cases, you might find a licensed Caregiver who is willing to do it all as long as the patient's condition permits.

Chef

A Chef can be a personal professional Cook that works in your home. He/she may charge by the hour, day, or by the meal that is being prepared. Chefs will charge various rates depending on expertise, the number of meals to prepare, and the number of people present. Do not underestimate the value of an experienced chef. Preferably, the Chef is a graduate of a culinary school, perhaps even specializing in macrobiotics, nutrition and gourmet cooking. Review one's education and, most importantly, the cooking itself by having the Chef make a few meals for you. Depending on the expertise of the Chef, the number of guests, the formality of your home, and if you have other staff members, you may ask other staff members to serve and to care for the kitchen after meals. If you have other staff members, you may ask your housekeeper to take care of the kitchen after meals. If the Cook/Chef is prepared to do the entire cooking, serving and cleaning function, this should be taken into consideration when discussing a salary.

Houseman

A Houseman is sometimes referred to as a Butler. A Houseman is capable of doing all a Housekeeper would complete and more. One exception is that a Houseman is "male only" and can often do heavy physical cleaning that some female housekeepers find challenging. A Houseman can clean, do errands, market and even cook. A Houseman who is multi-talented might even do other work around the house like gardening, pool care, washing of cars, and light maintenance chores that are considered duties of a handyman. Depending on how multi-faceted the Houseman, you may find him to be highly valuable to a household. He can go from the role of a Butler in greeting your guests at the door, to being a chauffeur, to cleaning and doing complete maintenance of the house, to marketing, to cooking and serving a gourmet meal. A Houseman usually will live-in; however, there are many Housemen who prefer to live-out. For many elderly widows, a Houseman also can serve as a bodyguard or security for the household. A Houseman can receive a salary up to $75,000 annually.

Chauffeur/Driver

This domestic title is self-explanatory. A Chauffeur/Driver solely drives for the employer. He/she can clean and take full charge of the automobiles as well as taking the vehicles for service and gas. Detailing and cleaning of the cars is often part of a Chauffeur's duties as well as running many errands for the employer. He/she is available at any time of the day during the designated work schedule to drive the employer or others wherever requested. He/she may work as a live-in or live-out on call, part-time or full-time and will charge anywhere from $20 to $25 per hour or a set salary per week. He/she may drive his/her own car; however, usually the employer provides the vehicle. The Chauffeur/Driver must have an excellent driving record and be insured and insurable. This position is very often combined with a Houseman position unless the employer requires a full-time driver.

House Manager/Major Domo

A House Manager, in more sophisticated terms, is known as a Major Domo. He/she must oversee all matters pertaining to the house. This person may organize and handle all party arrangements, do some light administrative office work, and handle any household matter. This includes managing other in-house staff members and outside household maintenance workers. This person should have excellent language skills and be experienced in management. Work experience in a previous home as a House Manager or Personal Assistant/Secretary would be important, since managing a home requires strong administrative skills. Depending on the sophistication of the household, this position could require at least 3-5 years of experience and pay $75,000 or more annually.

Personal Assistant

A Personal Assistant handles all administrative duties with respect to a household and/or outside office. The duties may include answering phones, making all travel and personal entertainment arrangements, conducting preliminary interviewing for all staff members, running extensive errands, performing light bookkeeping, working on a computer, coordinating social functions and sometimes serving as a chauffeur. This position requires an intelligent, multi-tasking person similar to an Administrative Assistant/ Secretary/Girl Friday. This position pays anywhere from $35,000 to $75,000 annually. A Personal Assistant has a demanding job and may be asked to travel with the employer and be on call 5-7 days a week. A person who does not have many other commitments is best suited for this very demanding position.

Couple

A Couple will work as either live-in or live-out, and is usually a man and a woman who are married to each other and work closely together as a team. A guesthouse for them or at least separate quarters with a separate entrance is preferable for living accommodations. The married couple will share together all the responsibilities for the household. For example, the wife might market, cook, clean and do the laundry while the husband will take care of the pool, garden, and automobiles, and perform heavy household maintenance, run errands, provide security and serve as a chauffeur.

Very often, you will find that a couple has one member who is hard working and terrific, while the other lacks in some area.

It is best when hiring a couple to be sure that they have previously worked together in a household; otherwise, they may end up killing each other over responsibilities. A couple may be eager to work together, but never having done it, may find it difficult. It is preferable that they are married; however, there are individuals who work together as a couple and are NOT married. Very often, you will find that a couple has one member who is hard working and terrific, while the other lacks in some area. This is common. Sometimes the man does more than his share, and the woman is the princess. On the other hand, the woman may be the hard worker, and the man is simply lazy and unskilled. You have to see the Couple working in action to know.

There are clearly many advantages to hiring a couple if you happen to find the right pair. First, you can get all household chores accomplished with a staff of two people. Second, if the couple is amenable to taking separate days off or at least taking only Sundays off, you can joggle the schedule so that you have most days of the week covered.

Couples are paid anywhere from $52,000 to $95,000 annually. The variation in salary once again depends on the sophistication and size of the household and the couple's skills and experience.

MATCHING DOMESTIC TITLE AND EXPERIENCE TO SALARY

Let's begin with highly experienced domestics.

An Executive Housekeeper, Professional Nanny, House Manager, Houseman, Personal Assistant, Chauffeur, and Certified Caregivers can demand top dollar - anywhere from $15 to $25 per hour - if they have the following qualifications as applicable to the position:

- *Fluent English (excellent reading and writing skills)*
- *Driver with good driving record*
- *Vehicle in good condition for use on job*
- *Full coverage insurance (above minimum limits)*
- *5-10 years of experience*
- *CPR certified*
- *Child development course graduate*
- *Nanny school graduate*
- *Good cooking ability and/or culinary course graduate*
- *Certified Nurse Assistant/Home Health Aide/LVN*
- *Excellent long term references*
- *U.S. resident or U.S. citizen*

Nannies, Housekeepers and Companions who have the following qualifications can demand anywhere from $12 to $15 per hour:

- *English is moderately fluent, communication and understanding good*
- *Driver with good driving record*
- *Vehicle (may or may not be used on job)*
- *Full coverage insurance (above minimum limits)*
- *3-5 Years of experience*
- *CPR certified*
- *Excellent references*
- *Work Permit/U.S. resident*

Babysitters, Nannies and Housekeepers who have the following qualifications are paid anywhere from $10 to $12 per hour:

- *English and communication skills are limited*
- *Non-driver or driver for transportation only*
- *1 – 3 years of experience*
- *References are good but minimal*
- *Work Permit*
- *CPR certified*

With all of this in mind, there is still another set of criteria that you must include as applicable to the position when determining the salary you offer in order to be fair and just to your employee. For example:

- *What is the size of your home; how many bathrooms and bedrooms are there to clean?*
- *Do you want **all** rooms and bathrooms cleaned daily, or just those that are **used** daily with the others cleaned 1-2 times per week?*
- *How many children are there in your family and how many are present*

throughout the day?

- *Do the parents work or is there a stay-at-home parent?*
- *Does another domestic work on the off days and clean 1-2 times per week?*
- *Are there other domestics working in the house sharing responsibilities simultaneously?*
- *Does the domestic need to walk your pets or do extra pet-care duty?*
- *Is the position "full charge"? (You expect the domestic to do all the housekeeping, childcare, driving and cooking)*
- *How much driving is needed? Is the domestic responsible for driving many other children in a car pool situation?*
- *Are you providing a car or using the domestic's car?*
- *Does the domestic do extensive cooking at your home, and for how many individuals, or does the domestic only need to assist?*
- *Is there heavy ironing and daily laundry (dress shirts/sheets included)?*
- *Does the domestic need to have the skills to tutor your child with homework?*
- *Does your domestic need to interact frequently with outside sources (service companies) coming to your home?*
- *Are you requesting that your domestic NOT take any other positions so as to be on call for you whenever you need extra days or hours?*
- *Do you insist that your domestic be available to travel anywhere (including outside the U.S.) and at anytime you need her/him? (For example, during the holiday season?)*
- *Do you need your domestic to stay-at-home and house-sit when you travel, even if she is normally a live-out employee?*

Many of these questions may or may not apply to your specific job. If any of these points are actually part of your job description, then you do need to consider the impact of this on the salary you are offering. The idea here is to pay properly and according to what is fair for the amount of work and requirements made by you. The more demanding your job, the greater the salary.

A LIVE-IN VERSUS A LIVE-OUT DOMESTIC

A "live-in" is a domestic who lives in your home (preferably in private quarters) from 2 to 7 days per week. This person may live-in during the weekends, weekdays or the complete week. A live-in is provided meals along with lodging and may or may not have use of your vehicle, depending on your arrangement.

A "live-out" is a domestic who *comes to your home on a daily basis* from 1 to 7 days per week and leaves at the end of the workday. All meals are usually not provided to a live-out unless the employer wishes to make them available. Some meals can be provided, such as lunch if the employer wishes. This is strictly discretionary. Most live-out personnel have their own vehicle to get to and from work. In some instances, a live-out will get to work by public transporation, in which case the employer can choose to pick up the employee or ask him/her to walk if the residence is in close proximity to the stop or station.

Every domestic title may work as a "live-in" or "live-out." There are definite pros and cons to hiring live-in or live-out. This is further reviewed in Chapter 2. The most confusing question for you is whether to hire a live-in versus a live-out. Many people believe that hiring a live-in is less costly. Years ago, that may have been true. However, as mentioned earlier, the labor laws have changed somewhat and the wages that can be deducted for providing room and board are no longer as significant. State by state, you can review all this information on an updated basis with the Employment Development Department (EDD) Pamphlet #1105, entitled Public Housekeeping Industry. Another reason why hiring a live-in can be just as costly as hiring a live-out is because a live-in is not easy to find. This is especially true when hiring a live-in that drives. Those who choose to work as a live-in demand a higher salary because they know that their day will be long and that if they drive, they are a hot commodity. The costs for hiring a live-in today can be the same as hiring a live-out if all other factors are equal.

You will need to consider some inherent differences in costs for a live-in, such

The costs for hiring a live-in today can be the same as hiring a live-out if all other factors are equal.

as the following:

- Providing a suitable room and bath (separate quarters)

- Furnishings (bed, sheets, dresser, television)

- Utilities (cable/electricity/telephone/water)

- Groceries (additional member eating 3 meals per day)

- Providing a car for use on/off the job (optional)

- Insuring your live-in employee for driving

As mentioned earlier, the room should be adequate and contain proper furnishings. When providing a separate telephone line, you would pay for the installation and the basic monthly charges. The domestic would pay for his/her own long distance and local toll charges. You may choose to pay local toll, and keep the long distance charge separate or pay all charges within reason. The advantage of providing a phone line is that your domestic is not on your private line, and you can easily keep track of the charges. A uniform, if required, may cost anywhere from $20 to $50; shoes are an extra $40-$50 (these are provided by the employer for live-in or live-out positions). The cost of groceries is relative depending on what the family eats and whether or not the live-in has special dietary requests. You may have a car for your live-in domestic to use, but you need to name her/him as an "additional named driver" on your insurance policy.

A live-in's room should be adequate and contain proper furnishings.

When hiring a live-out, the costs are less and limited. Although you would still pay extra for gasoline costs and mileage while driving for you on the job, most live-outs have their own vehicle. This amount for gasoline and mileage is explained earlier and can be combined weekly and paid separately. With a live-in situation, in most cases you are providing a car. The live-in may require use of the car on duty as well as off duty, whereas a live-out does not take your car home at night. A live-out usually will not eat at your home. You may supply lunch; however, the domestic usually brings it. If the domestic does bring a lunch, this avoids your needing certain lunch foods available in the refrigerator. My advice is to have your live-out domestic do just as any other employee position might require; bring a lunch and have a minimum 30-minute lunch break, depending on what has been decided earlier.

Overall, hiring a live-in may appear to cost you less, especially when hiring a non-driver, but in reality, you make up most of the difference with all the extras that a live-in requires when residing with you.

Most live-ins work 5 days and 5 nights.

WHAT IS THE BEST WORK SCHEDULE FOR MY HOUSEHOLD?

Let's begin by breaking this down between a ***live-in*** and ***live-out domestic***.

Scheduling a Live-in Domestic: Most live-ins work 5 days and 5 nights. Many prefer to leave the last night of the workweek instead of the morning after. If the live-in owns a car, or someone can pick her up, then she can leave once you get home. This works out fine as long as she is flexible to baby-sit as late as you need her on the last night of the workweek. However, without a car or ride, it may NOT be safe to send her off late at night. In this case, sending the domestic home the next morning is preferable. This is not an issue when the domestic makes the workplace a permanent residence 7 days per week.

Here are the various weekday work schedules in order of employee preference:

a) **Monday to Friday**
   (Leaving Friday night or Saturday morning)

b) **Tuesday to Saturday**
   (Leaving Saturday night or Sunday morning)

c) **Wednesday to Sunday**
   (Beginning Wednesday morning through Sunday night)
   (Beginning Wednesday morning through Monday morning)

d) **Weekends**
   (Beginning Saturday morning to Sunday night)

(Beginning Friday night through Sunday night)
(Beginning Friday night through Monday morning)

One of the main reasons more and more domestics do not want to work as a live-in is because of the long hours that employers demand without taking into consideration overtime. An employer normally wants a live-in because it is a known fact that most employers can get the maximum time out of their employee when they work as a live-in. Live-ins will work a 12-hour shift with breaks and are usually paid a lump weekly salary for a very long day. (A live-out *rarely* works a 12-hour shift and is almost always paid by the hour.)

For example, an employer will ask a live-in to wake up early in the morning with the children and work until they are done with dinner and/or have put the children in bed to sleep. This could be anywhere from 6-9 AM to 6-9 PM, which constitutes approximately 12-hour days with perhaps overtime. However, unless the employee takes the necessary breaks, the employee will be exhausted and eventually become completely burned out on the job. It would be your responsibility as an employer to be sure that your employee works no more than 12 hours and follows through taking all necessary breaks for meals and time off.

An employer with a live-in domestic situation has the advantage of a built-in babysitter since most live-in domestics stay on the premises in the evenings. You may ask your domestic to put the children to bed and/or keep an eye on them when they are sleeping. If the extra time is over and above the number of hours you agreed on, then you should compensate her extra for babysitting.

Be sensitive to the issue of potentially overworking your live-in domestic. Accordingly, you will be able to keep your live-in employee happy. Never have your employee work more than a 12-hour shift, unless she/he agrees and you are paying overtime. Be sure that the necessary meal and other breaks are being taken. If you need that extra time during the day and the employee is in agreement, then you should calculate the salary accordingly. Be clear in the beginning as to the hours and how many nights you might need her for extra babysitting. If you have parties and require her to work the party, be sure that she takes an extra break in

One of the main reasons more and more domestics do not want to work as a live-in is because of the long hours that employers demand without taking into consideration overtime.

Be sensitive to the issue of potentially overworking your "live-in" domestic.

the day so that she will not be exhausted in the evening. An extra bonus for working hard at a party should also be considered.

Remember: Do not take advantage of your live-in employee. Calculate her schedule at no more than a 12-hour day with the necessary breaks. Pay her extra for anything above and beyond your set schedule. If you burn out your live-in, you will lose your employee before you know it.

Scheduling a Live-out Domestic: Live-out domestics normally ONLY like to work Monday to Friday during daytime hours and are not as flexible with their evenings. However, you *can* find live-out domestics who are willing to work any schedule, including weekends. Remember, a normal workday for a live-out is anywhere from 8-10 hours. Beyond a 10-hour day, there are fewer prospective live-out applicants.

You can *find live-out domestics who are willing to work any schedule.*

In light of the above discussion, sit down and think about your day and when you need your employee the most. You may need someone to come early and help you with the children so that you can get out the door to your workplace. If another parent in the household cannot help you handle the children in the early morning, then you have no choice but to hire a person who will arrive as early as 7:00 or 7:30 AM. Hopefully, you can somehow get home at a decent hour so the domestic's day is not running longer than 10 hours. Decide on how many hours you absolutely need. Take into consideration your budget and whether you should hire a live-in to accommodate a longer schedule.

Live-outs charge by the hour and will want to be paid by the clock. Design the schedule for your live-out indicating when you would most need her services. Calculate the hourly wage based on what the going rate is for a live-out and the amount of work she is required to do. It may be harder to find someone to work a longer shift. However, there are live-out domestics who would welcome the extra pay. Try to find what you need the most first. If you find that there are fewer people available who are interested in the schedule, then you may need to alter it somewhat. As long as you are paying fairly and complying with the current labor laws, then there is a person out there for every job.

Here are the various workweek hourly schedules for live-out domestics in order of employee preference:

Most domestics prefer working an 8-hour day (40-hour week) with the following schedules:

- 1st Choice
  - 8:00 AM - 4:00 PM
  - 8:30 AM - 4:30 PM
  - 9:00 AM - 5:00 PM

- 2nd Choice
  - 7:00 AM - 3:00 PM
  - 10:00 AM - 6:00 PM
  - 12:00 PM - 8:00 PM

For those of you who are working parents and need more than a 40-hour week to cover getting to and from work, then you may need to hire a person to work 45 hours, 9 hours per day as follows:

- 1st Choice
  - 8:00 AM - 5:00 PM
  - 8:30 AM - 5:30 PM
  - 7:30 AM - 4:30 PM

- 2nd Choice
  - 9:00 AM - 6:00 PM
  - 10:00 AM - 7:00 PM
  - 11:00 AM - 8:00 PM

An employer commonly requests a schedule that requires 10 hours (50-hour week). While a 10-hour day totaling a 50-hour week is difficult for many domestics who may have their own family obligations, it is commonly worked with schedules as follows:

WHERE DO I BEGIN?

- 1st Choice
  8:00 AM - 6:00 PM

- 2nd Choice
  7:00 AM - 5:00 PM

- 3rd Choice
  9:00AM - 7:00 PM
  10:00AM - 8:00 PM

Think carefully about the schedule you absolutely require. Remember that anything over and above a 40-hour workweek is considered overtime according to the labor code in many states. (Be sure to check the labor code in your state regarding this issue) If you need a 50- to 60-hour workweek, you may be better off with hiring a live-in.

Remember that anything over and above a 40-hour workweek is considered overtime according to the the labor code in many states.

Chapter Two

CHOOSING THE RIGHT DOMESTIC FOR ME

CHOOSING THE RIGHT DOMESTIC FOR ME

ADVANTAGES AND DISADVANTAGES TO HIRING A
LIVE-IN OR LIVE-OUT

The very first question that you will ask yourself and your family is, "Should we hire a live-in or live-out domestic?" The decision is not an easy one, unless, of course, you do not have the room for a live-in, in which case you will have no choice. Many people try live-in help and hate it, while others could not survive without it. We have already discussed the cost and schedule differences. Let's review some of the advantages and disadvantages to having a domestic work on a live-in versus live-out basis.

Advantages to a Live-in

The most obvious advantage to hiring a live-in is that a live-in is there 24 hours a day until it is time to leave the premises at the end of the workday when the workweek has ended. If you schedule this person to work Tuesday morning until Sunday morning, then you can take full advantage of having a "date night" both on a Friday AND Saturday. So a live-in virtually is there the whole time. She/he may live-in 5, 6 or 7 days, and may be available to you at all times during the workweek. You also have the advantage of going out spontaneously during the set hours that your live-in is scheduled to work. Depending on the arrangement you make with your live-in, you may never need to seek another person to do extra babysitting. This is an important advantage for most employers. *NOT ONLY do you have a weeklong employee, you have a live-in babysitter to facilitate a spontaneous and/or planned social life.*

For those new mothers who have a tough time with getting up at night to feed the baby, you may welcome a live-in there to assist with night feedings. Remember, however, you will need to let your nanny sleep as well and alter feeding shifts so that she gets her rest at some point along with you. For parents who have to leave very early in the morning to get to work, another advantage to having a live-in is that the domestic is in your home ready to work as early as 6 AM. You need not worry every morning about whether or not she will arrive daily at your home on time. Also, with a live-in, there is always an extra pair of hands to help during

NOT ONLY do you have a weeklong employee, you have a live-in babysitter to facilitate a spontaneous and/or planned social life.

those difficult hours of the day and early evening when most live-outs are not there. It is most felt during the so-called "witching hour" from 5:00 PM to 8:00 PM.

Additionally, a live-in can get closer to the family by spending more personal time with family members. Children in particular sometimes get very attached to live-in domestics who are there to bathe them, read a story and put them down to sleep each night.

If you have pets and like to travel, but find it difficult to leave because there is no one to care for those little darlings who are often like children to you, you will welcome a live-in who can guard the house and be there at all times with your pets.

If you have more than one child and especially if they are under 5 years of age, the more likely choice for you during the early years of their lives will be to have live-in assistance.

Disadvantages to a Live-in

The down side to having a live-in is *just that* – this person will be living with you 24 hours per day and in some cases, 7 days per week. *Your privacy will be invaded.* Your house is not just your home. Your personal life may be exposed, and you may not like the fact that you can't walk around "half naked." Although you can deal with this "invasion of privacy" by having certain rules that would apply, your options are limited.

For example, you can instruct your live-in domestic to go to her room after dinner so that you and your family have privacy. You may ask her to eat separately so that your family eats privately together. You may warn your live-in domestic to knock before entering a room. However, overall, you must understand that this domestic is under your roof and your personal life is exposed. When you have private conversations and potential family arguments, a live-in domestic will be privy to such a thing. In my experience, I have found that men, in particular, do not like the idea of hiring a live-in. Yet, when they realize how much freedom there is with a live-in that will help with dishes after dinner and be available to baby-sit on a whim, they usually come around and decide a live-in is best. Therefore, if you relish your privacy, you will detest the idea of a live-in, but if you have an active household, tough work schedule and busy social life, you will love having a live-in.

Along with the concept of losing your privacy is the other closely related issue of *overstepping boundaries*. It is easier for this to occur in a live-in situation with both the employer and the employee due to the fact that the employee is there 24/7 or 24/5. There is just so much time spent together during off and on hours that sometimes the employee tends to feel like a family member and the employer tends to feel obligated to treat the employee like a family member. Well, we all know what happens with family members. They tend to tell us their opinions and their problems and expect us to be there for them 100% of the time. This might be OK when it's your mother or brother, but when it comes from a person who is, no matter what, still an employee, you may tend to resent the familiarity over time. Some of you reading this may have had nothing but terrific experiences with live-in employees who have ultimately become like wonderful family members. May you never know what it is like to have an employee who thinks and acts as though she deserves special entitlements, meddles into your private affairs and/or tries to be your best friend. It will be up to you to be sure that boundaries are not crossed, and that you maintain a professional relationship.

Another possible disadvantage to having a live-in is dependent on the size and configuration of your home. If you have a small house and/or do not have separate quarters, *the house can get a bit crowded*. A shared bathroom or bedroom could upset someone in the family. Most domestics would not be happy without a private room and bath. A household that is spacious, where the premises have private, separate quarters, will make it easier on everyone but can still feel a bit crowded if you yearn for privacy. Lack of space and privacy can definitely cause problems and ultimately lead the live-in domestic to soon become a live-out.

The last point that is most significant when describing the disadvantages to hiring a live-in is that you *may not encounter the same longevity* with a live-in as

*The greatest
turnover in
domestic jobs has
always been when
live-in help
is hired.*

you might with a live-out. The greatest turnover in domestic jobs has always been when live-in help is hired. Many domestics who work as live-ins become "burned out" from the extensive hours and extra workload that seem to come with the territory. Employers are less likely to observe the need for down time with the live-in employees. The result is no surprise. No matter how wonderful the family thinks they have treated the live-in employee, the fact remains that there is always more work and less time off in a live-in situation, resulting in the employee counting the days to escape the prison and work like any other normal employee on a "live-out" basis. Whether they have been terminated or simply decide to quit on their own accord, there is a higher percentage of change when it comes to live-in help.

Advantages to a Live-out

A live-out arrives when you need her/him to work, and leaves at the end of the work day. Privacy is not an issue.

A live-out normally does not eat 3 meals per day at your home, use your utilities, or require a car or other special amenities. Extra financial costs are limited. A live-out doesn't spend as much time at your house or with you; hence, there is less opportunity for personality clashes and overstepping boundaries. It is easier to maintain a professional employer/employee relationship.

A live-out gets paid an hourly rate calculated on a daily basis. It is a simple, straightforward calculation. *There is less confusion regarding hours, wages and scheduling.* A live-out has a set schedule that is usually kept consistently.

Live-out employees tend to last longer at their jobs and are happier since they have the ability to enjoy their own families and private lives at the end of the work day.

Another advantage to hiring live-out help as opposed to live-in help is something that is normally not observed until you begin the interview process and work with the employee. Often, but not always, live-out domestics will have reached *a higher level of qualifications.* As we all know, domestics are usually immigrants. They have come to the United States to find a better life for themselves. Their English skills may not be good, and education in their field of study may not be transferable. The line of work they can do as a domestic may require no education, sometimes only some English, and as little as one year of work experience. Often due to not having a place to live or the ability to drive and purchase a car, these domestics will first take live-in positions with lower salaries. Once they have gained experience and elevated their level of English, they usually change from a live-in to a live-out position. My point here is that live-out domestics very often have gained most of their experience through the live-in positions and the *majority* of your high-end qualified domestics will be those who ultimately work as live-outs. As in everything, there are always exceptions. You will also find wonderful experienced domestics who simply have always preferred to work as live-ins. However, today finding one who is very experienced, skilled as a driver, speaks excellent English, and is content to work as a live-in is truly rare. Unfortunately, the ratio of live-in versus live-out employees is changing dramatically. Nine out of ten domestic employees prefer to work as a live-out.

There are no disadvantages to hiring a live-out other than not getting the number of hours and availability that a live-in provides.

Let's move on to another commonly asked question when choosing a domestic.

DO I NEED A DRIVER?

A domestic who drives can cost more, but is very useful. If you are a working mom or just a very busy mom and cannot make yourself available to drive your children and/or complete all those tedious errands, it will be a blessing to have a driver. If you have small children who will soon start pre-school while there is a baby at home, you may want a driver to help you so that you do not have to take the baby everywhere. You may also want a driver before your child starts school in order to take your child to doctor appointments, play dates, and other activities. You may want the domestic to do your marketing for you, or simply be able to drive in the event of an emergency. Many new mothers will mention that they would NEVER have the Nanny or Housekeeper take their new baby or child in a

A domestic who drives can cost more, but is very useful.

CHOOSING THE RIGHT DOMESTIC FOR ME

car. This is an understandable concern and fear for all mothers and fathers. If someone is not a good driver, you would want to be extremely cautious about putting your child in this person's car, whether it be your employee, your relative, neighbor or friend.

The idea here is to review an applicant's current driving record to help verify whether or not the person is a good driver, and go out test driving to be sure. You may want to do this several times prior to allowing this person to drive your child. You obviously want the caretaker to have the same sense of responsibility as you when any child is in the car. Without a doubt, there are childcare providers out there who are excellent drivers. There may be childcare providers who are better drivers than their employers. However, until you check them out, you really cannot tell anything about their driving ability. Even then, there are no guarantees that this driver will be able to avoid an accident anymore than you can. It is just another risk we must take to accommodate our needs.

If you do decide to hire a person who drives, take the necessary precautions and you might increase your child's safety. Consider the following:

Do everything in your power to lessen the risk when hiring a driver.

- Check for a valid driver's license
- Check driving record for violations and accidents
- Check amount of experience driving in the U.S.
- Check insurance coverage
- Check applicant's vehicle for safety
- Do several driving test runs
- Map out the various destinations with safe routes

If you do all of the above, you have done everything in your power to lessen the risk when hiring a driver.

DO I NEED PART-TIME OR FULL-TIME HELP?

To answer this question, you must think about how much assistance you

CHOOSING THE RIGHT DOMESTIC FOR ME

require to accommodate your needs and keep you stress-free. For those of you who are planning to be stay-at-home mothers or fathers, you may only need a few hours per day or perhaps two to three full days per week. This decision will come down to economics and personal needs. One way of figuring out your needs might be to try a person out a few days per week to see if that appears to give you sufficient help and/or time for yourself. As long as you mention this to your prospective part-time employee, this will give you a good opportunity to test the situation out.

On the other hand, for those of you who are working mothers and fathers, the answer is clear. You obviously need full-time help. The question now is how many hours in the day you need. Most parents will need the extra time in the morning to get to work and to return back home. It would be ideal to have a parent work a schedule so that one parent can be home with the children earlier in the morning. It is always a shame to see a family where both parents are working very long days and rarely home to be with the children. We all understand what it takes to survive in this world. Very often, parents have no other choice but to work very long hours. Choosing between work and home is only a problem for those who have the choice. If there is a choice to be made, my best and most sincere advice is that you would opt to **work less, make a little less, but spend a little more time with your family.**

Basically, without offending all of you very bright, hard-working parents who have struggled through so many years of education and/or years of work to get where you are today professionally, I would like to voice some further opinions on the subject of scheduling your work day. When you make the sound decision to have a baby, it is a bigger undertaking than you ever imagined before. The early years are the most crucial in any human being's life. The nurturing, loving bond that a mother or father can give a child can never be matched by any Nanny, no matter how good the Nanny appears. This period in your child's life comes and goes in a blink of an eye. If you can financially afford to take a break from work the first year or so, do it. If you *must* work, then at least limit your day to part-time or at least no more than a normal 8-hour day so that you can spend more time with your child. If your boss can't accept this arrangement, then find another boss. If your budget can't accept this arrangement, then cut something out that is less important. If your career can't accept this arrangement, then wait to have children for a time when you can put as much effort into child rearing as into your career. You will miss out on so much if you don't.

WHAT TYPE OF DOMESTIC IS MOST SUITABLE FOR MY HOUSEHOLD?

Now you know the various domestic job titles, schedules, salaries and responsibilities. You also know the advantages and disadvantages to hiring live-in and live-out help. Let's try to pull this all together and see which scenario works best for you. You will want to answer the question: *"What type of help should I hire to fulfill my needs within my budget, ensuring my children are not neglected and my household runs smoothly and efficiently?"* Here are a few scenarios. See which one might relate to your life.

Scenario 1 - You are a princess and have money to burn. You live in a large, luxurious home of at least 8,000 square feet. You have either a new baby or several children at home. You may or may not have to work, but one thing you do have is a very busy social life.

Under these circumstances, you need a staff. First, you should hire a Nanny, who may or may not do light housekeeping, primarily to care for the baby and/or other small children. In addition, you need (a) separate Housekeeper(s) who strictly cleans and who works 3 to 5 days per week, depending on the size of your home. If you are a real live princess, you probably are not well-versed in the kitchen and/or do not have time to waste doing the marketing and cooking. You may want to a hire a Chef or have your Housekeeper be a "Housekeeper/Cook." You will probably want your Nanny to live-in so that you can enjoy your busy social schedule. The Housekeeper, Chef or Housekeeper/Cook does not have to live-in. However, if you have two separate rooms for help, you may prefer that all your help lives in, making them available at all times. If you only have one room

What type of help should I hire to fulfill my needs within my budget, ensuring my children are not neglected and my household runs smoothly and efficiently?

for live-in help, choose the Nanny to be your live-in and have the the other staff members work as live-outs. You may also want to have a House Manager to run the house and staff.

You may ask yourself, why couldn't I just hire a full-charge Housekeeper/Nanny/Cook? Well, you probably could. But considering the size of your home, your social schedule, and *the amount of attention needed to care for your family,* your *one* domestic would probably only stay until she drops dead in your very large foyer.

Scenario 2 – You are on a strict budget. You live in a medium-sized home (approximately 2,500 to 4,500 square feet) and have one child under 5, or perhaps you are expecting another. The good news is that you do not have to work. Therefore, there is a non-working mother or father at home who participates in the care of the children. You want to maximize your money because you have a limited budget since you are a one-income family. You do not want to bother with the cleaning and need help with the childcare.

You would be best in finding a full-charge Housekeeper/Nanny who is capable and experienced in both areas, but who is flexible to work in either capacity as you require. The key here is that you are there to assist. You may want her to clean more on one given day, while you spend more time with the children, or you may need her the entire time with the kids, if your schedule that week calls you away too often. This domestic may still be better in one area than the other, but what is important is that she has performed both responsibilities in previous jobs and is capable in both areas. She may be paid slightly more for doing both jobs, especially if she cooks and drives. Full-charge means this domestic can do anything from cooking, cleaning, driving, marketing, and errands to caring for children of any age. This would be the most economic route for you, and you can choose how many days to hire this domestic to work, depending on your budget.

Whether you choose live-in or live-out truly depends on you. It is a personal choice. Since you are a stay-at-home mom, the likelihood is that you do not need a live-in unless you have several children mostly under the age of 5 and you need a lot of help in the early hours and late evening.

Scenario 3 – You are a family in which both parents work a somewhat long day. You must leave in the morning early and do not get home until after 6:00 PM. Your child is either an infant/toddler who needs tremendous care, or maybe even a school age child needing to be picked up from school, driven to sports activities, and helped with homework. You live in a normal-size home with room for a live-in. What you need depends partly on your budget, the age of your child and what is most important to you. If the child is small, hire a live-in Nanny/Light Housekeeper. If the child is older and in school, hire a live-out Housekeeper/Nanny who gets them from school and watches them until you get home. This Housekeeper/Nanny could be an afternoon part-time worker spending a few hours each day cleaning and the rest of the time doing the various activities with the child. Or, if you need to save money, you might consider an afternoon Nanny who comes when it is time to pick up the child from school and stays with him or her until you get home. This would be the most economical.

As mentioned earlier, it is rare to find someone who is a professional cleaner *and* an excellent Nanny. A wonderful Nanny who loves to take special care of children, playing with them, reading to them, etc., will hardly want to take the necessary time to do the heavy cleaning. Conversely, an excellent cleaner who loves to see the house sparkle will hardly like to make it messy while playing with the children. If you need sole devotion to the baby or children, and you would also like your house to be spotless, then hire a Nanny or Nanny/Light Housekeeper and hire a separate housekeeper to come in as many times as you can afford.

With respect to live-in versus live-out, if both parents work very long hours because your careers are terribly demanding, then you would be better off with a live-in person who can stay with you and work those late nights when you get home from work exhausted or simply need a break to go out for the evening. Otherwise, find a live-out who can work a schedule to accommodate you.

Scenario 4 – You are a mother of a new baby. You have decided to quit your career to have this baby, and you want to be the integral part of this baby's life. You

CHOOSING THE RIGHT DOMESTIC FOR ME

are truly blessed because you can afford to do this, or you are making the necessary financial sacrifices. However, you find yourself needing a little break from time to time so that you can go to lunch with a friend or even just get some errands done that are difficult to do with a child. You have a medium-sized home that is manageable for the most part; however, you would like to have someone do the heavy cleaning.

The best bet for you would be to hire a part-time live-out person to come perhaps one to three days per week. A good choice for you would be to hire a Nanny/Light Housekeeper to work either one day per week or more. Perhaps, Mondays, Wednesdays, and Fridays or Tuesdays and Thursdays would be sufficient. You might then want someone to come and clean one day per week. If you hire a Nanny/Housekeeper, you could have the domestic work as a Nanny on the days you need to go out of the house and then hire her as a Housekeeper one day per week where she is solely devoting her time to cleaning. If she is excellent at both functions, then you have it made, since it is always preferable to have one person capable and willing to do it all.

When trying to select the right domestic for you consider the following:

- What is your budget?
- How many children are present?
- How large is your home?
- How busy is your social life?
- What is your work schedule?
- Is there a stay-at-home parent?
- How much work can you give one person?
- Is the house cleaning compromising the safety and care of your child?
- Are the childcare needs leaving little time to clean?
- Are you able to relieve the domestic, enabling her to do the childcare and cleaning separately?

CHOOSING THE RIGHT DOMESTIC FOR ME

- Who will do the marketing and errands?
- Do you need assistance with cooking?
- Do you need a person who drives?
- How much driving is required?
- Do you need a live-in or a live-out?
- Do you need 5-day or 7-day help?
- Do you need part-time or full-time help?

This criteria will assist you in putting together the job description for choosing the right domestic for you and your household.

Chapter Three

WHEN AND WHERE TO FIND MY DOMESTIC

WHEN DO I NEED TO BEGIN MY SEARCH?

The appropriate time to begin your search to find a suitable domestic varies depending on the method you use. If you are doing this on your own, without an agency, then you will need more lead time to find the right person. There is no telling how long it will take when you do the search on your own. You may get lucky right away, or it may take you months.

If you choose to use an agency, the preference would be to inform the agency of your needs and have a work order in place anywhere from one to four (1-4) weeks prior to the hire date. However, if it was an emergency and you needed an agency to find you someone immediately, you could call an agency and be prepared to meet applicants right away. That is the beauty of utilizing an agency. An established agency will have a good pool of personnel ready to go on interviews and be ready to work immediately.

One thing you do not want to do is begin interviewing applicants too far in advance from the start date. Most of the domestic workers need to begin work soon and will not want to wait more than 4 weeks to start a job. If you interview many people and find someone you want, but cannot hire that person for at least 2 months, you may lose that person to another job that starts sooner. Try to limit the window of time for interviewing to no earlier than 4 weeks prior to the start date. Otherwise, you may be wasting a lot of time.

WHAT ARE MY RESOURCES FOR FINDING HELP?

There are various methods to approach the search. All methods are time-consuming and require patience and due diligence. Some are practically free, while others can be quite costly.

Word of Mouth

Word of mouth is always a great way to find someone and certainly the most economical and can be the most reassuring. This is usually the first way one tries to find one's help. However, keep in mind that you still need to perform the required due diligence that entails all the background checks on anyone you hire.

There are various methods to approach the search. All methods are time-consuming and require patience and due diligence.

WHEN AND WHERE TO FIND MY DOMESTIC

Someone you know very well may highly recommend a person. However, the referrer possibly may not have completed the necessary background investigation on this person. There could be some information about this applicant that your friend, neighbor or relative never knew or thought about checking. Background checks can cost up to $100.00 for a full credit, driving record, Social Security Verification and Criminal Report. (Chapter 6 will provide more detail regarding background checks.)

Check the person out thoroughly, consider the person who gives the referral and try the candidate for a day up to one week before making a sound judgment.

The advantages of finding someone through "word of mouth" are you won't be paying the fee to an agency and/or spending the time and trouble finding an employee through an ad. Another advantage is if a friend is referring someone who was a former employee, you will most likely get an honest reference from this person. Keep in mind, however, that it is possible that not everyone holds the same standards as you. A measurement of excellence by one person could be simply mediocre to another. (This is important to keep in mind when checking references.) If you try a person out who has been referred by a good friend and find that this employee was not what you expected, you will find it difficult telling your friend what a mistake it was hiring her. This could create a sore spot in the friendship. You might want to consider how your friend keeps and runs his/her household before hiring his/her former employee.

Do as you would with any employee, no matter what the source may be- check the person out thoroughly, consider the person who gives the referral, and try the candidate for a day up to one week before making a sound judgment.

Placing an Ad in a Local Newspaper

If you try to do this on your own, running an ad will cost you anywhere from $25 to $100 depending on the newspaper you choose, the length of your ad and the number of days you run it. You should strive to be very descriptive about the position in your ad to avoid calls from unqualified people. The major paper for your city will provide you with various regional locations so that your ad is run in your part of town. Local papers will be less expensive but may not have the widespread readership. Since many immigrants come to this country seeking domestic positions, you might want to place your ad in certain newspapers generally read by immigrants. For example, the majority of Nannies in the Los Angeles area are Hispanic. Accordingly, you might check out the Spanish speaking papers like *La Opinion* or *El Informador*.

Sunday is absolutely the best day in the week to run an ad. You may want a résumé before you make any calls. Therefore provide in your ad a fax number or e-mail address with a request for résumés only. Or, you might ask for the résumé to be sent to a P.O. Box. The individuals who will take the time to put their résumé together with their entire job experience and qualifications are usually very professional employees. Once you review the résumés, you can begin making your calls and screening these potential applicants by telephone first. This will narrow your choices and save you time.

Posting an Ad at a Local College

Many college students who are studying child development, psychology, sociology and other related subjects would like to work as a Babysitter/Nanny as it fits with their school schedule. You may find someone who will be available afternoons, mornings, evenings or weekends. You may or may not get a college student to do your housekeeping, but many are willing to do light housekeeping while working as babysitters, tutors and drivers. College students are as expensive as domestics who do this on a regular basis. Sometimes they may even request more money. However, the standard salaries should apply, unless, of course, they are also tutoring.

The only caveat to using a student is that their schedules will change after each semester or quarter, in which case, if you want to keep the same student, you may need to request that they take classes that correspond to your needs. If you don't work and can be flexible, then this won't present a problem. Otherwise, you will be searching again. Most colleges will not charge you to put an ad in their local school paper. They may, however, ask for a small donation. You could also put your ad on a job placement board that is available at the various schools.

An example of an ad might look like this:

Nanny/Light Housekeeper needed for Live-in position Monday to

Friday for family w/ 2 children in Beverly Hills. Must have 3-5 years experience w/ newborns and toddlers, references, speak excellent English, drive w/car, Salary $600/week. Send résumé via fax (818) 784-3213.

Internet

Another resource for finding prospective applicants is **www.craigslist.org.** Craigslist has job listings for all types of employment.

Local Hospitals

If you are looking for a Baby Nurse or Doula or a Certified Nurse Assistant, maternity departments in certain hospitals will provide you with a list of those they recommend. Also, some hospitals will offer four hours of complimentary doula services for their maternity patients.

Local Religious Institutions and Women's Organizations

Certain institutions and organizations can be a good networking source. They may have a job placement board where you could leave your information. You may even try to speak with the head of the religious institution or organization to discuss your job opening and inquire if they might be helpful in getting the word out.

Being a Host Family for an Au Pair

If you are looking for a Nanny, another way to find one would be to become a "host family" for an Au Pair. An Au Pair is an international Nanny who comes to this country with some very specific training and on the job experience. They are usually women anywhere from 18 – 26 years of age. There are companies that strictly place Au Pairs from countries all over the world. An example of one such company that is a wonderful source for this is Cultural Care Au Pair, a division of EF Au Pair. The entire program costs approximately $6,000.00 for the placement. There is a non-refundable registration fee of $250.00 to apply to be a host family. This includes the following: recruitment, screening and preparation of your Au Pair by experienced staff; your Au Pair's training at the Cultural Care Au Pair school; host family and Au Pair orientations; international airfare and the visa paperwork; a full year of medical and travel insurance; training materials; and year-long support from the Cultural Care office staff and a local childcare coordinator. You must pay a weekly stipend directly to the Au Pair for 52 weeks, which includes two weeks of paid vacation. The Department of Labor sets the weekly stipend. The amount is determined by using a formula based on the federal minimum wage. Any increase in the minimum wage will result in an increase in the stipend. Since tax laws are different in every state, you would need to consult a tax professional regarding filing requirements. In addition, federal regulations require you to provide a $500 educational allowance per Au Pair to enable your Au Pair to attend post-secondary educational courses during the program year. The commitment is for one year.

An Au Pair can provide a very interesting international influence in your household.

An Au Pair can provide a very interesting international influence in your household. Although the Au Pair must speak fairly good English, she will also be fluent in her native language. You may choose someone from a particular country who can speak her native language with your child.

Enlisting an Agency

You may ultimately prefer going through an agency that will do the search and necessary background checks on each applicant. There are fees associated with enlisting an agency. These will vary anywhere from 50% of one month's gross salary all the way up to 18% of the annual gross salary. Along with the fee comes a replacement guarantee 30 days up to 12 months.

Some people are adverse to utilizing an agency because they think they have been taken by an agency for their money when an employee does not work out properly. Truth be known, there are many agencies that don't deserve to be in business. Cheating, lying and manipulating a situation so as to receive a fee has no place in any business. Certainly there is plenty of that going on in *all types of businesses* in the world, not just domestic agencies. If you work with a top agency that has good business ethics, great follow-through, due diligence on every applicant presented, and is there for you if any problems occur, it can make finding your domestic a positive experience. So now that I have suggested to you

WHEN AND WHERE TO FIND MY DOMESTIC

How will you know which agencies are efficient?

that there are reputable agencies out there, let me help you to choose a good one.

Choosing a Good Agency

There are many agencies dying to have your business, many of which you probably will not want to know, and many of which you will find quite efficient. The question is, how will you know the difference without finding out the hard way? Ideally, if a friend of yours has utilized the agency and had a good experience, you may find that comforting and choose to call that agency based on this referral. Otherwise, you can find the various agencies listed on the Internet or in your local yellow pages. Agencies also advertise in the newspaper and in various family magazines.

The first thing you will want to know is how long the agency has been in business. If an agency is new, it is uncertain if it will remain in business for the duration of the replacement guarantee that you obtain from them. New agencies, while they may be good, might not have the pool of people that you will want to see. Remember that agencies are no longer regulated and do not need to be licensed. If an agency tells you that they are licensed, you are already starting with an agency that is not telling you the truth.

Ask the agency how they find their people. Do they advertise and/or is it through word of mouth, referrals and other networking methods? Most agencies in business a long time do not need to advertise for employees or employers because their pool of people is quite extensive as a result of many years of networking. Next, ask the agency what their requirements are for accepting applicants. Do they have a set of criteria necessary for placement?

Ask the agency what their requirements are for accepting applicants.

The criteria for screening should include the following:

- Applicants must be legal to work in this country

- Work experience should be minimum of 2 - 5 years

- English should be sufficient to communicate

- Applicants must have references that are reachable

- Applicants have reference letters

- Applicants must agree to any background checks

- Drivers should hold a valid driver's license

- Drivers have evidence of car insurance

- CPR/Infant CPR/First Aid is required

- Nannies can be registered with *Trustline*

If they do not mention some of these factors, you may question their screening process and approach for placing personnel.

The next question to ask is ***does the agency have an office*** where you can come and meet the counselor and see the operation? You may question whether the agency meets each and every applicant who is in search of employment.

Does the agency check references and are you given the references so you may check them as well? Certainly, this is the top priority for any prospective employer. If the agency does check references, you should also check them. If they do not allow you to check the same references, then you should be suspicious. Ask how the agency checks the references. Do they keep a sheet with questions for each reference detailing the answers? Does the agency, if asked, provide you copies of this reference check for your review?

Be sure to call each reference that is provided. Sometimes, a reference will not be honest with the agency and will be more frank with a prospective employer. An agency is sometimes surprised by the fact that the response given to a client for a reference on an applicant conflicts with the one provided to the agency. It could be that the previous employer providing a reference may feel concerned about the information being given to the agency since it might lead to the agency's tossing the applicant's file. If the bad reference check is revealed to the applicant, it might be of concern to the previous employer. By law, you cannot sabotage one's ability to get a job by giving a bad reference. However, you must verify employment; simply state the dates that the employee worked and duties performed. There is a

WHEN AND WHERE TO FIND MY DOMESTIC

limit to what one can say when providing a less-than-glowing reference. The key here is that if a previous employer is vague and not willing to provide a lengthy, wonderful reference, you immediately can surmise that there must have been a problem. Sometimes, the reference provider will explain the problem "in confidence" and tell you that "apart from that, the employee was terrific." This is the optimum situation when speaking to a reference. You want to hear everything and hope that the reference will be completely honest so that you can make a good decision. This is why it is very important that you call the references yourself.

Another question to ask the agency is **do they investigate what might appear to be a phony or bad reference?** A very high percentage of references are phony. It is not difficult to tell whether a reference is real or not; a skilled and trained consultant at an agency should know just how to do this. For example, sometimes a reference will seem like it could be the applicant's relative or friend. In some cases, the applicant indeed worked for a relative. Or, the reference could be completely made up. Sometimes the applicant will say that the previous reference moved and is not reachable. If you can get the complete information on this reference, you will sometimes be able to track this reference down, only to find out that the reference is still in town but simply not willing to give the applicant a good recommendation. Find out the reasons why the previous employer won't provide a reference. Note: many good employees have been loyal to a family for many years, only to find themselves unemployed and without a reference because of some "personality issue." People can get "burned out" on each other and need a change. However, this should not mean that the employee should be left with an unjust recommendation or no recommendation at all.

When you work with an agency, the most important issue is that you are receiving all the facts and that the agency is completely honest with you.

Does the agency do background checks on the applicants? These background checks can include the following:

- Criminal checks for misdemeanors and felonies
- Social Security verification

> *A very high percentage of references are phony. It is not difficult to tell whether a reference is real or not.*

- Credit history
- Driving check
- Personal history check

In order to receive these reports, the agency must get approval from the applicant to do so. This approval is a "Disclosure and Release Authorization" in order to perform a consumer report on an individual. Without this authorization, signed by the applicant, you cannot get a random consumer report on anyone for employment purposes. This discussion is reviewed in greater detail in Chapter 5. These reports are costly and sometimes the prospective employer assumes the cost. However, most agencies cover the cost of these reports. The agency might provide the prospective employer these reports subject to hiring an applicant. Be sure to ask, once these reports are completed, if you can receive copies. (Keep in mind that the employee must also be able to receive a copy of whatever report was performed on your behalf.)

In order to receive these reports, the agency must get approval from the applicant to do so.

Does the agency comply with the I-9 regulation? The I-9 Employment Eligibility Verification form is generated by the **U.S. Department of Justice, Immigration and Naturalization** and requires that every employer obtain copies of all the necessary identification. The employee, employer and/or agency who has verified the identification of the applicant signs this form. It is kept on file in the agency and/or the employer's residence. Necessary documentation for this:

- California driver's license
- Social Security card
- Work Permit, Resident Card, citizenship, or U.S. passport
- State identification card.

Other documentation that agencies may require includes the following:

- Photo of applicant
- CPR card
- Medical test results

- Letters of reference
- Current DMV driving report
- Auto insurance
- Set of fingerprints for *Trustline* registration

In California, it is mandatory that all child care providers are registered with Trustline.

Does the agency register their Nannies with* Trustline?** Certain states make it mandatory for you to register your Nanny with *Trustline*. In California, it is mandatory that all child care providers are registered with *Trustline*. *Trustline* was created by the California Legislature to offer parents, employment agencies, childcare resource and referral programs, and child care providers access to a background check conducted by the **California Department of Social Services (CDSS).** This includes checks of the **Criminal History System and Child Abuse Central Index (CACI)** at the **California Department of Justice (DOJ)** and a check of **Federal Bureau of Investigation (FBI)** records. The ***Trustline Registry is maintained by CDSS and may be checked through the **California Child Care Resource and Referral Network** by calling 1-800-822-8490.

The *Trustline* Registry is made up of childcare providers who have submitted an application to CDSS along with a set of their fingerprints to the Department of Justice background clearance process. Individuals listed on Trustline do not have 1) disqualifying criminal convictions listed on the Criminal History System; 2) substantiated reports of child abuse listed on the CACI; and 3) disqualifying criminal convictions listed on the FBI criminal history system. All reports of child abuse found in the CACI will be confirmed with local child protective agencies before they are used to evaluate a *Trustline* applicant.

Trustline is for parents who use in-home and license-exempt childcare providers, employment agencies, in-home educators and in-home counselors. An in-home childcare provider provides care in the child's home (i.e., Babysitters, Nannies, and Au Pairs). A license-exempt childcare provider is an individual who provides childcare in his or her own home and is not required to be licensed by CDSS. An employment agency (as described by CDSS) places individuals in home-based settings to care for children.

Does the agency tell you about payroll taxes? As will be mentioned in Chapter 5, domestic employees ARE NOT independent contractors. Therefore, under certain circumstances as described in the same chapter regarding your obligations under tax laws, you are required by law to file payroll taxes quarterly or annually on any qualifying domestic employee.

Does the agency provide you with a Contract for Placement Services? An agency that is professional will give you an agreement that stipulates for what service you are hiring (a complete job description), the fee you have paid for such a service, and the replacement guarantee being offered for such a fee. Both parties should sign the contract. This way you have *in writing* what you are hiring, paying and receiving as a replacement guarantee from the agency. You should also receive a résumé on the applicant, copies of letters of reference, and copies of identification and all other documentation for your records.

Will the agency provide you a trial period? There are many agencies that want you to pay for the employee being hired on or before the date the employee begins employment with you. In some instances, this is appropriate. If, in fact, an employee is hired several weeks prior to the "start date," you may need to sign the contract and pay the fee to secure the applicant. It is advisable to try to have a trial day or two prior to the long wait for the employee to begin working. This way, both parties have not waited this period of time only to find out on the first week of employment that things are not working out. This would be a great waste of time for you and the prospective employee. If you are hiring someone very shortly after having gone through the interview process, then you should squeeze in some "trial period" to solidify your belief that this employee is your best choice. An agency that is clearly interested in making a happy marriage should be amenable to this. The agency may still want you to sign their contract stipulating this "trial period" and its length while receiving your promise to pay the agency fee if you decide to hire the employee.

It is advisable to try to have a trial day or two prior to the long wait for the employee to begin working.

Let us assume that you want to hire someone who is currently working as a Nanny for someone else. This person would have to give notice and actually leave a place of employment to take the position you are offering. In this case, you most definitely would want a trial period of at least a day before the applicant leaves the old job. You could squeeze in the time by having the person work evenings or on the weekend. Once the trial time is completed to your satisfaction and the employee has been given the go-ahead to give notice to the previous employer, then you have offered this position to the prospective employee. It would be your responsibility as the employer to judge whether or not you had enough time to try out the prospective employee before asking her to leave her prior job for your position. It would clearly be an act of hire if you tried this employee and then requested that she provide notice to her prior employer. This employee now is counting on your job to begin at a given date. The agency at this point would require that you sign the contract for placement services and pay the fee. Ethically speaking, you are now bound to the employee and the agency.

> *Remember:* **Ask the agency what their policy is about a trial period prior to hiring an applicant. The agency might agree to a one-day trial period up to a one-week trial period. This shows that the agency is NOT just interested in getting their fee, but truly wants to help you find the right person for you and your family. Be sure that the applicant that you are hiring knows that there is a trial period and that ONLY if that trial period is completed to everyone's satisfaction will the applicant be hired.**

Visit the agency and have a private meeting with the owner to get a better sense of the quality of the agency and its personnel.

Having reviewed the above-mentioned, you may still question whether the agency is the one for you. Let us assume that the agency qualifies with all the criteria as mentioned, but somehow you are still uncertain that you made the right choice. If you need more reassurance, you may want to ask the agency for a referral list of clients to whom they have provided their service. Call a few of these clients and have a discussion regarding the service the agency provided. If there was a need for a replacement guarantee, how quickly did the agency respond? Did they send the same quality of people for a replacement as they did when the client first contracted? Another suggestion would be to visit the agency and have a private meeting with the owner to get a better sense of the quality of the agency and its personnel. Just as "chemistry" is important when hiring personnel, it is equally important when contracting with an agency. If, after all this, you are still uncomfortable with the idea of using that particular agency, then you had better move on to another one. If you find yourself still uncomfortable with the next agency, then it may well be that you just have a bad feeling about using an agency.

No doubt, there have been many abuses with employment agencies. There are those who choose to lie, cheat and basically do whatever it takes to make the placement. If you have been taken by one of these agencies, then you certainly have reasons to have trepidation over the process.

Let me simply say this: there are good and bad businesses in every line of work. You do not need to generalize that, as a result of one bad experience, each and every agency must be the same. You are approaching the process with very negative thoughts, and you will most likely fail in your outcome.

If you can see that previous bad experiences with agencies and/or household help do not necessarily mean all agencies and domestics are total nightmares, then your positive approach will bring about a positive outcome.

WHAT ARE THE FEES AND TERMS FOR AGENCIES?

Agencies will charge many different rates. A smaller operation may charge you as low as 50% of the first month's salary. This salary is calculated by taking the weekly salary and multiplying it by 52 weeks and dividing it by 12. You must then multiply this amount by the percentage charged, as in this case 50%. This is the accurate method of calculating the fee structure for any percentage of one month's salary all the way up to 100% of one month's salary. Some agencies may even ask the applicant to pay for the job they have acquired through the agency, lowering your fee. Other agencies who have been in business many years will charge anywhere from 10% to 18% of the gross annual salary. This means that you are taking the gross annual salary (before taxes) and multiplying it by the percentage charged.

All fees to the agency are usually paid in full when or before an employee begins working. Some agencies will give you a trial period ranging from one day up to one week and request the fee to be paid once the trial period is over. The fees range, depending on what type of domestic(s) you hire and the monthly and/or annual salary paid.

These fee structures will also provide a variety of replacement guarantees that range from 1 month to 12 months. The replacement guarantee promises to find you a replacement that meets the requirements for the original position within a specified period of time without any further fees. Most agencies will provide an unlimited number of replacements within the given replacement guarantee.

The replacement guarantee promises to find you a replacement that meets the requirements for the original placement within a specified period of time without any further fees.

If you are searching for a Nanny and would like the Nanny to be checked through *Trustline,* most agencies in certain states where it is required will register the Nanny subject to being hired. It costs $130 and takes up to 20 days to get results. This includes fingerprinting that must be done digitally. The agency may or may not include these costs as a part of their placement fee. Some agencies will pay for the fingerprinting ($87) and pass on to the client the fee ($43) to register the Nanny with *Trustline.* Other agencies will pass on to the client the full fee to fingerprint and register the Nanny, separate from the placement fee. Check with each agency to see how the costs for *Trustline* registration are handled. More detailed information about *Trustline* is found in Chapter 6.

Do not be alarmed by the wide differences in fees from agencies. You may be on a tight budget and prefer using an agency that is more economical. Keep in mind that this agency may or may not represent the person of your choice. It would be a better approach to check out the agency and its people before you concern yourself with the fee. Hiring an employee to care for your child and/or home is too important a decision to cut corners. If you find the choice candidate from a higher-charging agency, it may be well worth the higher fee.

Once again, keep in mind that no agency likes to have provided excellent to a client only to be left waiting week after week to receive payment on a contract. The agency does not like calling the client on this matter. By doing this, you leave the agency in a very bad state of mind, one that may remain in their memory when it comes to servicing you again. Once you have passed the trial period and have started the employee on a permanent basis, the contract is complete and the fee must be paid. If you are stalling to pay the agency because you still have some doubts, then remember that is why you have a "replacement guarantee" for any changes needed thereafter.

Remember: Fees can run anywhere from 50% of the employee's first month's salary (usually calculated on a 52 week per year basis) up to 18% of the gross annual salary. Some agencies will negotiate a flat rate for placement. Replacement guarantees are anywhere from 30 days to 12 months. A standard replacement guarantee is 90 days.

YOUR RELATIONSHIP WITH AN AGENCY

From an agency's perspective, it is always preferable that the client uses them exclusively. Certainly, any business owner that knows that you are only using his or her service would be very pleased. Clients will often choose to use several agencies simultaneously with the thought: "I want to meet as many people as possible, and by using several agencies I open up my choices and potentially expedite my search." This is all very true. Especially if you are in a hurry to find someone, you may need to do this if the one agency you normally use does not have a lot of personnel that meet your requirements at that time. The best answer to this question of whether or not you should use more than one agency is "yes." It is always to your advantage to do so. Although most agencies do not like it, they are accustomed to the practice. What is important for you to do, however, is to inform the agency that you are calling upon other agencies to assist you. This way, the agency knows what they are up against. It soothes the pain for the agency when you have to make that call telling them, "Thank you very much for all your hard work, but we have selected someone from another agency."

Once you have found the right agency for you, then your experience can be very pleasant. You will want to make every effort to maintain a good relationship. Here are a few suggestions for being ensured the best possible service:

WHEN AND WHERE TO FIND MY DOMESTIC

- Treat the agency as you would want them to treat you. Just because you had a previous bad experience with another agency, does not mean that the same thing will occur with the new one. Don't begin the relationship with a major chip on your shoulder. An agency will sense it immediately and misconstrue you as a difficult client with a major grudge and then choose not to work with you.

- Be honest with the agency and let them know if you are using more than one agency to make the search. There is no problem with doing this. What can be upsetting is if the agency is not aware of this fact and thinks you are exclusively searching through them.

- Call the agency after every interview and give them feedback so they know just how you feel about each candidate. This will assist them in knowing what you like and don't like as they continue the search for you and hopefully get closer to finding you the perfect match.

- If the agency calls you, try to return their calls in a timely fashion just as you would anyone else you cared about. Don't wait a week to get back to them. Be courteous.

- If you have chosen someone from another agency, inform the other agencies you are using immediately so that they do not continue working unnecessarily for you.

- When your agreed-to trial period for their candidate is completed to your satisfaction, and you decide to hire the applicant, complete the contract and pay the fee in a timely manner. Do not make the agency wait to be paid because you simply hate paying bills or only pay your bills on the first of the month. If you have a business manager who pays the bills for you, instruct the office to get this bill paid quickly. Agencies, like most businesses, do not like to wait for their money after their job is completed. Do not make them call you incessantly for their money. If you happen to need to call upon your "replacement option" in your contract, the agency that you made wait 4 weeks for its money may also return the favor by making you wait for the replacement.

Remember: **Agencies do not forget the clients who are kind, professional and who abide by the terms of their contract. A good agency can pick and choose their clients. If you want to seek their assistance again, my advice is to conduct yourself in a manner that makes them remember you fondly instead of as "the client from hell."**

Chapter Four

MEETING AND
INTERVIEWING APPLICANTS

MEETING AND INTERVIEWING APPLICANTS

HOW MANY APPLICANTS SHOULD I MEET?

This is a question that truly is subjective. You may be very new to this entire process. A "new mother" usually translates to a very concerned and somewhat fearful mother who will most likely want to meet a dozen people, if not two dozen people, before she feels comfortable enough to hire anyone. This is not unusual, and it is very understandable. Other employers who are old pros at this might meet one qualified person and hire instantly. Once you are used to hiring help over the years, you might be as savvy as any agency owner when choosing the right applicant for you. So the answer to this question is: you should meet as many people as you need to until you feel 100% comfortable with your choice.

An agency may only have a few candidates available who fit your needs exactly at the time you call. You may have a schedule that most domestics are less likely to take. It is better to meet three good candidates that qualify and meet all your requirements than ten candidates who have not been screened properly and ultimately do not meet your needs. If all three candidates the agency sent you have the exact qualifications you have requested and agree to your schedule and salary, then you now only have to choose based on their individual personality and the chemistry between you. Do not be worried that you have rushed into hiring someone because it was the first person you met. It could well be that the first person you met is the best person for you. It doesn't have to be difficult.

In the case of hiring live-in help, you may not have as many choices available to you simply because the demand is greater than the supply.

In the case of hiring live-in help, you may not have as many choices available to you simply because the demand is greater than the supply. As discussed earlier, there are not as many domestics who prefer to live-in. You may want to know why. In my opinion, this is as a result of three important factors:

- *Immigration is tighter these days (doors have been closed since April 2001).*

- *Those domestic workers who started out by working as live-ins for many years have now advanced themselves by speaking better English and learning to drive. Now having transportation makes it easier for them to work as live-outs.*

- *Many domestics working as live-ins have been taken advantage of by their employers by being overworked and underpaid without any consideration for overtime. This deters many domestics from ever working as a live-in again, even if their livelihood depends on it.*

Therefore, if you are hiring live-in help, you may not have the opportunity to meet as many candidates. If you only meet one great candidate and are worried that you are acting hastily by hiring this person immediately, think it over carefully. You may need to respond quickly so as not to lose this candidate. Highly qualified domestics who work live-in are hard to find and are hired the quickest.

Although there will always be more live-out personnel at your disposal, keep in mind that the same rule applies. Act quickly on a terrific candidate. If you interview for a very lengthy period of time, you might end up losing someone good who will go elsewhere and be offered a job instantly. Try to complete the interviewing process within two weeks. Keep in touch with any candidate you liked and tell the candidate of your interest, especially anyone that you met early on in the interview process. As a suggestion, you might request a trial period with the candidate of interest right away. This way you can check the candidate out while looking at other individuals until your decision is made. You may not be able to do this for a very long period, but an interested applicant will be amenable to the process of a trial period.

Always act quickly on a terrific candidate.

WHERE IS IT BEST TO MEET APPLICANTS?

Unless you have a concern with privacy, it is recommended that applicants coming from an agency interview directly at your home. This way, the applicant actually drives to the location and knows just how far or close the job is located. The applicant can observe the work environment immediately. Also, it is quite different to tell an applicant your home is 4,800 square feet than it is to show the applicant the actual size of the home. The applicant may find that 4,800 square feet is much bigger than imagined and ultimately too much work. There is an aura and energy in every home. Certainly, when hiring any live-in, it would be mandatory that they see the living quarters prior to accepting a position. Many applicants will walk away from an interview at a client's home simply stating that they did not like the environment. It is a fair consideration for anyone working 40 or more hours in one place.

The other way of handling the interviews if working with an agency is to do the first interview at the agency and then set up a second interview at your home with those applicants that interest you. This may be more time-consuming but would be the most private approach.

If, however, you are doing this on your own and your resource is, for example, the newspaper, it would be preferable to meet your applicants in a neutral location like a restaurant or your office. After you have checked out the applicants thoroughly, and you narrow your decision to one or two candidates, then bring them individually to your home to see the environment where she/he will be working. At that point, you would have your family present and take the time to see how they interact with the applicant. Remember to also have those furry little critters present, since they are also members of the family and need to be considered.

COMPLETE AN EMPLOYMENT APPLICATION

It is very important to have your applicant fill out an application for you, no matter how you found the person. Even if this applicant is coming from an agency, have her/him fill out your own application. This way, you can observe the applicant's reading and writing skills. You can put an application together yourself. Also, you may want to utilize the application included in this book as a sample of one that is tailored for a domestic position. Remember, if you do construct your own application, be careful not to include questions that, by law, are not acceptable.

Make sure you have an I-9 form as part of your application.

Make sure you have an I-9 form as part of your application so that if your applicant is an immigrant, you have covered your bases with respect to the applicant's legal status in this country. By having your applicant fill out and sign this form, it shows that you asked for her/his legal status and have verified proof of the work authorization, resident card or proof of citizenship. This form is signed both by you and the employee.

Also, be sure that your application includes a form requesting the applicant's approval to complete a background check for purposes of hiring this individual. Without this approval, you are not allowed to do a consumer report and would be breaking the law by doing so. You must also provide, upon request, copies of a background check completed on the applicant.

Be sure to get copies of letters of reference and any identification that is available for you to keep on file. Copies of a CPR card and any other certifications should also be attached to the application.

Here is a sample application for a household employee. Within the interview itself, there are ways of getting pertinent information to help you make a sound decision. The subsequent application analysis and suggested questions for the interview will show just how you can get all the information you need without violating any labor laws.

MEETING AND INTERVIEWING APPLICANTS

Visit **www.domestic-connections.com** *to download a printable pdf version of this form.*

HOUSEHOLD EMPLOYEE APPLICATION

Name _____

Alternate Name _____

Address _____

City/State/Zip Code _____

Home Phone# _____ Cell phone# _____

Emergency Phone# _____

Whom do we contact in case of an emergency? _____

Date of Birth (optional) _____ Birth Country (optional) _____

Social Security#_____ DL/ID# _____ Expiration _____

What Position are you Seeking? _____

Are you looking to work: (circle)   Live-In   Live-Out

What is your legal status? _____

How long have you been in this area? _____

How long do you plan to stay in this area? _____

What is your minimum salary requirement? _____

What was your last salary in your previous job?_____

Are you flexible with your work schedule?_____

What hours do you want to work? _____

Are you flexible to work overtime?_____ How late?_____

Do you drive?_____ Do you have a vehicle?_____ How long have you been a licensed driver?_____

Did you drive in your last job? _____ If the job requires it, would you use your car? _____

What kind of car do you drive?(year/model/make) _____

Do you have car insurance? (circle)   Minimum Limited Coverage   Extended Coverage

MEETING AND INTERVIEWING APPLICANTS

Do you like to work with children? _____ What ages? _____

Do you have child experience of your own? _____

Do you take medication? _____ If yes, describe _____

Do you swim? _____ Do you have CPR certification? _____ Date certified? _____

Do you have any Allergies? (please list) _____
_____

Do you like pets? _____ Will you take care of them? _____

Do you do any cooking? _____ (If yes, explain what type of cooking) _____
_____
_____

Are you good at Laundry? _____ Can you iron? _____

If ironing is required at a job, will you iron? _____

Is there anything in the housekeeping or childcare line of work that you DO NOT want to do? _____
If yes, explain? _____
_____

Have you had, or currently have, any condition, illness, or disability, either temporary or permanent, which may affect your ability to do domestic work? _____ If yes, explain _____
_____
_____

Describe in a few sentences your best qualities: _____
_____
_____

If you are working with children, what are your most favorite activities? _____
_____
_____

How is your English? (circle)   EXCELLENT   MEDIUM   LITTLE

Do you read and/or write English? _____

What other languages do you speak? _____

WORK REFERENCES (Most recent job first)

Name _____

Address _____

Home and Work Telephone #'s _____

Salary at Start _____ Final Salary _____ Date of Hire _____ Date Job Ended _____
Reason for Leaving_____

Ages of the children when you started the job _____

Job Responsibilities _____

_____

Name _____

Address _____

Home and Work Telephone #'s _____

Salary at Start _____ Final Salary _____ Date of Hire _____ Date Job Ended _____
Reason for Leaving_____

Ages of the children when you started the job _____

Job Responsibilities _____

_____

Name _____

Address _____

Home and Work Telephone #'s _____

Salary at Start _____ Final Salary _____ Date of Hire _____ Date job Ended _____
Reason for Leaving_____

Ages of the children when you started the job _____

Job Responsibilities _____

_____

MEETING AND INTERVIEWING APPLICANTS

PERSONAL REFERENCE:

Name and Address_____

Telephone Number _____

Relationship _____

Please write down as best you can the reasons why you enjoy doing the type of work that you are seeking.

_____

_____

_____

_____

_____

_____

_____

_____

EDUCATION:

Did you graduate High School?_____ Where?_____

Did you graduate College? _____ Where?_____

Have you taken any College courses?_____

Have you attended any other schools or courses?_____ If yes, explain _____

_____

I understand that any omission or misrepresentation of any fact in this application may result in refusal of, or separation from, employment. I hereby authorize and give permission to any police department or agency to provide information in their possession regarding my background in connection with the application for employment. I hereby authorize and give permission to do a full investigation of my background.

Signature of Applicant _____ Date Signed:_____

MEETING AND INTERVIEWING APPLICANTS

APPLICATION REVIEW

Now let's review the application. The questions being asked are all pertinent to an applicant that is applying for a domestic position. None of the questions have a discriminatory intent. If the applicant perceives it as such, then you already have a problem that you do not need. Let us examine the questions so that you understand why each of them is relevant to hiring a domestic employee.

- The ***Name and Address*** should be current and match with some other form of identification. If the address is new, the applicant should also have it changed on his/her identification or driver's license. You will need a current address when doing the full background check on the applicant.

- Obviously, ***Telephone Numbers*** are important so that you can contact this applicant. Many people today have cell phones; be sure to get all numbers clearly.

- The ***Emergency Telephone Number and Contact*** are very useful in the event numbers on the application become disconnected. It is also always nice to have the number in case there is a medical or other emergency and you need to contact an applicant's close relative or friend.

- The ***Date of Birth*** is optional; however it is necessary to have one to do a complete background check. Again, make sure that the date matches other identification, such as the driver's license/resident or work permit card or U.S. passport. Only after an offer of employment is extended to the applicant can you request the date of birth to do a necessary background check. (Note: The Age Discrimination in the Employment Act of 1967 prohibits discrimination on the basis of age with respect to individuals who are at least 40 but less than 70 years of age.) Try not to judge someone based on age. Try to put age aside and focus more on one's capabilities. Certainly, you may think you prefer, for example, a younger Nanny to play with your children. However, there are many

You will need a current address when doing the full background check on the applicant.

wonderful, experienced older applicants who have high energy and make great Nannies. No one wants to be judged by age.

- The **Birth Country** is optional but important only because sometimes when you have multiple employees in your home, it is helpful to have them from the same country. Due to the animosity amongst certain Central American countries, it is not uncommon to see workers from one country NOT getting along with workers from another country. For the most part, this is purely informational to ask the country of origin. Please note that if, in the past, you happen to have had a bad experience with a person who was from a particular country, this does not mean that every domestic employee from that country will be a problem for you. Try not to make generalizations.

- The **SSN** represents the social security number. It is necessary to have a social security number when completing all background checks. Check the social security number against the actual social security card. Be sure the card is real. If the applicant has a legal work permit and/or resident card, the social security number will be valid for employment. You can check on the social security number to see if it is valid and was issued to the person as listed on the card by calling the Social Security Office and/or doing a Social Security Verification through a background check.

- The **Driver's License / Expiration Date** should be from the state where the applicant plans to drive. Normally, the state where you are driving will require that you be licensed in that state within a certain short period of time. For example, you are not allowed to drive in the state of California with an out-of-state license for more than 12 months. You cannot insure a driver in the state of California who does not have a valid California driver's license. If the applicant tells you that they have an international license and can drive with that, the information is correct but only until a certain period of time, at which point the DMV requires you to convert it to a valid local license. Check the expiration

It is necessary to have a social security number when completing all background checks.

date. If the license has expired, the applicant should have a temporary driver's license from the Department of Motor Vehicles to serve as a temporary driver's license until the new license arrives. Check for a current address and a birth date that coincides with the application.

- The *Job Title* that the applicant writes tells right off the bat what they are looking for and what position they are seeking. If an applicant writes "Housekeeper," she/he probably ONLY wants to do housekeeping. If an applicant writes "Nanny/Housekeeper," he/she has probably done both jobs together in prior positions and is amenable to performing either function or both simultaneously. If the applicant writes ONLY "Nanny," he/she will probably have little to no interest in doing housekeeping other than the "light housekeeping" that is required by most Nanny positions. If the applicant writes "any job," there is a sense of desperation there to get any kind of employment. This still does not mean that the applicant is qualified for all domestic positions. If the applicant says "full-charge domestic," he/she is basically able to work as a Nanny, Housekeeper, Cook, and Driver all in one.

- The question of whether the applicant wants to work as a *Live-in or a Live-out* is crucial. You never want to hire a live-in that prefers to work live-out. You can be sure that what she/he really means is that this applicant will take the position of live-in because there is NO current live-out position, but as soon as one appears, it's *"Adios amigos."* If you question the applicant carefully on this point, you will get to the honest answer. On the other hand, you will not have the same problem when an applicant answers "live-out." An applicant who wants to work "live-out" is rarely ambivalent about the choice. If the applicant writes in both answers "live-in or live-out," you must be sure that this person is truly amenable to a live-in position and is not simply desperate to take any position. Check to see if prior positions were also live-in. The goal here is to avoid hiring a person who does not want to accept the living circumstances that come with your job description. You will be saving a

You never want to hire a live-in that prefers to work live-out.

lot of time and headaches if you get complete, accurate assurance that the applicant is being fully honest when describing what job the applicant prefers.

Sometimes, although rarely, a household could hire the applicant to work either way (live-in or live-out) and find it perfectly doable. However, if you are set on needing one OR the other, you need to be sure that your applicant is in full agreement.

- *Legal Status* is absolutely mandatory. You may only hire applicants who are legal to work in this country. This is a federal law punishable by severe penalties if you violate it. Be sure the applicant has a work authorization, resident card, or proof of U.S. citizenship. Check to see that the cards are valid and active. The application also has an I-9 Form that the Immigration and Naturalization Service requires every applicant who is applying for work to fill out. The numbers on the work authorization, resident card, U.S. passport and all other identification must be listed on this I-9 Form. (More information regarding the I-9 Form is provided at the end of the application.)

- *How long the applicant has been in this area* is important in terms of knowing how many years the applicant might have been here working. Perhaps the applicant only worked 5 years as a domestic but has been here 10 years. This is a good time to ask what the applicant did during those other 5 years and where the applicant was living (this is good for tracing previous whereabouts for a criminal check).

- *How long the applicant wants to stay in this area* is relevant to a prospective employer who might want his/her employee to work for a lengthy period of time. Perhaps the applicant only plans to stay one year in the area and then return to her/his respective country. This may work for the employer and may not. Either way, it is nice to know what the applicant's future plans are with respect to residing in the city where she/he is applying for employment.

- The question of **Salary** is tricky. The salary an applicant wishes to make on a particular job should coincide with what the job market pays for the work performed. An applicant might expect to be paid top dollar. Certainly, if he/she is worth it and you can afford it, you may want to consider meeting the applicant's demands. What the applicant made in the previous job should also be taken into consideration. Unless he/she was grossly underpaid or overpaid, you might want to stay close to a previous salary so that you have some room to offer a raise. Basically, by asking the applicant what salary they are seeking, you simply know what is expected. Perhaps you are far off from the amount that this applicant needs in order to make ends meet. Perhaps you planned to pay less, but are willing to meet these salary demands if everything else checks out. It is important to know the applicant's expectations with respect to salary so that you have a starting point from which to begin your negotiation.

- **Flexibility** in a job is important. Let us say that you work and you might have a late meeting. If the applicant is NOT flexible, he/she might not be too happy when you consistently come home late due to traffic or being held up at the office. Find out what hours the applicant absolutely CAN work and **how late is too late** for the applicant.

- **Driving** is not always necessary for every domestic position. However, if the applicant is a driver and will be driving for you, it will be important to know many facts. You will want to know how long the driver has driven. Is he/she a new driver or experienced? You will want to know about the driving record. Are there many violations and what kind of violations? (You can get a driving record at any local DMV office.) You will want to know if the applicant drove in the last job. The previous employer may also be informative about the applicant's driving skills. If you are using the applicant's car for the position, it will be important to know the type of car that is being used. Is it in good condition? If this would be applicable, is it safe for carrying children on board? Does the applicant carry insurance on the car? Is the insurance coverage the

If the applicant is NOT flexible, he/she might not be too happy when you consistently come home late due to traffic or being held up at the office.

You can get a driving record at any local DMV office.

required "minimum limited liability" or is it "extended coverage?" If you do ultimately hire the applicant to drive, be sure to go for a test run in the car to check out driving skills.

- If your job description requires a domestic who works as a Nanny to care for your children, you will want to know whether this applicant actually *enjoys working with children and of what ages.* Many domestics prefer working with babies. Everyone loves babies, but not everyone has references working with babies. Some applicants prefer to work with babies and do not like it when the children grow up since they become more difficult to manage and require a different set of skills. In this case, the Nanny may prefer to move on to work with another baby with a new family. Be sure the applicant is comfortable working with children of all ages, especially children as old as your children at the time of hiring.

- It is nice to know if the applicant has children. However, it is not mandatory for the applicant to answer this question. If the applicant chooses to answer this question and happens to reveal some information regarding the applicant's family, you will want to *be sure there is childcare present for those children under 12.* (Again, you cannot discriminate against an applicant because they have or do not have children. It is simply nice to know if the applicant has any maternal or paternal experience.) Some clients in the past have requested to hire an applicant who "does not have small children" for fear that the Nanny's children will interfere with the job. You should not make this generalization because it is highly discriminatory.

Many of us who work also have families. Can you imagine if you didn't get that fabulous job you wanted because the prospective employer thought your baby would interfere? The domestic applicant seeking work is no more irresponsible than you would be under the same circumstance. If anything, being a parent tends to make you more responsible. Reviewing the applicant's family life should not be for the purpose of discrimination but simply to get to know the applicant.

- If the applicant is taking any *medication,* you should be aware of it. This does not mean that the taking of medication should inhibit the employee from working. It is simply a good idea to be aware of the kind of medication being taken and what reaction the medication could cause in an emergency situation. It is important that this information is discussed in light of the fact this person is working for you in your home, and may be taking care of children. (The domestic should keep all medicine away from small children.)

- *Knowing whether or not your applicant swims* is important when you have children in the house. You certainly do not want to leave your domestic with the children at a pool if the domestic does not swim. You also should be concerned for the safety of the domestic, who could also drown if she/he should fall into a pool unattended.

- *CPR (Infant or Adult) and/or First Aid* are important and mandatory when caring for children or anyone in general. Anyone caring for an infant should be certified in Infant CPR. You can obtain certification from many hospitals, the Red Cross and private instructors. An applicant that you want to hire might have taken CPR previously and have a general idea of what to do. However, you should have the applicant update the certification on a yearly basis. It is best to have the procedure fresh in your mind, to be better prepared for an emergency situation.

You should have the applicant update the CPR certification on a yearly basis.

- *Allergies* to pets should be discussed with the applicant. If there are any cats, dogs or birds present, this might cause an applicant serious medical problems if allergic to these animals. These allergies might be treatable by medication and NOT present a problem. Some animals have hair that is non-allergic. Check to see if your pet can cause any problem to an allergic person. It is also a good idea to be aware of anyone's food or other type of allergy, especially if the employee is going to live and eat with you. Food allergies can be as deadly as animal allergies. If a domestic already working for you becomes allergic, be sure to have this person see a doctor. As mentioned, the allergic reaction might be suppressed with the help of medication.

- The question pertaining to *liking animals* is only relevant if animals are present or are planned for the near future in the household. Some domestic jobs require *caring for the animals.* It would be good to know whether the applicant likes animals or is afraid of them. Some applicants may like the animals but refuse to care for them. Not everyone wants to be responsible for walking a dog or "poop detail." If that is one of the responsibilities, you better find out if the domestic is ready, willing and able.

- *Does the applicant cook, and if so, what kind of cooking?* This is nice to know in case you need your domestic to make a meal for you. What a luxury it is to come home from a long day at the office and have your dinner waiting for you. If the domestic is a live-in, it is nice to know that the breakfast can also be handled. If the applicant knows nothing about cooking, ask her/him if there is any willingness to learn and make the best effort at it.

You might be surprised to find out that many domestics do not like to iron.

- *Laundry* is important since every household needs some laundry to be handled by the Nanny and/or the Housekeeper. Even Nannies who ONLY do light housekeeping will need to do the laundry for the baby. Ironing, on the other hand, is something that not every domestic enjoys or is willing to do. Be sure to find out about the applicant's ironing capability. If there is a lot of ironing at the job, you certainly do not want to hire a person who finds ironing a dreadful chore.

You might be surprised to find out that many domestics do not like to iron. Some perceive the duty of ironing to be tedious and not something they particularly care to do. Some domestics will not iron because of a myth circulating in some Latin American countries. The myth is that if one works with water all day long and then proceeds to iron, arthritis will set in. There has never been any proof of this, and most American doctors find it humorous; however, the myth lives on.

- Asking whether or not there is *anything in the housekeeping or childcare line of work one does NOT want to do* will most likely not be answered truthfully. However, it is worth a shot. If one does answer it honestly, you may find out something very important to help you decide if this person is right for you. Have you ever heard the expression, "I will not do windows, floors, toilets..." This is often heard in jest when describing how ludicrous it is for a domestic "housekeeper" to declare such a statement. The normal response is to ask, "Well, then *what do you do?*" The point here is that if there is in fact any duty the applicant will not perform, you want to know this NOW. You may find this acceptable or you may find it impossible to overlook.

- Any *illnesses or past conditions* that might affect his/her ability to work should not be a deciding factor as to whether or not you hire someone. It is purely informational and may help you decide which household /childcare chores should not be given to this person. You also want a disclosure of past illnesses such as a back condition, etc., so that someone does not spring a lawsuit on you for a back injury that might have been previously sustained. (You may want to do a worker's compensation history check to see if there have been previous injuries and complaints.)

You may want to do a worker's compensation history check to see if there have been previous injuries and complaints.

- *Describing one's qualities* is a good question to discover self-observation. A very detailed response will indicate that this applicant is very well aware of the skills and services that she/he can best provide in a job. It is impressive to read a lengthy and descriptive response. If one's writing skills inhibit the applicant from being expressive and detailed, take the time to discuss this response in person.

- *Favorite activities working with children* tell you so much about the

MEETING AND INTERVIEWING APPLICANTS

Nanny's skills. Once again, the more one writes about his/her abilities, the more you understand his/her qualifications. If a Nanny does not have any favorite activities but responds "I love to do everything with children," try to get the Nanny to be more descriptive. Maybe the Nanny responds, "I love to play different games, do arts and crafts and teach the child the alphabet." Whatever the response, it will indicate to you the Nanny's level of communication and child development skills.

- ***One's level of English*** is usually very hard to measure. If an applicant considers his/her level of English to be excellent, it is probably very good and passable. Most applicants are modest about their English skills and will check off "medium." Some will indicate they speak very little English; yet when testing them, they seem to know more than you expected. This is often the case because people who learn a foreign language tend to have less self-confidence discussing their proficiency. They may underestimate their true ability to speak. The true test is in your discussion with the applicant. Does the applicant seem to understand most, if not all, of your questions? When you ask a question, are you getting an answer that you can understand, or do you have to repeat yourself several times? To further your analysis of the applicant's language skills, have the applicant read for you a children's book at grade level 3-4.

- ***References*** are self-explanatory and each part of this section should be answered carefully and accurately. Note that the most recent job is listed first. This makes it easy for you to see one's most recent experience. Did this applicant work with children recently, or was her child experience several years prior to the most recent job? You will later compare these answers to those answers received from each reference you contact. It is always preferable to obtain letters of reference as attachments to the application.

- ***Personal References*** are important to have in order to obtain additional information regarding the applicant. Also they are useful to have in case you need to contact someone close to your applicant if there should be an emergency.

- *Why you enjoy this line of work* is helpful to know the applicant's aspirations. Some will tell you they sincerely love to work with children or love to clean or cook, etc., while others might say they simply need a job and need to make money. Again, this answer helps you see the applicant's motivation for employment.

- *Educational* questions give you an idea of the applicant's level of education and perhaps objectives for the future. If the applicant is looking for a job between finishing high school or college, you may get an idea of how long they plan to work in this capacity. The applicant may be in the middle of a child development course of study at a school. Certainly, any and all education is helpful with any position. However, in this case, most Nannies and domestics get their experience from on-the-job training. Many people who come to this country seeking employment have come from impoverished countries where education is a true luxury. Do not be surprised if many applicants do not have the equivalent of a high school diploma. In other cases, you will find highly educated applicants seeking domestic work because they cannot work in their fields of expertise until they get certified in the States.

- *The final statement* verifying the applicant has not lied about any facts listed is important. Also, what follows is an authorization to run a criminal check. In addition, it would be a good idea to have a more thorough "Consumer Notification and Authorization Form" signed as well. Be sure to have the application signed and dated.

Most Nannies and domestics get their experience from on-the-job training.

MEETING AND INTERVIEWING APPLICANTS

Visit **www.domestic-connections.com** *to download a printable pdf version of this form.*

EMPLOYMENT ELIGIBILITY VERIFICATION (FORM I-9 page 1)

U.S. Department of Justice
Immigration and Naturalization Service

OMB No. 1115-0136

Employment Eligibility Verification

INSTRUCTIONS
PLEASE READ ALL INSTRUCTIONS CAREFULLY BEFORE COMPLETING THIS FORM.

Anti-Discrimination Notice. It is illegal to discriminate against any individual (other than an alien not authorized to work in the U.S.) in hiring, discharging, or recruiting or referring for a fee because of that individual's national origin or citizenship status. It is illegal to discriminate against work eligible individuals. Employers **CANNOT** specify which document(s) they will accept from an employee. The refusal to hire an individual because of a future expiration date may also constitute illegal discrimination.

Section 1 - Employee. All employees, citizens and noncitizens, hired after November 6, 1986, must complete Section 1 of this form at the time of hire, which is the actual beginning of employment. **The employer is responsible for ensuring that Section 1 is timely and properly completed.**

Preparer/Translator Certification. The Preparer/Translator Certification must be completed if Section 1 is prepared by a person other than the employee. A preparer/translator may be used only when the employee is unable to complete Section 1 on his/her own. However, the employee must still sign Section 1.

Section 2 - Employer. For the purpose of completing this form, the term "employer" includes those recruiters and referrers for a fee who are agricultural associations, agricultural employers or farm labor contractors.

Employers must complete Section 2 by examining evidence of identity and employment eligibility within three (3) business days of the date employment begins. If employees are authorized to work, but are unable to present the required document(s) within three business days, they must present a receipt for the application of the document(s) within three business days and the actual document(s) within ninety (90) days. However, if employers hire individuals for a duration of less than three business days, Section 2 must be completed at the time employment begins. **Employers must record: 1)** document title; **2)** issuing authority; **3)** document number, **4)** expiration date, if any; and **5)** the date employment begins. Employers must sign and date the certification. Employees must present original documents. Employers may, but are not required to, photocopy the document(s) presented. These photocopies may only be used for the verification process and must be retained with the I-9. **However, employers are still responsible for completing the I-9.**

Section 3 - Updating and Reverification. Employers must complete Section 3 when updating and/or reverifying the I-9. Employers must reverify employment eligibility of their employees on or before the expiration date recorded in Section 1. Employers **CANNOT** specify which document(s) they will accept from an employee.

- If an employee's name has changed at the time this form is being updated/ reverified, complete Block A.

- If an employee is rehired within three (3) years of the date this form was originally completed and the employee is still eligible to be employed on the same basis as previously indicated on this form (updating), complete Block B and the signature block.

- If an employee is rehired within three (3) years of the date this form was originally completed and the employee's work authorization has expired **or** if a current employee's work authorization is about to expire (reverification), complete Block B and:
  - examine any document that reflects that the employee is authorized to work in the U.S. (see List A **or** C),
  - record the document title, document number and expiration date (if any) in Block C, and complete the signature block.

Photocopying and Retaining Form I-9 A blank I-9 may be reproduced, provided both sides are copied. The Instructions must be available to all employees completing this form. Employers must retain completed I-9s for three (3) years after the date of hire or one (1) year after the date employment ends, whichever is later.

For more detailed information, you may refer to the INS Handbook for Employers, (Form M-274). You may obtain the handbook at your local INS office.

Privacy Act Notice. The authority for collecting this information is the Immigration Reform and Control Act of 1986, Pub. L. 99-603 (8 USC 1324a).

This information is for employers to verify the eligibility of individuals for employment to preclude the unlawful hiring, or recruiting or referring for a fee, of aliens who are not authorized to work in the United States.

This information will be used by employers as a record of their basis for determining eligibility of an employee to work in the United States. The form will be kept by the employer and made available for inspection by officials of the U.S. Immigration and Naturalization Service, the Department of Labor and the Office of Special Counsel for Immigration Related Unfair Employment Practices.

Submission of the information required in this form is voluntary. However, an individual may not begin employment unless this form is completed, since employers are subject to civil or criminal penalties if they do not comply with the Immigration Reform and Control Act of 1986.

Reporting Burden. We try to create forms and instructions that are accurate, can be easily understood and which impose the least possible burden on you to provide us with information. Often this is difficult because some immigration laws are very complex. Accordingly, the reporting burden for this collection of information is computed as follows: **1)** learning about this form, 5 minutes; **2)** completing the form, 5 minutes; and **3)** assembling and filing (recordkeeping) the form, 5 minutes, for an average of 15 minutes per response. If you have comments regarding the accuracy of this burden estimate, or suggestions for making this form simpler, you can write to the Immigration and Naturalization Service, HQPDI, 425 I Street, N.W., Room 4034, Washington, DC 20536. OMB No. 1115-0136.

EMPLOYERS MUST RETAIN COMPLETED FORM I-9
PLEASE DO NOT MAIL COMPLETED FORM I-9 TO INS

Form I-9 (Rev. 11-21-91)N

HELP!

MEETING AND INTERVIEWING APPLICANTS

EMPLOYMENT ELIGIBILITY VERIFICATION (FORM I-9 page 2)

U.S. Department of Justice
Immigration and Naturalization Service

OMB No. 1115-0136
Employment Eligibility Verification

Please read instructions carefully before completing this form. The instructions must be available during completion of this form. **ANTI-DISCRIMINATION NOTICE:** It is illegal to discriminate against work eligible individuals. Employers CANNOT specify which document(s) they will accept from an employee. The refusal to hire an individual because of a future expiration date may also constitute illegal discrimination.

Section 1. Employee Information and Verification To be completed and signed by employee at the time employment begins.

Print Name: Last   First   Middle Initial   Maiden Name

Address (Street Name and Number)   Apt. #   Date of Birth (month/day/year)

City   State   Zip Code   Social Security #

I am aware that federal law provides for imprisonment and/or fines for false statements or use of false documents in connection with the completion of this form.

I attest, under penalty of perjury, that I am (check one of the following):
☐ A citizen or national of the United States
☐ A Lawful Permanent Resident (Alien # A _____)
☐ An alien authorized to work until ___/___/___
(Alien # or Admission #)

Employee's Signature   Date (month/day/year)

Preparer and/or Translator Certification. (To be completed and signed if Section 1 is prepared by a person other than the employee.) I attest, under penalty of perjury, that I have assisted in the completion of this form and that to the best of my knowledge the information is true and correct.

Preparer's/Translator's Signature   Print Name

Address (Street Name and Number, City, State, Zip Code)   Date (month/day/year)

Section 2. Employer Review and Verification. To be completed and signed by employer. Examine one document from List A OR examine one document from List B and one from List C, as listed on the reverse of this form, and record the title, number and expiration date, if any, of the document(s)

List A	OR	List B	AND	List C
Document title: ___		___		___
Issuing authority: ___		___		___
Document #: ___		___		___
Expiration Date (if any): ___/___/___	___/___/___			___/___/___
Document #: ___				
Expiration Date (if any): ___/___/___				

CERTIFICATION - I attest, under penalty of perjury, that I have examined the document(s) presented by the above-named employee, that the above-listed document(s) appear to be genuine and to relate to the employee named, that the employee began employment on (month/day/year) ___/___/___ and that to the best of my knowledge the employee is eligible to work in the United States. (State employment agencies may omit the date the employee began employment.)

Signature of Employer or Authorized Representative   Print Name   Title

Business or Organization Name   Address (Street Name and Number, City, State, Zip Code)   Date (month/day/year)

Section 3. Updating and Reverification To be completed and signed by employer.

A. New Name (if applicable)   B. Date of rehire   (month/day/year) (if applicable)

C. If employee's previous grant of work authorization has expired, provide the information below for the document that establishes current employment eligibility.
Document Title: ___   Document #: ___   Expiration Date (if any): ___/___/___

I attest, under penalty of perjury, that to the best of my knowledge, this employee is eligible to work in the United States, and if the employee presented document(s), the document(s) I have examined appear to be genuine and to relate to the individual.

Signature of Employer or Authorized Representative   Date (month/day/year)

Form I-9 (Rev. 11-21-91)N Page 2

EMPLOYMENT ELIGIBILITY VERIFICATION (FORM I-9 page 3)

LISTS OF ACCEPTABLE DOCUMENTS

LIST A		LIST B		LIST C
Documents that Establish Both Identity and Employment Eligibility	OR	Documents that Establish Identity	AND	Documents that Establish Employment Eligibility

LIST A — Documents that Establish Both Identity and Employment Eligibility

1. U.S. Passport (unexpired or expired)

2. Certificate of U.S. Citizenship (INS Form N-560 or N-561)

3. Certificate of Naturalization (INS Form N-550 or N-570)

4. Unexpired foreign passport, with I-551 stamp or attached INS Form I-94 indicating unexpired employment authorization

5. Permanent Resident Card or Alien Registration Receipt Card with photograph (INS Form I-151 or I-551)

6. Unexpired Temporary Resident Card (INS Form I-688)

7. Unexpired Employment Authorization Card (INS Form I-688A)

8. Unexpired Reentry Permit (INS Form I-327)

9. Unexpired Refugee Travel Document (INS Form I-571)

10. Unexpired Employment Authorization Document issued by the INS which contains a photograph (INS Form I-688B)

OR

LIST B — Documents that Establish Identity

1. Driver's license or ID card issued by a state or outlying possession of the United States provided it contains a photograph or information such as name, date of birth, gender, height, eye color and address

2. ID card issued by federal, state or local government agencies or entities, provided it contains a photograph or information such as name, date of birth, gender, height, eye color and address

3. School ID card with a photograph

4. Voter's registration card

5. U.S. Military card or draft record

6. Military dependent's ID card

7. U.S. Coast Guard Merchant Mariner Card

8. Native American tribal document

9. Driver's license issued by a Canadian government authority

For persons under age 18 who are unable to present a document listed above:

10. School record or report card

11. Clinic, doctor or hospital record

12. Day-care or nursery school record

AND

LIST C — Documents that Establish Employment Eligibility

1. U.S. social security card issued by the Social Security Administration (other than a card stating it is not valid for employment)

2. Certification of Birth Abroad issued by the Department of State (Form FS-545 or Form DS-1350)

3. Original or certified copy of a birth certificate issued by a state, county, municipal authority or outlying possession of the United States bearing an official seal

4. Native American tribal document

5. U.S. Citizen ID Card (INS Form I-197)

6. ID Card for use of Resident Citizen in the United States (INS Form I-179)

7. Unexpired employment authorization document issued by the INS (other than those listed under List A)

Illustrations of many of these documents appear in Part 8 of the Handbook for Employers (M-274)

Form I-9 (Rev. 10/4/00)Y Page 3

EMPLOYMENT ELIGIBILITY VERIFICATION (I-9 FORM)

This form is available at the U.S. Department of Justice, Immigration and Naturalization Service. It is mandatory that this form is filled out by the employee upon being hired. The employee must provide his/her correct name and any names that differ from the present name because of marriage or other reasons. The employee must also provide current address, date of birth, social security number and verification of all identification. The following important notice is written on this form:

The I-9 Form is available at the U.S. Department of Justice, Immigration and Naturalization Service.

Authority for collecting the information on this form is in Title 8, United States Code, Section 1324A, which requires employers to verify employment eligibility of individuals on a form approved by the Attorney General. This form will be used to verify the individual's eligibility for employment in the United States. Failure to present this form for Inspection to officers of the Immigration and Naturalization Service or Department of Labor within the time period specified by regulation, or improper completion or retention of this form, may be a violation of the above law and may result in a civil money penalty.

If the form is being prepared by someone other than the employee, the preparer must certify the form by signing it and printing or typing his or her complete address.

The employer (this refers to employers of the applicant as well as those who recruit or refer the applicant for a fee) must complete section 2 by examining evidence of identity and employment eligibility. Copies of documentation presented by an individual for the purpose of establishing identity and employment eligibility may be copied and retained for the purpose of complying with the requirements of this form and no other purpose. Any copies of documentation made for this purpose should be maintained with this form.

This Employment Eligibility form must be retained by the employer for three (3) years after the date of such hiring; or one (1) year after the date employment is terminated, whichever is later.

Visit **www.domestic-connections.com** *to download a printable pdf version of this form.*

CONSUMER NOTIFICATION & AUTHORIZATION

This is used to inform you that a Consumer Report/Criminal Report is being obtained from a consumer-reporting agency(ies) for the purpose of evaluating you for employment. By signing below, you hereby authorize _____ to retrieve such information from any agency or agencies and authorize release of said information to a prospective employer.

EMPLOYEE

I hereby authorize and request any police department or agency having knowledge about me, to furnish bearer with any and all information in their possession regarding me in connection with an application for employment including consumer report information that may include motor vehicle records.

I understand that any prospective employer will have the right to make employment determinations based on this information.

I authorize that a photocopy of this authorization is accepted with the same authority as the original and I understand that this authorization is to be made part of the written employment application, which I have signed.

Print Name _____ Former Name(s) _____

Date of Birth _____ Social Security Number _____

Signature _____

OBTAINING AUTHORIZATION FOR BACKGROUND CHECK

The applicant's authorization is mandatory prior to completing a background check.

The applicant's authorization is mandatory prior to completing a background check. The applicant must be aware that the investigation will be conducted and utilized by the potential employer to determine the individual's viability for employment. It would be crucial to know whether this applicant has been convicted for drunk driving or possession of drugs. You would certainly want to know if the applicant has a history of crime or violence. This sounds a bit scary, doesn't it? Well, it *is* frightening. You have every right to know everything you need to know about a person you are hiring to work in your private home to care for it and/or your children. It is completely legal to obtain a "consumer report" from any prospective employee as long as you obtain his/her authorization to do so and provide the employee with a copy of this report upon request.

MEETING AND INTERVIEWING APPLICANTS

HOW TO HANDLE THE INTERVIEW AND SUGGESTED QUESTIONS

After taking a few minutes to carefully review and analyze the application, you will want to sit down with your prospective employee with a list of questions for discussion. It is a good idea to take notes on the responses provided. The applicant may come from another country where the first language is not English, you may find this a bit of a language barrier. The applicant may feel nervous and freeze up in the interview. Be sensitive to this by asking the questions slowly. You may even have to repeat the question or ask it in a different way so that the applicant understands. Be relaxed so you make the interview comfortable for you and your applicant.

Sit in a quiet room, preferably where there are no children present, for the first part of the interview. Later, once you have asked all of your questions, bring in the rest of the family to meet the applicant. Observe the interaction between the applicant and each family member. If you have an infant, it would be a good idea to have the applicant hold the baby. By having the applicant take a few minutes to care for the baby, you will have an instant idea of how comfortable and experienced the applicant is with infants.

The "chemistry," for lack of a better word, between you and the candidate will be half the battle when choosing among qualified candidates. Their experience and references will reflect the balance of your decision. In the end, your decision will be made based upon your due diligence and your good instincts.

Once you have had sufficient time together (anywhere from 20 minutes up to an hour), you can thank your applicant for her time and inform her that you will be interviewing other applicants for whatever duration of time you decide. Tell your applicant that, one way or another, you will be contacting her with your final decision. If you are particularly impressed with this person, you may want to emphasize your interest so that the candidate does not accept another job. You may want to call soon after the interview to inform the applicant of your plans to pursue a reference check rather quickly and make a decision. (If you are working with an agency, protocol requires you to call the agency with your feedback and ask them to contact the applicant.)

MEETING AND INTERVIEWING APPLICANTS

In addition to the application, interview questions are an excellent way to discover more information regarding the applicant and her level of communication. Such information could be very telling about the person's character and background, and tremendously helpful in knowing whether this person is right for you.

Here are some questions for a personal interview with a domestic applicant. Keep in mind that some of these may or may not apply to your particular position.

- *What is it about this line of work that you love the most?*
  Note: This is a good opening question because it allows the applicant to be openly expressive about his/her expertise. This question is on the application as well. If the position is for "cleaning," the applicant will hopefully talk about the fact that he/she loves to clean and is highly organized. Or, the candidate applying to work with children may tell you about her child development skills and how much she loves working with kids. Hopefully the applicant will go into detail about his/her experience and desire to work in this capacity.

- *Have you ever considered doing any other type of work?*
  Note: An applicant may be attending classes in a chosen field and may leave domestic work upon being awarded a degree. If this question is answered honestly, it will give you an idea as to this person's goals and plans for the future.

- *Is there any domestic duty that you absolutely refuse to do?*
  Note: In the case of hiring a "housekeeper," you may discover that some housekeepers do not want to do things such as windows, outside barbecue, the car, etc. These duties are not necessarily standard tasks; however, if your particular job demands these kinds of duties, then it would be a good idea for you to find out now whether or not the applicant will do them.

- *Are you flexible with your time if I were to need you for some overtime hours?*
  Note: Overtime may never be required, but it is good to know ahead of

Interview questions are an excellent way to discover more information regarding the applicant and her level of communication.

time if someone is flexible to work extra hours if necessary. If this applicant has a family to attend to, or perhaps goes to school at night, he/she will most likely need to leave work on time. What you want to ascertain is the applicant's flexibility in an emergency or unusual situation.

- *If I needed to travel during the week or weekends for business, vacation or an emergency, would you stay and care for the house, pets or perhaps children?*

Note: One of the worries when traveling is leaving your house, pets or especially children in the hands of a trusted soul. It is ideal to have your household employee be that person. Having someone available to pick up the mail and newspaper and check on the house each day is very comforting when you go away. Hiring a live-out Housekeeper or Nanny who is willing to stay with the children if you need to leave town is a great advantage. When hiring a live-in, this question would be relevant because some domestics do not feel comfortable being alone in a house whether or not children are present. Sometimes a family will choose to have a friend or relative stay in the house alongside the domestic when they go away, just to keep an eye on things, and provide an extra pair of hands in case of an emergency.

- *What ages of children do you feel most qualified to care for at this time?*

Note: Although a childcare provider may have worked many years with children of all ages, he/she may at this point prefer, and be most capable of, caring for only infants or school age children. Experience is one thing; having the requisite energy and patience for certain age groups is another.

- *Do you like to wear a uniform at work?*

Note: This question only pertains to a household where a uniform is required. Many employers prefer a uniform because it looks very professional. On the other hand, many employees do not like to wear one because it takes away their individualism and makes them feel like a servant. My take on the subject is that a uniform on a domestic is no more condescending than one on a policeman, fireman or doctor. The employee comes to work looking like a professional. No offense should be taken when asked to wear a uniform. However, you may feel that your household is casual and that a domestic in a uniform might make *you* feel uncomfortable. Decide on this issue ahead of time. One thing for sure, you do not want to spring it on an employee several weeks into the job. *Remember: The employer is responsible for purchasing all uniforms used on the job.*

- ### *Do you have family here?*

Note: You cannot ask the question of "Marital Status" on any application for employment; however, you can get around the question by asking about one's family life in an informal interview. The applicant may tell you about family members. If an applicant chooses not to answer this question, that is his/her prerogative. It certainly should not be used to decide whether an applicant qualifies for your position. The truth of the matter is that whether or not a person is single, married, divorced or widowed, with or without children, should NOT make any difference when choosing an applicant. Many times, a client will specifically ask for someone who does not have a family, or who has grown kids. Although probably not intended, its impact could be terribly discriminating. Whether a person has any of the above does not make her/him less or more responsible. If their previous references have clearly stated that this employee was fabulous and was always on time and highly reliable, then the marital and family status wouldn't matter. Another concern often shared is that if they have small children, what would happen if their child gets sick? Well, let me ask you this: if your child got sick, would you take the day off? Probably not, that is why you are hiring a Nanny, correct? Would you want your prospective employer to pass you up for another employee who was single and without children? I don't think so. Understanding a person's family background may be informative to you as you get to know your applicant but should not prevent you from making an offer.

- *How often do you go back to your country to visit your family?*
Note: Many domestics come from different countries to work in America. They often leave behind children and parents, sometimes even a spouse. On a routine basis, they may want to go home to visit their relatives at least once a year during their vacation time. This is all feasible as long as it coincides with the allowed vacation time. The likelihood is that the applicant will want to go during the holidays. Be sure that this coincides with your plans so that you do not have any problems down the road. Please, please, please, do not say "Oh, I couldn't possibly hire this person who has children in her country. It would be too sad for me to hire someone like that." You need to understand that most immigrants who come here to work very often do so in order to send money back to their countries so that their children and families can live a better life there. Sure, they miss their families, and sure, they would like their lives to be different, but thousands upon thousands of immigrants do this. They come here because they can get work here. The only reason you want to know about their trips back home to visit family is to know just how often they actually go home and how this would coincide with their vacation time. Try not to get emotionally involved in the ramifications of having family elsewhere. There are also thousands upon thousands of immigrants who work here in hopes of becoming residents and then bringing their family here to be with them. In some cases, this can take years. Every domestic has a story and a plan with respect to his or her family, none of which should keep you from hiring this employee.

- *If you have been given an instruction, but you do not understand it completely, is it your inclination to try to do it in spite of your uncertainty, or will you ask your employer to go over it once more? (In simpler form, you may ask the question as follows: Will you ask me to repeat something if you do not understand what I am saying?)*
Note: One of the main reasons there is so much frustration when hiring

domestic help is that domestics tend to fear questioning a directive. It is due to the language barrier and culture difference. They do not want to admit that their English might not be as good as you thought. They do not want to admit that they did not get the instruction in the slightest. They are afraid to ask you to repeat it, so they nod their heads and say "yes, yes, yes." This problem is endless. To be sure that an employee actually understood what was said, you might want to ask the employee to repeat the directive so that you are sure it was understood. It may appear as though you are talking to your child, but when you ask the employee to repeat something, it will ensure that the directive is understood.

- *If I instruct you to handle something with respect to my child in a manner of which you personally do not approve, will you have difficulty implementing my instruction?*
  Note: The assumption here is that this particular instruction would not be something unreasonable. The response from the applicant should be that the parent is the one who makes the decisions and rules for the child. The childcare provider should do as the parent wishes without making any personal opinions unless the parent welcomes suggestions.

- *Have you ever had an emergency occur in a workplace? If so, what was it and how did you handle it?*
  Note: This question will be one that you will also ask the reference. The focus of the question is not about the emergency itself, it is about how the domestic handled the emergency. Did the domestic call 911 and/or the parents immediately? Did the domestic stay calm and controlled so that she/he could attend to the safety of the children, pets and/or household? Was it necessary to administer CPR? You may find out that this domestic tends to panic in an emergency or is very steadfast and controlled.

- *If you are alone in the house and someone knocks on the door, what would you do?*
  Note: A Housekeeper should know NOT to answer the door under any

A Housekeeper should know NOT to answer the door under any circumstances UNLESS instructed to do so by the employer.

circumstances UNLESS instructed to do so by the employer. In today's world, unfortunately, we have to be very cautious. Home invasions usually occur when someone in the household lets the "bad guys" in. It is well documented that some very professional criminals have posed as policemen, utility workers and the like, only to lure their way into someone's home. Even if you live in a gated community, you need to be cautious. It is always best to ask who it is and what the person wants. Then the domestic should contact the homeowner and discuss the situation; otherwise, one might be opening the door to a real threat.

- *If my child is misbehaving and you have tried everything possible to stop what he/she is doing, how would you handle the situation?*
  Note: The caregiver should be aware that the first reaction should be to quietly tell the child to stop his/her behavior or there will be consequences. The child may continue misbehaving, at which point the second warning can be given. Finally, the caregiver can opt to give the child a time out or tell the child that now a certain privilege will be taken away. If all else fails, the parent(s) should be called. Parents do not want to be called every time their child does something wrong. The caregiver must gain the child's respect without the parents' constant intervention. A call to the parent should be the one that truly concerns the child if all else fails. If the applicant gives you a response that shows some patience, methodology and control, then you are headed in the right direction. Every family will have its own ideas of how to handle discipline. Certainly under NO circumstances should the caregiver be allowed to shake or hit your child. Abusive language can be very damaging. A caregiver should not use profanity or yell at the child. Any threats that involve scaring the child are also unacceptable.

- *What are your favorite things to do with a child who is (my child's age)?*
  Note: Each age from newborn to teenager will warrant a different answer. A caregiver might love to walk the baby and take the baby to the park or

sing to the baby. A caregiver might love to read books to a toddler and teach the child new things and/or play with various toys. A caregiver might love to do arts and crafts with a school age child or play sports outside. A caregiver will most likely not have much of an answer with teenagers because most teenagers do not want much to do with their parents, let alone their Housekeepers or Nannies.

- *If you are stuck in traffic and are running very late to work, what would you do?*
Note: The right answer here is to get out of traffic and call the employer to inform him/her of the problem. Fortunately, today almost everyone owns a cell phone. There should be no excuse for NOT making a call. If the employee ultimately uses "traffic" as an excuse each and every time he/she is late, you might get a bit suspicious. By the first few weeks of any employment, the employee should figure out how long it takes to get to work, with or without traffic, and leave at the same time each day. It is always better to arrive early or on time than late with an excuse.

- *How would you describe your personality?*
Note: Putting aside the credentials and qualifications, 50% of why you choose to hire a person will be the chemistry you have with this employee. A person may be aggressive, hands-on and very take-charge. This personality may be exactly what you want, especially if you are a working mother and need to feel the confidence that this caretaker will know exactly what to do at all times. Perhaps the employee is soft spoken, subdued and even somewhat subservient. You may find this personality more suitable in your home. The applicant's perception of her own personality will give you an inkling of what she is like; however, only time will help you establish a comfortable knowledge of this person's true personality and character.

50% of why you choose to hire a person will be the chemistry you have with this employee.

- *What kinds of activities do you like to do on your time off from work?*
Note: This response tells you a lot about a person. He or she may like to

play a sport, read, and go to church or study. He or she may like to go out dancing, spend time with family, or go away for the weekend. Extra-curricular activities may tell you something interesting about the candidate. This question does not have a perfect answer. It simply allows you to know your applicant better by the activities he or she enjoys most.

- ***How much television do you think a child should watch?***
  Note: As a parent, you may not mind television. You may think it is an excellent babysitter and use it often yourself when you are alone with your child. This is strictly a personal view. However, you may be adamantly opposed to overexposure to television and want to know that your child's caretaker is in agreement. Or you may simply hope that the response is something like this: "I will allow your child to watch ONLY as much television as you deem appropriate." If the television were used for educational purposes, then the use of the television would be good for the child's stimulus and growth. If you have educational products for television use, you may want these utilized on a daily basis for a specific period of time. Be clear about your views with respect to this matter.

- ***How do you take constructive criticism? (Simpler form: If I tell you I do not like the way you are doing something, would you be offended?)***
  Note: You may need to explain "constructive" criticism. Constructive does not mean to criticize a person gratuitously, but to give criticism that will assist in the betterment of one's behavior and workmanship. This may apply to one's abilities, work ethics, common sense, and organizational skills. As an employer, you need to be sensitive as to what you say as well as how you say it. There may be things about your employee that you want to change, but at this point are impossible to change. However, you might be successful in making a person a more professional employee and improving upon his/her skills by teaching the employee through constructive criticism. For example, a housekeeper cleans over and over with the same rag. This rag is too dirty to be reused. You tell the employee that she should take rags that are dirty and toss them in the rag pile for

cleaning while frequently using new rags on new surfaces. This way you ensure that she is not cleaning with dirty rags. This may seem a simple, "common sense" issue. However, you will be surprised to discover many times over that "common sense" is not always used in many circumstances. So you directly tell your employee to proceed as follows. The employee has a choice of getting upset and annoyed that she is being told what to do after so many years of experience. She becomes irate and cops an attitude that you have not seen before. Your criticism is sound and one that can only help her in cleaning of the house. If she takes this criticism in the right light, she will only improve her housekeeping skills and should be thankful for the advice.

An example where criticism may not be so "constructive" would be if your housekeeper tends to be soft spoken and shy. You tell her "why are you so quiet, open up your personality and get with it." She looks at you like you just turned into an eight-foot gorilla. She becomes even more introspective, somewhat offended, and now finds it hard to look at you in the eye. A personality is virtually formed at a very early age. There is no way in heaven's name you are going to start reshaping one's very nature so late in the game. If you want an outgoing, bubbly employee, be sure to hire an outgoing, bubbly employee in the first place. Choose your criticism carefully and be sure that it is over something that the employee can change. Say it in a positive and gentle manner without hurting one's self-esteem and self-respect. If your applicant responds to this question somewhat adversely, you will have a clue that she/he may be a bit damaged from many years of criticism either from family members, personal relations, or employers. Perhaps this employee is excellent at her work and needs very little direction. Although this scenario is possible, it is very *unlikely* that you will never have to give constructive criticism. It is an art to know how to give constructive criticism and a blessing to know how to take it.

• *Would you agree to an AIDS, TB and/or hepatitis test?*

TB testing is important when hiring applicants to work with children, infants in particular. Many applicants come from countries where TB might be prevalent. Many of these applicants may not have had the vaccine. The disease might even be dormant. It would be important to have your domestic tested. If the results are positive, but there is no sign of current symptoms, the doctor will recommend that chest X-rays be taken to be assured that the disease is not present. There have been many cases where a person has been tested for TB with positive results and negative chest X-rays. The chest X-rays will be the determining factor as to whether the person is positive for TB.

AIDS, TB and hepatitis testing may be important when children of all ages are present. However, by law, you cannot refuse a person employment based on the results of this testing. There might be other reasons for not hiring someone, but they cannot be related to medical test results.

There are many more questions that you may have for your prospective employee as they pertain to your particular household and family. Have them ready for the interview and take notes for you to review later.

Many applicants come from countries where TB might be prevalent.

By law, you cannot refuse a person employment based on the results of this testing.

MEETING AND INTERVIEWING APPLICANTS

Visit **www.domestic-connections.com** *to download a printable pdf version of this form.*

REFERENCE CHECK FOR: _____ Date Information Provided: _____

Reference Name/Phone/Address _____

Title/Duties _____

Job Performance _____ Date Job Started and Ended _____

Attitude _____ Honesty _____ Reliability _____

Any problems or issues that you can discuss? _____

Did employee take direction well and follow it? _____

Did the employee drive for you and how were his/her driving skills? _____

How was this employee with the children? _____

_____

Reasons for Termination _____ Salary at Termination _____

Comments: _____

_____

_____

REFERENCE CHECK FORM

A reference for an applicant may not be as candid to an agency as to a prospective employer.

This form is a guideline of questions that you can legally ask a former employer. There are many other questions that you may want to discuss with a former employer. When it comes to checking a reference for someone that you are taking into your home, it would appear to me that many questions should be asked. Most parents and homeowners who are former employers of domestics would agree. Keep in mind that a reference for an applicant may not be as candid to an agency as to a prospective employer. Therefore, it is important that you, as a potential employer, speak to each reference personally, to obtain an honest and thorough reference check.

MEETING AND INTERVIEWING APPLICANTS

HAVING A TRIAL PERIOD WITH THE APPLICANT

Since we are not dealing with widgets, and we do not have Consumer Reports to provide us with any idea of a domestic's quality assurance, the truth of the matter is that *we do not know whether we have hired the right domestic for our family until we have had this person work on a trial basis.*

We are often dealing with people with vast cultural differences. Their work ethics and former conditions are sometimes very different from ours. There are those applicants who know how to work in a very sophisticated home because they themselves were raised in a higher socio-economic environment, and others who were raised in humble abodes. Therefore, you will need to do some training and be patient as you show them the way in which things are handled here.

For those applicants who have worked here many years and are seemingly experienced, you may still be shocked by their performance. Sometimes references will be excellent, and yet the employee doesn't perform at that type of level for you. Do not be surprised at this revelation. Every family runs their house differently and has a different set of standards for childcare as well as for housekeeping. Your standards may simply be different than those of the previous employer.

Bottom Line: Try each applicant for a minimum of one week to get to know her skills and work ethics. A trial period is mandatory for any applicant. By all means, be patient during the trial and training period.

HOW DO I KNOW I HAVE SELECTED THE RIGHT APPLICANT?

Some employers, new mothers in particular, have great trepidation over the process of hiring and ultimately leaving a first-born child with anyone. This could be your first time at hiring. You may feel terribly insecure about your choice as well as the very concept of leaving your child with anyone. This is very normal. A new mother is going through a lot of different emotions, many of which are a direct result of sleep deprivation, separation anxiety, and postpartum depression. If this is you, be aware that your sensitive state of mind is normal. Try not to second-guess yourself. Go with the best choice by analyzing all the facts carefully. Have a family member or friend help you in making a sound decision, and then give the employee a try. If you really like this person, all the reference and background checks are good, and the "trial period" went well, then the chances are that the choice was a good one. If you feel you need more time with the prospective employee before offering the job, then ask the employee if she/he will agree to another week's trial period. If you are working with an agency, ask the agency to accommodate you. Little by little, you will feel comfortable and secure with your decision. The chemistry you feel with someone will be 50% of the equation. Go with your gut instincts. Do not feel uncomfortable asking many questions of the person over and over until you feel completely confident that you have made the right choice.

If you are not a new mother, but have been burned in the past by other employees that you thought were going to be terrific and ended up being a nightmare, you may be very hesitant and distrust your instincts. You are just going to have to bite the bullet and keep an open mind with the next situation. Do all your due diligence, learn from your past mistakes and make every effort to make a sound decision. Try to treat every new person that you interview fairly and without presuming that this person will behave exactly the same as the last person. Generalization of people and situations will only make it more difficult for you to find a good employee.

It is impossible to know whether the person you selected is truly going to work out, until you take the chance and try the person out. Once all the necessary checks have been made, the designated trial period is complete, and you have spent sufficient time to observe the employee, you now must trust that you have done everything possible to be assured of having made a good choice. Your job now is to be an observant employer.

Chapter Five

MY OBLIGATIONS
AS AN EMPLOYER

MY OBLIGATIONS AS AN EMPLOYER

Now we get to what some people may consider as *tedious,* but is important to a successful hire. There are many obligations that you should be aware of as an employer. These cover the Immigration and Naturalization Service, Internal Revenue Service, and Labor Commission issues. This chapter will give you a summary of these laws that pertain to hiring domestic help. Please note that this discussion is a brief overview of the area. It is not intended, nor should it be considered by you as legal advice for any specific issues that you may have. The discussion is only intended to identify the issues for you.

WHY IT IS BEST TO HIRE A LEGAL DOMESTIC EMPLOYEE

The fine for employing an undocumented worker is currently $3,000 per worker and up to six months in jail. First-time offenders will most likely get off the hook with a lesser fine and perhaps no jail time, but why bring about this aggravation and grief in your life? When you hire an illegal, you are potentially eliminating an opportunity for someone who has worked hard to become legal and who desperately needs a job. The legal immigrants who work in the domestic field are often not trained in any other line of work. They are the ones who should get the domestic jobs. Otherwise, these legal domestics will turn to the system and find a way of using our system to survive. There is no question that it is always a shame to pass up a great, experienced prospective employee only because she/he is undocumented. The authorities think otherwise. Until the law changes and allows for work permits to all aliens living in the United States, you can only employ a person who has legal documentation to work in this country.

WHAT DOES IT MEAN TO BE LEGAL TO WORK?

The Federal Immigration Reform and Control Act requires that ALL employers must verify the identity and work eligibility of all persons hired. You are required to check the status of your employee through an I-9 form, Employment Eligibility Verification that is kept on file for every employee.

An employee should have one of the following items to be legal to work:

• An active **Work Authorization Card** will have an expiration date on it.

When you hire an illegal, you are potentially eliminating an opportunity for someone who has worked hard to become legal and who desperately needs a job.

MY OBLIGATIONS AS AN EMPLOYER

Check the date. If the applicant has applied for renewal, the INS will send a letter stating the application has been received and approved, and the applicant should be receiving a renewal card within 90 days. However, it may take longer. The important point is whether the petition for renewal is approved. Sometimes a person holding an expired work permit will not get approved for renewal. An employee with a work permit cannot leave the country, but can travel freely within the United States. If the employee leaves the country, there is a risk of losing the work permit and not being able to re-enter the country. If the work authorization (work permit) is not renewed, you may not employ this person further.

- **Legal Resident** Card confirms that the immigrant has been approved to live in the United States legally. He/she can benefit from most of the services provided by our country. This immigrant can travel in and out of the United States. This immigrant is also eligible for citizenship.

- A legal **U.S. Citizen** will either have a U.S. passport, a certification from INS, or a card that actually indicates citizenship.

A legal U.S. Citizen will either have a U.S. passport, a certification from INS, or a card that actually indicates citizenship.

Although many people flat-out disagree, the consensus has it that you should not hire anyone who is illegal to work. It can potentially cause you problems down the road. To begin with, you cannot do complete background checks without legal documentation. Some employees who are not legal to work have received a social security number and a valid driver's license. These are important pieces of identification necessary for a background check as long as they are valid. If a person has this type of documentation but does not have a work permit, resident card or proof of citizenship, then the employee is still not eligible to work in this country. The social security number in this case very often has a message directly on it stating "not valid for employment without work authorization." When the employee does not have any documentation, there would be no way of tracking this person in the event of a serious problem. You may also risk losing an illegal employee to deportation.

- Check for legitimate resident card, work permit or U.S. citizenship

MY OBLIGATIONS AS AN EMPLOYER

- Verify the number and active status with INS
- Be sure the applicant has a social security card issued to the applicant and valid for employment
- Applicant may also have an identification card and/or a valid driver's license

People are often confused about the alternative sources (other than a work permit, resident card or citizenship) that constitute proof of the legal right to work in this country. For example, if you hire an employee with a visa or a work authorization/sponsorship in process, is that legal?

A student visa does not qualify a person to work for a salary. It merely allows a person to stay in this country while studying for a given period of time. A (J1) Nanny visa for an Au Pair does allow the Nanny to come from overseas to work for a period of one year while living with the family and working a limited number of hours. The salary paid is minimal, and there are several other requirements attended to this particular visa issuance. Any other visa might allow a person to stay in the U.S. for up to 10 years, but it does not allow the person the right to work for a paid salary.

An applicant who does not have a work permit but is in process to receive one DOES NOT qualify to work. Back in 1989, a democratic gubernatorial candidate, Jane Harman, thought that her English nanny was hired legally because she was going through the sponsorship process. In reality Ms. Harman was violating U.S. immigration laws by employing the Nanny before the application process was complete. Since 1986, federal law has provided for fines of up to $3000 for employers of undocumented workers. Years ago, the government did not require people to check their worker's work authorization status. Now with the mandatory I-9 forms, no excuses are accepted for not knowing what makes a person legal to work.

HOW DO I MAKE MY EMPLOYEE LEGAL?

If your domestic qualifies under the immigration laws to become legal in this

MY OBLIGATIONS AS AN EMPLOYER

country through sponsorship by an employer, then you can do so through the services of an immigration attorney.

If you do decide to call an attorney to help assist your domestic in getting a work permit or residency, keep in mind that a good immigration attorney will check one's file carefully to see the options and possibilities for making one legal before any fees are required. Be sure to check on the credentials of any attorney you choose. There have been many immigration lawyers who have taken a client's money and either quickly closed shop or have done absolutely nothing for the client, knowing that the case is not headed for success, while continually requesting more fees.

This process of obtaining residency may take an undetermined amount of time depending on the quota for unskilled workers from a particular country.

According to a prominent immigration attorney, Dan Korenberg of Korenberg, Abramowitz & Feldun, "The sponsorship quota for unskilled workers has fluctuated continuously over the years. There is no way of knowing whether or not a person has a chance of obtaining labor certification without first seeking the advice of an immigration attorney. Only if the quota is current for unskilled labor at the time one files a petition for permanent residence does one qualify."

If your employee has an ***active work permit,*** and you want to sponsor this person to obtain residency, you will still need to contact an immigration attorney to see if the employee actually qualifies to be a resident. This process of obtaining residency may take an undetermined amount of time depending on the quota for unskilled workers from a particular country. This area of the law is so complicated and ever-changing that it would be well beyond the scope of this book to describe each and every circumstance that might be the basis for approval. Sometimes it is only a matter of such criteria as the birth country and the date of entry. In other cases, the question of legalizing an employee is a major, lengthy, and costly undertaking.

Certainly the concept of sponsoring an individual is a wonderful gesture. By obtaining an excellent immigration attorney, you will determine immediately the probability of success. Under all circumstances, you need to know that there may be a chance that the process cannot be successfully completed. Speak with an experienced and well-respected immigration attorney to get all the facts before you agree to go forward with a sponsorship.

THE CONSEQUENCES OF HIRING UNDER THE TABLE

You may ask yourself the question: "What are the chances of anyone finding out I have hired an illegal?" Or let us say that you think you are doing the right thing because you have hired a legal person; however, you do not choose to pay this person legally by doing payroll taxes. Since so many people pay their employees in cash, "under the table," the likelihood of getting caught may appear slim. However, consider the following remarks made by Robert E. King, who is the founder of Legally Nanny (http://www.legallynanny.com), a company providing legal and tax advice for clients in connection with hiring nannies and other household employees:

"There are various ways that even an amicable parting between you and your employee could result in you facing investigation. Some ways of getting caught are as follows:

- *Unemployment:* You terminate your employee. She is now out of work and files for unemployment benefits. When asked about her last place of employment, she names you. There are no records of you paying employment taxes.

- *Workers Compensation:* Your employee gets hurt while working in your home. Now she can't work but still needs to pay her bills, so she files for worker's compensation insurance, and she reports you in order to obtain benefits.

- *Social Security:* Your employee is older and wants to retire. Upon retiring, she claims social security benefits. Her benefits are lower than she expected, and she realizes that for the time you employed her illegally, she wasn't contributing to social security. To obtain more benefits, she reports

"There are various ways that even an amicable parting between you and your employee could result in you facing investigation."

MY OBLIGATIONS AS AN EMPLOYER

her employment with you to the Social Security Administration.

- **Taxes:** You think you are smart and describe your employee as an independent contractor responsible for her own taxes. Then your employee's tax bill comes due and she realizes that she's responsible for both the employer's and employee's share of social security and Medicare, resulting in a much larger tax bill than she expected. She complains to the IRS about the unfairness of it all and has now turned you in."

It is clear that you could potentially ruin your reputation and career, especially if you are an attorney, accountant, financial advisor, or any professional who trades on integrity. We recently saw an example of this with Bernard Kerik and his nomination for Secretary for Homeland Security being withdrawn.

You may also be interested to know that if you have been paying payroll taxes previously on any household employee, it will be a "red flag" if you stop doing so. The IRS has threatened to audit all agencies to identify those employers who have hired domestic employees and who failed to report income. To date no evidence of the IRS raiding agencies has materialized. Unless you enjoy taking risks and living on the edge, it is advisable to pay your employee properly and not be at risk.

THE ADVANTAGES OF HIRING LEGALLY

If you decide to hire a legal worker, but choose NOT to pay the necessary taxes, you are still breaking the law.

The vast majority of families with domestic employees do not pay taxes on their help. The Census Bureau reports about 2 million household workers in the country. The Bureau of Labor Statistics counts even more. Many of these domestics work in several homes simultaneously. The Internal Revenue Service has made a rough calculation that well over 3 million people should have paid taxes on their domestic employees.

Some employers are content with hiring a legal employee but refuse to put them on payroll due to the attendant costs. If you decide to hire a legal worker, but choose NOT to pay the necessary taxes, you are still breaking the law.

So, let's consider the reasons why it makes sense to hire legally. There are a number of advantages to hiring a household worker legally. Robert King continues:

- **Dependent Care Account:** Save taxes by putting up to $5,000 pre-tax per family per year into a Dependent Care Account if applicable and offered through your employer. Depending on your effective tax rate, this could save you hundreds or even thousands of dollars in taxes while you use this pre-tax money on eligible dependent care expenses, including paying your nanny.

- **Child Care Tax Credit:** You may be eligible to claim the federal child care tax credit. For 2005, this credit, if applicable, allows you to receive a minimum tax credit of 20% for the first $3,000 in qualifying expenses for each of your first two children per year.

- **Cash Flow:** You can actually improve your cash flow by hiring your nanny legally. By withholding your nanny's personal income and employment taxes, your weekly out-of-pocket cost to pay your nanny legally is often lower than what you would have paid under the table. Thus, although you ultimately will pay your taxes annually, you can reap the time value of this money and improve your weekly cash flow.

- **Peace of Mind:** You can spend more time with family and sleep well at night knowing that you've done everything legally. Don't underestimate how worrying about getting caught and the consequences of hiring legally can take a toll on you personally and professionally.

The bottom line is that after calculating potential tax advantages, hiring a nanny legally typically adds approximately 4% - 5% to your cost. On a $20,000 annual salary, that's roughly an additional $800 - $1,000. Social Security, Medicare and state and federal unemployment taxes add approximately 9% of a worker's salary to a typical household employer's costs. However, by making the most of tax advantages available to you, the true burden of hiring a nanny can be substantially less," King concludes.

MY OBLIGATIONS AS AN EMPLOYER

WHAT ARE MY OBLIGATIONS UNDER TAX LAWS?

Many employers are completely unaware of the fact that that a household employee is NOT considered an independent contractor. If you are NOT an independent contractor, then you are an employee. Let's break it down.

Many employers are completely unaware of the fact that that a household employee is NOT considered an independent contractor.

According to the Employment Development Department, a domestic worker who works in a house is called a "household employee." A *"household"* is defined as follows:

- A house
- An apartment
- A mobile home or boat
- A summer or winter home
- A condominium
- A hotel room
- A fraternity or college club

"Household Employees" are as follows:

- Babysitters
- Butlers
- Caretakers
- Chauffeurs
- Cooks (unless employed by a catering service)
- Crews of private yachts
- Gardeners (unless employed by a gardening service)
- Governesses/Governors
- Nannies
- Handy-persons (unless employed by a handyman service)
- Home Health Care Workers

- Janitors
- Housekeepers/Maids
- Laundry Workers
- Pilots of private planes for family use
- Pool Maintenance People (unless employed by a pool company)
- Valets
- Waiters/Waitresses (unless employed by a catering service)

If you are uncertain about whether or not the people who work for you are considered "household employees" then you can call the Employment Tax Call Center for your state. The number in the state of California is (916) 653-7795 or go online to www.edd.ca.gov.

If you qualify as hiring a household employee in your home, then you may also qualify for registration with the Employment Development Department (EDD). The reason you need to register with EDD is because you will need to report payroll taxes on your employee. This is a very complicated area that many employers would rather leave to their tax accountant or a payroll service. On the Internet, you can find many payroll services who specifically work with household employees. Check out www.4nannies.com or www.legallynanny.com.

On the Internet, you can find many payroll services who specifically work with household employees.

The amount you pay your household employee in a given quarter will determine whether or not you need to register with the EDD and pay taxes. (This information can be found in the pamphlet entitled "Household Employer's Guide" put out by the Employment Development Department.) For example, for the state of California:

- If you pay less than $750 to your employee(s) in cash wages in a calendar quarter and provide meals and lodging valued at $150, you are NOT required to register, report employee wages, or withhold pay or any state payroll taxes because you have paid less than the cash wage limit of $750 in cash wages. (The value of lodging and meals is not considered when evaluating the $750 cash wage limit for SDI.)

MY OBLIGATIONS AS AN EMPLOYER

- If you pay $750 or more to your employee(s) in cash wages in a calendar quarter and provide meals valued at $75, you must register, report employee wages, and withhold SDI on the entire $825. You are not liable for UI and ETT taxes because the cash wage limit of $1,000 in a quarter has not been met.

- If you pay $900 to your employee(s) in cash wages in a calendar quarter and provide meals and lodging valued at $150, you MUST register, report employee wages and withhold SDI on the entire $1,050. You are not liable for UI and ETT taxes because the cash wage limit of $1,000 in a quarter has not been met.

- If you pay $1,000 to your employee(s) in cash wages in a calendar quarter and provide meals and lodging valued at $100, you MUST register, report employee wages, and pay UI and ETT taxes and withhold SDI on the entire $1,100 because you have met the $1,000 cash wage limit.

HOW TO REGISTER AS AN EMPLOYER WITH THE EMPLOYMENT DEVELOPMENT DEPARTMENT

To register as a household employer with EDD, obtain a "Registration Form for Employers of Household Workers" (DE1HW) in any of the following ways:

- Call the Employment Tax Call Center at (888) 745-3886
- Visit your local Employment Tax Office
- Call the EDD Forms Warehouse at (916) 322-2835
- Download the DE1HW form at www.edd.ca.gov/taxform.htm
- You can fill out this form by contacting www.edd.ca.gov/txfilfrm.htm.

When you have completed this form (DE1HW for the state of California), you then send it via fax or mail to the following address:

**Employment Development Department
Account Services Group, MIC 28
P.O. Box 826880**

Sacramento, CA 94280-0001
Fax: (916) 654-9211

You will be issued an employer account number. This number is on all pre-printed forms sent to you. You can get an employer account number immediately by calling (916) 657-0529. You still need to mail or fax a completed DE1HW form to EDD.

WHAT ARE PAYROLL TAXES?

Payroll taxes vary from state to state. You can call the IRS at (800) 829-1040 or log onto www.irs.gov and get a tax schedule for your state. Mandatory federal payroll taxes include Social Security and Medicare. As an example, in California, additional payroll taxes as of 2005 are paid as follows:

Payroll taxes vary from state to state.

- *Unemployment Insurance (UI)* – is paid by the employer. The rate changes each year based on an employer's UI experience. The EDD informs employers of their new rates each December. Generally a new employer's UI tax rate is 3.4% (.034) for the first three tax years.

- *Employment Training Tax (ETT)* – is paid by the employer. This rate is set by statute at 0.1% (.001) of UI-taxable wages for employer with positive UI reserve account balances.

- *State Disability Insurance (SDI)* – is paid by the employee. The employer must withhold SDI from the employee's wages. The 2005 SDI tax rate is 1.08% (.0108). This is set by the California State Legislature, and SDI may change each year. EDD notifies employers of the new rate each December.

- *California Personal Income Tax (PIT)* – is paid by the employee. Household employers are not required to withhold personal income taxes from employee wages unless BOTH the employer and employee agree to withhold the tax. The employee, however, is still responsible for reporting and paying the taxes due to the IRS and State Franchise Tax Board. The

MY OBLIGATIONS AS AN EMPLOYER

California PIT is withheld based on the employee's W-4 or the DE 4 form.

HOW CAN I MAKE PAYROLL TAXES EASY?

There are various payroll services that you can utilize to do the tedious task at hand. Check out the following site on the Internet:

www.4nannytaxes.com – *Homework Solutions* offers household employers a selection of service plans that include the following service:

NaniTax – a tax preparation service that is perfect for employers who want to write their own paycheck and let *Homework Solutions* prepare the tax returns. This includes complete preparation of signature-ready quarterly and annual payroll returns, full account set-up and the staff support of *Homework Solutions*.

There are additional tax service plans that include debiting directly from your checking account or charging the taxes to your credit card. Also, through electronic funds transfer from your checking, employees may also be paid by direct deposit or by NaniPay checks.

This site has a wonderful feature called "free tax calculator." This provides a very useful instant calculation for payroll taxes by inserting the weekly gross amount, pay frequency, filing status and withholding allowances. You will instantly be able to see what a $500/wk gross amount will cost you in payroll taxes as well as what the deductions are for the employee. You can print this out and hand it to a prospective employee so that she/he will automatically know what her/his paycheck will look like each week.

www.legallynanny.com - **Legally Nanny** also provides legal tax advice on completing all the start-up paperwork and showing you how to handle the ongoing tax and reporting issues yourself.

Your very own tax accountant may or may not wish to handle this for you, but might also refer you to a good local service who does handle this on a regular basis.

So let's review:

MY OBLIGATIONS AS AN EMPLOYER

- If you hire a Nanny, Babysitter, Housekeeper or any other person who qualifies under the title of a "domestic employee" and pay that person $750 or more in one calendar quarter, then you must register your employee with EDD and pay payroll taxes.

- Ask for a Social Security Number or the ITIN (to apply use form SS-5 or Form W-7, respectively).

- Get a Federal Employer Identification Number (Form SS-4).

- Pay taxes according to the current EDD payroll tax laws. Remember social security tax may be split 50-50 with the employee.

- Withhold federal and state income tax, if the employee requests it (Form W-4).

- File a quarterly tax return (Form 942) and Wage and Tax Statement at year-end (W-2 Form).

- Give the employee a Wage and Tax Statement (W-2) by January 31st of each year.

IMPORTANT LABOR ISSUES TO KEEP IN MIND

The Labor Code for Household Occupations varies from state to state. Although many states have adopted various sections of the California Labor Code, you will need to check the labor code for your state by calling the U.S. Department of Labor or your State Labor Commissioner's Office. In the state of California, there is a pamphlet put out by the Department of Industrial Relations written by the Industrial Welfare Commission regulating wages, hours and working conditions in the "Public Housekeeping Industry." These laws are in accordance with the Labor Code and the Constitution of California. It has been amended as of January 1, 2001. Here are some important labor issues as they relate to domestics.

For all employees who are 18 years of age and over, a working day constitutes eight (8) hours and workweek constitutes forty (40) hours.

- ***Hours and Wages*** - For all employees who are 18 years of age and over, a working day constitutes eight (8) hours and workweek constitutes forty

(40) hours. An employee shall not be employed more than forty hours in any workweek unless the employee receives one and one-half (1 1/2) times such employee's regular rate of pay for each additional hour. No overtime pay shall be required for hours worked in excess of any daily number.

- *Minimum Wages* - Every employer shall pay to each employee wages not less than six dollars and seventy-five cents ($6.75) per hour for all hours worked effective January 1, 2002. Every employer shall pay to each employee on the established payday for the period involved, not less than the applicable minimum wage for all hours worked in the payroll period.

- *Reporting Time Pay* - Each workday an employee is required to report for work and does report, but is not put to work or is furnished less than half of said employee's usual or scheduled day's work, the employee shall be paid for half the usual or scheduled days work, but in no event for less than two (2) hours nor more than four (4) hours, at the employee's regular rate of pay, which shall not be less than minimum wage.

If an employee is required to report for work a second time in any one workday and is furnished less than two (2) hours of work on the second reporting, said employee shall be paid for two (2) hours at the employee's regular rate of pay, which shall not be less than minimum wage.

The foregoing is not applicable if operations cannot commence due to threats to employees or property; public utilities failing to supply electricity, water, gas or sewer system; and if the interruption of work is caused by an Act of God or other cause not within the employer's control.

None of the foregoing applies to an employee on paid standby status that is called to perform assigned work at a time other than the employee's scheduled reporting time.

- *Records* - Every employer shall keep accurate information with respect to each employee including full name and address; occupation and social security number; birth date; time records showing time employee works, meal periods and authorized rest periods; total wages paid each payroll period including value of board, lodging or other compensation actually furnished to the employee; and total wages paid each payroll period.

Employer shall at the time of each payment of wages furnish each employee either as a detachable part of the check draft or voucher paying the employee's wages, or separately, an itemized statement showing (1) all deductions; (2) the inclusive dates of the period for which the employee is paid; (3) the name of the employee or the employee's social security number; and (4) the name of the employer.

All required records shall be in the English language and in ink or other indelible ink form, properly dated, showing month, day and year, and shall be kept on file by the employer for at least three years at the place of employment or at a central location within the state of California. An employee's records shall be available for inspection by the employee upon reasonable request.

- *Cash Shortage and Breakage* - No employer shall make any deduction from the wage or require any reimbursement from an employee for any cash shortage, breakage or loss of equipment, unless it can be shown that the shortage, breakage, or loss is caused by a dishonest or willful act, or by the gross negligence of the employee.

- *Uniforms and Equipment* - When uniforms are required by the employer to be worn by the employee as a condition of employment, such uniforms shall be provided and maintained by the employer. The term "uniform" includes wearing apparel and accessories of distinctive design or color.

When tools and equipment are required by the employer or are necessary to the performance of a job, such tools and equipment shall be provided and maintained by the employer.

- *Meals and Lodging* - (a) "Meal" means an adequate well-balanced serving

When tools and equipment are required by the employer or are necessary to the performance of a job, such tools and equipment shall be provided and maintained by the employer.

of a variety of wholesome, nutritious foods. (b) "Lodging" means living accommodations available, decent, and sanitary according to usual and customary standards. Employees shall not be required to share a bed. (c) Meals or lodging may not be credited against the minimum wage without a voluntary written agreement between the employer and the employee. When credit for meals and lodging is used to meet part of the employer's minimum wage obligations, the amounts so credited may not be more than as stipulated in the Labor Code.

Lodging:

Room occupied alone ....$31.05 per week
Room shared...$26.20 per week
Apartment 2/3 of the ordinary rental value........$381.20 per month
Where couple are both employed by the
employer 2/3 of the ordinary rental ....$563.90 per month

Meals:

Breakfast ....$1.95 per day
Lunch ....$2.75 per day
Dinner ....$4.30 per day

Meals that are evaluated as part of the minimum wage must be bona fide meals. Deductions shall not be made for meals not received or used. If, as a condition of employment, the employee must live at the place of employment or occupy quarters owned or under the control of the employer, then the employer may not charge rent in excess of the values as listed.

Every employer shall authorize and permit all employees to take rest periods.

- **Rest Periods** - Every employer shall authorize and permit all employees to take rest periods, which insofar as practicable shall be in the middle of each work period. The authorized rest period time shall be based on the total hours worked daily at the rate of ten (10) minutes net rest time per four (4) hours or major fraction thereof. However, a rest period need not be authorized for employees whose total daily work time is less than three and

MY OBLIGATIONS AS AN EMPLOYER

one-half (3 1/2) hours. Authorized rest period time shall be counted as hours worked for which there shall be no deduction from wages.

If an employer fails to provide an employee a rest period in accordance with the applicable provisions of this order, the employer shall pay the employee one (1) hour of pay at the employee's regular rate of compensation for each workday that the rest period is not provided.

Although the Labor Code is quite extensive, the above information applies specifically to "Household Help." It would be prudent to get a copy of the latest edition of the Official Notice on the Public Housekeeping Industry to check on any changes and get a complete view of each Labor Code. If you have any questions, you can also contact the Industrial Welfare Commission in California as follows:

> **State of California**
> **Department of Industrial Relations**
> **Industrial Welfare Commission**
> **320 West 4th Street, Suite 450**
> **Los Angeles, CA 90013**
> **(213) 620-6330**

For labor law requirements, log onto www.dir.ca.gov/dlse or call DIR's Labor Standards Enforcement Division (refer to the government listings in your local telephone book).

WORKER'S COMPENSATION FOR HOUSEHOLD EMPLOYEES

It is mandatory in many states, as in California, that you have worker's compensation insurance for your household employee(s). Therefore, one of the first calls you make after hiring your domestic employee will be to your insurance agent. It is very important that you be covered for any potential bodily harm that your employee may suffer, especially if it is as a result of negligence on your behalf.

If you own a home, you probably have homeowner's insurance. Most

It is very important that you be covered for any potential bodily harm that your employee may suffer, especially if it is as a result of negligence on your behalf.

MY OBLIGATIONS AS AN EMPLOYER

homeowner's insurance policies have automatic coverage for household employees who work up to 20 hours per week. This would cover any housekeeper who might come to work in your home from 1 to 3 days per week at an average of approximately 6 1/2 hours per day. However, if you are employing anyone beyond 20 hours per week, you will need to notify your homeowner's insurance company so that you can obtain a separate worker's compensation endorsement that will cover a full-time employee. The cost of this is very minimal. For example, your employee is cleaning your windows and falls off a ladder that was not stable enough to hold your employee. If this person breaks an arm and cannot work for 8 weeks, who is responsible for all the medical bills? The employer may be held responsible. Another example would be that one of the duties your housekeeper must complete is to take the groceries from the car into the house. Each week, cases of water are purchased. Your housekeeper moves the large case of water and pulls her back. She needs x-rays and therapy. Who is responsible for these bills? The employer is responsible. Perhaps you will ultimately not want to use the worker's compensation coverage, but you certainly want the option. You may also need to check into your "personal excess liability insurance" to see what it will cover for any incidents caused by a household employee.

For worker's compensation requirements, access www.dir.ca.gov/dwc for the state of California or call Department of Industrial Relations (DIR) Worker's Compensation Division in your area.

Chapter Six

BACKGROUND INVESTIGATIONS

BACKGROUND INVESTIGATIONS

N ow that you have gone through the painstaking process of interviewing prospective candidates for your position and you understand your legal obligations as an employer, you may have found a prospective employee that you wish to hire. Assuming you have taken the next step of checking references, your last step before offering this person the job will be to get a background investigation completed. An immediate name match can be obtained by some background search firms (check out the web site: http://www.proeaccess.com). A more in-depth search will cost $20 to $100. Be sure to input all names that the applicant holds and has held in the past. If the name match exists, this does not necessarily mean that it is for the same person you are investigating. Many people have the same names. You will need to do a further search in the county or counties where the name match appeared by inputting the social security number and the date of birth. The turnaround time is 24-48 hours for results. Professional search firms are able to access their data from more than 65 proprietary sources and from every court in the United States and most foreign countries.

If you are eager to hire this person and fear losing her/him before the criminal check can be performed, then you can offer the position subject to the results. Let us assume that you are very short on time and need to get this person started ASAP. Perhaps based on the references, you feel 99% sure that this person's criminal record will be clean. Go ahead and set up a trial day (with you being present) so that you can observe this person's performance and not lose time. Naturally, it is still a risk to have anyone in your home prior to receiving a full criminal check; however, you will need to go on your gut instinct on this one.

There is a possibility that a person might have a criminal record that does not pertain to the person you have just investigated. That sounds terribly confusing, doesn't it? This is because of a very popular crime called "identity theft." If this is the case, the applicant may be completely in shock when she/he sees the rap sheet for crimes that this person swears she/he never committed. If this is the case with one of your prospective applicants, you will need to make the decision on how to proceed.

Assuming you have taken the next step of checking references, your last step before offering this person the job will be to get a background investigation completed.

BACKGROUND INVESTIGATIONS

There are many companies available to do background investigations. Their rates are competitive. If you are not going through an agency, you must have the "consumer notification release" form signed by anyone that you plan to investigate. This form notifies the individual that you are doing a background check and with their signature gives you their approval that you can perform this check. By law, you are also required to provide copies of any check performed on the individual upon request.

THE FAIR CREDIT REPORTING ACT

The federal Fair Credit Reporting Act (FCRA) is designed to promote accuracy, fairness and privacy of information in the files of every consumer reporting agency (CRA). Most CRA's are credit bureaus that gather and sell information about a person, such as whether this person pays bills on time or has filed bankruptcy – to creditors, employers, landlords and other businesses. You can find the compete text of the FCRA, 15 U.S.C. 1681-1681u at the Federal Trade Commission's web site (http://www.ftc.gov). The FCRA gives you specific rights. You may have additional rights under state law. You may contact a state or local consumer protection agency or an attorney to learn those rights. Some of those **employee** rights are as follows:

- You must be told if information in your file has been used against you. Anyone who uses information from a CRA to take action against you, such as denying an application for credit, insurance or employment, must tell you, and give you the name, address, and phone number of the CRA that provided the consumer report.

- You can find out what is in your file. At your request, a CRA must give you the information in your file.

- You can dispute inaccurate information with the CRA. If you tell a CRA that your file contains inaccurate information, the CRA must investigate the items (usually within 30 days) by presenting to its information source all relevant evidence you submit, unless your dispute is frivolous. The

BACKGROUND INVESTIGATIONS

source must review your evidence and report its findings to the CRA.

WHAT IS A CONSUMER REPORT?

A consumer report consists of information deemed to have a bearing on job performance, and may include information from public and private sources, public records, former employers and references. All pre-employment inquiries are limited to information that affects job performance and the workplace. It must be conducted in accordance with applicable federal and state laws, including the Fair Credit Reporting Act (FCRA). The scope of the reports may include information concerning driving records, civil and criminal court records, credit, worker's compensation records, education, credentials, identity, past addresses, social security number, and previous employment and personnel references. This report may also include reference checks from former employers or references provided by the applicant. Any reference check is strictly limited to job-related information. This type of report is known as an "investigative consumer report." This type of report is legally defined as a report based upon interviews that may contain information relating to the applicant's character, general reputation, personal characteristics or mode of living. The employer has a right to request additional information or to inspect any files concerning such a report with the prospective employee's permission.

A consumer report consists of information deemed to have a bearing on job performance, and may include information from public and private sources.

This Disclosure and Release Authorization must be signed and dated by the applicant prior to proceeding with investigation. To obtain a complete consumer report, the applicant must provide the following:

- Name (former names)
- Current and former address in last 7 years
- Social security number
- Driver's license number and state it was issued
- Date of birth

USING CORRECT NAME(S) AND DATE OF BIRTH

It is recommended that you check the formal name of the individual as listed

It is recommended that you check the formal name of the individual as listed on his or her driver's license, passport or identification card.

on his or her driver's license, passport or identification card. If the person has a known legal nickname, you will also want to check this name. Say, for example, the person's legal name was William Smith. You would want to also check Bill Smith. If there is middle initial, check the report under the name with and without the middle initial. If there are other forms of identification with different names, be sure to do a criminal check on each name.

Using the correct date of birth for each applicant has become essential in order to complete criminal background verifications. You can still run a preliminary name search; however, if the check is inconclusive, then the date of birth and the social security number must be submitted for any further search.

CRIMINAL HISTORY

Felony and misdemeanor records search for convictions are completed by county. A county search for misdemeanor (municipal court) and felony (superior court) convictions can be conducted anywhere in the United States. Sometimes a reading of original court documents at the appropriate court will be necessary to verify identification of the subject and determine the disposition of the case. Most preliminary hearings for felonies are first heard in municipal court. If there is sufficient evidence to support the felony charge, the case is then sent to superior court for trial. It is recommended that you review both municipal and superior court records. Note that misdemeanor crimes include, among other things, petty theft, assault and battery and certain drug-related offenses. Felony charges include grand theft, sale and transportation of drugs, embezzlement and armed robbery, among other more serious crimes.

SOCIAL SECURITY TRACE

Frequently, a social security trace will reveal names or addresses not listed by the applicant on his or her application form. Due to the general reliability of the social security trace, if additional addresses and/or names (for example, an AKA or maiden name) appear on a social security trace, there is a high likelihood that the applicant has lived at such alternate addresses or gone by such alternate names. A social security trace also verifies that the number provided by the applicant is a valid one issued by the Social Security Administration and that the applicant is reporting this as his/her number. It is considered best practice to do the following:

First run a social security trace and compare the names and addresses on the report with those reported by the applicant, and

Second, run county criminal searches on additional addresses and names that appear to be associated with the applicant. On average, when checking alternate counties and names, you will see a criminal hit rate increase 3-4 percentage points. This is because criminals often "conveniently" omit a place of residence where they were convicted of a crime.

A social security trace verifies basic personal data, which may be covering larger problems. You will get 10 years of residence addresses as reported by the credit bureau subscribers; lists of all aliases and AKA's used; and a more thorough criminal check.

A social security trace verifies basic personal data, which may be covering larger problems.

EMPLOYMENT VERIFICATION

The employment verification report verifies dates of employment and previous job titles. It also verifies rate of pay, reason for leaving and eligibility for re-hire. It can reveal lapses in employment and exaggerated experience levels. This is by far one of the most important elements to a background investigation.

EDUCATION VERIFICATION

Verifying basic education credentials for domestics may not be as necessary as when hiring executives and the like; however, when this information is provided, you will want to verify that it is true. Dates of study, types of major, degrees received are verified. Background Investigation Services finds that over 8% of applicants exaggerate education credentials.

DEPARTMENT OF MOTOR VEHICLES REPORT

This report verifies the validity of a license and reveals information regarding

BACKGROUND INVESTIGATIONS

moving violations, convictions or accidents. This report will show drunk driving, reckless driving, outstanding traffic warrants, suspensions, penal code violations, probation and/or revocations. If you plan to have your employee driving for you, this report is mandatory.

WORKER'S COMPENSATION HISTORY

A search can be made with the Regional Worker's Compensation Board indices to determine whether these boards have any records on the applicant. If found, this file would reveal previous employers, hourly rate, and the nature of termination. This could identify employers that the applicant failed to list on the employment application.

TRUSTLINE

According to the California Department of Social Services, the following is a clear description of *Trustline*.

A search made with the Regional Worker's Compensation Board would reveal previous employers, hourly rate, and the nature of termination.

"*Trustline* is a California Registry of In-Home Child Care Providers. This was created by the California Legislature to offer parents, employment agencies, childcare resource and referral programs, and childcare providers access to a background check conducted by the California Department of Social Services (CDSS). This includes checks in the Criminal History System and Child Abuse Central Index (CACI) at the California Department of Justice (DOJ) and a check of Federal Bureau of Investigation (FBI) records. The *Trustline* Registry is maintained by CDSS and may be checked through the California Childcare Resource and Referral Network (CCRRN) by calling 1-800-822-8490.

The California Department of Social Services and the CCRRN along with local child care resource and referral programs and parents and child care providers have all worked together to develop the *Trustline* Registry. It is made up of childcare providers who have submitted an application to CDSS and their fingerprints to the Department of Justice background clearance process.

BACKGROUND INVESTIGATIONS

Trustline benefits parents by providing one more tool to use when it comes time to choose a child care provider. It benefits the child care provider in that by being listed on the Trustline Registry, you offer added reassurance and demonstrate to parents that you are serious about your profession as a child care provider. If no disqualifying criminal convictions are found on the California Criminal History System, and no reports of substantiated child abuse are found on the Child Abuse Central Index, the applicant's name will be placed on the Trustline Registry pending the FBI check." The current cost for digital fingerprints is $87 and to register the applicant is $43.

CAN I BE ASSURED MY DOMESTIC IS HONEST?

The answer is obviously and definitively "NO." Some people will lie and perceive the lie to be so minimal in their mind that they would not even consider it a problem. Even if an employee thinks that a "white lie" is best, it is vital that you tell your employee that any lie is unacceptable. You need to stress that being honest is so important to you that lying under any circumstance would be enough cause for termination.

Then you have the question of stealing, another form of dishonesty. Is there a way to lessen your chances of any potential theft? The answer is "probably," but there is never any 100% assurance that someone will not randomly choose to take something that belongs to you. We cannot be sure of anything except death and taxes. We can, however, be 90% sure that a person who has a clean criminal record and a history of having worked in various people's homes with longevity and without ANY incident would most likely continue to be an honest employee in your home. However, people can change and circumstances can make a person desperate. Someone whom you would think would be the very last person to ever take anything from you or lie to you could very likely surprise you. You must conduct your due diligence on every prospective employee, but do not think that this necessarily means you are completely in the clear.

People can change and circumstances can make a person desperate.

When you bring a person into your home, you are taking a risk with your belongings, your children and your well being. Case in point: There was an incident where dishonesty was revealed after 7 years of loyalty. A Housekeeper who was excellent at her profession and had developed a seemingly wonderful relationship with her employer, suddenly decided that it was her right to own some of the precious possessions at her employer's residence. The employer, somewhat elderly, did not notice the items were missing right away. Granted, the employer had an abundance of things ranging from silver to crystal to fine linens and jewelry. One day, however, the employee took something that was noticeable. The employer never imagined that it was her loyal Housekeeper of 7 years until another item of importance was missing. Soon after, the employer began to check all of her belongings, only to find that *several* were missing. She was finally led to believe that it could not have been anyone but the Housekeeper. She was able to obtain a warrant and go with the police to the Housekeeper's home. As she entered her Housekeeper's apartment, she was aghast and heartbroken to find each and every item that was missing from her home.

This is not about accusing all domestic employees of being potentially dishonest. This is about human nature. Theft occurs in all professions and even with some very high-ranking white-collar employees, as we have seen as of late. Some of the most honest people in the world are the poorest. But since we can no more generalize about the poor being honest nor the rich being dishonest, we are left with the conclusion that we are simply all prone to dishonesty. The difference is the type of items that are available to a particular employee. In an office setting, you might have an office employee take office supplies right under your nose and never know it. In a home, you are dealing with so many more personal, expensive items that can be removed swiftly. Whether or not you lose a roll of paper towels will be of little concern to you. However, a diamond ring is another story. Sometimes, employees will think they have the right to take a small, insignificant item because they worked there for so many years and they see how much money and possessions their employer has available. They have rationalized the situation to believe that it should not matter if they took that very insignificant item. This is where the problem begins. You can rationalize anything in life if you simply want to believe that you are not in the wrong. The fact remains: Stealing is stealing. A roll of paper towels that does not belong to you is just as significant in principle as a sterling silver fork. So what can we do to prevent any of this from happening to us?

HOW TO PROTECT YOURSELF FROM THEFT

There are some precautions an employer can take to keep a close watch on the situation. Here are some ideas:

- Do not leave your money and jewelry lying around all over the house. Why make it tempting for someone? Whether you have a permanent employee or workmen that frequently enter the premises, keep your wallets and purses in a private place. Store all excess money in a safe. After using your fine jewelry, remember to place it back in a locked safe at all times. The point here is: Do not dangle a carrot in front of someone's eyes.

- Keep a list of all of your expensive possessions. Photograph the items such as paintings, mink coats, jewelry, silver, china, antiques, etc. Keep a log and photographs of all your possessions. This is also important and suggested by your homeowner's insurance company in the event of theft or fire.

- Be aware of your possessions and what might be missing. Regularly observe your possessions, count your silver, and check your jewelry. Know how much money you carry in your wallet. If you keep a petty cash box handy for use by the domestics, then check it periodically and be sure the receipts match the amount taken.

- Take notice if your employee is suddenly carrying large, unusual bags out of your home. You may want to ask what is in bag. Don't be afraid to question your employee in a casual manner.

- Know where your employee resides. If you are suspicious, make a surprise visit to the employee's home, stating that you just happened to be in the area.

Do not leave your money and jewelry lying around all over the house. Why make it tempting for someone?

Know where your employee resides.

BACKGROUND INVESTIGATIONS

- Some employers like to test their employee by planting money in a hidden but somewhat obvious location to see if it is taken. It has been reported to me that this is often a good method for testing one's integrity. For example, let us say that money is planted by the employer in the pocket of a pair of jeans going into the washer. (Your Housekeeper may and actually should check pockets of clothing for items that do not belong in the washer.) If she does her job right, she would find the money and have two choices. Hopefully, the choice she makes is to hand it over to you, letting you know that it was found in the pocket of your jeans.

Video surveillance is often used in homes to observe all types of care providers.

- Video surveillance is often used in homes where there are many expensive possessions such as paintings and artifacts. It is also used to observe all types of care providers. It is expensive to install, but is most useful for those who are very concerned about theft and/or child abuse. The cameras, of course, cannot be placed in the bathrooms or the employee's private quarters; however, there are plenty of other locations where they can be strategically placed for your observance.

- Finally, make it clear from the very beginning that you do not tolerate any form of theft or dishonesty. No matter what the item, whether it is an ornate rubber band or a piece of fine jewelry, you will terminate the person instantly, and if you have the necessary proof, you will prosecute accordingly. Let it be known from the beginning that, although you have no reason to believe that this new employee will take anything from you, just the same, you will not tolerate any form of dishonesty.

THE USE OF NANNY-CAMS TO ENSURE CHILD SAFETY

The images of the "nanny-cam" past where we saw two separate child-care providers on television who had been caught on nanny-cam tape shaking a baby and hitting a baby over the head with a wooden spoon will never leave our memories. Those incidents were the ones caught on tape. Imagine how many more there might be that have gone unnoticed. The use of a nanny-cam is a great tool for keeping a close eye on your Nanny; however, it will require proper positioning of the nanny-cam and your taking the time to periodically review the tapes to make it worthwhile. You will need to inform your Nanny of the fact that you have nanny-cam in your home; however, you do not need to inform them of the locations of the cameras. To be absolutely sure of your rights to videotape an employee, you should first consult with an attorney, who may insist that you have a signed agreement with the Nanny acknowledging the right to videotape your residence.

HOW DO I HANDLE MY SUSPICION OF MISCONDUCT?

Making an accusation of theft or any misconduct without proof can land you with a nice lawsuit and perhaps a problem with the Labor Board. Do not be quick to accuse and be very careful what you say to your employee about your suspicion unless you are absolutely sure and can support the charges. Very often, when an employer is sure of the misconduct, the employer will elect to simply terminate the employee without revealing the actual cause for the termination. Depending on the severity of the offense, this may be the right approach to the problem. Employers are often concerned over what may happen after confronting their employee with a serious offense such as stealing. If you do not have proof, and the employee is deeply offended by the accusation, you may find the employee taking action against you. Depending on the value of what is missing, your level of proof and your decision to follow through and press charges, you may insist on accusing your employee and taking the matter to the authorities. Please be sure to immediately consult with an attorney and /or your local police department before discussing the matter directly with your employee. Keep in mind that if there are several employees working at the residence, it will be difficult to accuse one person over the next. Be sure to have all your facts, witnesses and evidence in place prior to involving the authorities or they will not be of much use to you.

If the accusation is one of lying, you will most likely approach your employee with greater ease. Sometimes sitting down with your employee and laying out all the facts that clearly present the lie will force your employee to divulge the truth. The employee may be very apologetic and plead for forgiveness. Your choice to

To be absolutely sure of your rights to videotape an employee, you should first consult with an attorney, who may insist that you have a signed agreement regarding acknowledgement of the nanny-cam.

keep an employee who has broken your trust will be a personal decision. You may give the employee a warning and leave it at that. The issue revolves around the type of lie, the employee's decision to admit to the lie, the employee's explanation for the lie and your belief that it will never happen again.

An accusation of hurting your child will be the worst and most serious offense.

An accusation of hurting your child will be the worst and most serious offense. If the Nanny spanked your child and thought it was O.K. because she had seen you do the same, then you will need to review what type of disciplinary actions she is allowed to use. This kind of discipline may be used by a parent, but should never be used by an employee. If you already made this clear to your domestic and she took it upon herself to physically discipline your child, this would be grounds for termination. You might even feel enough anger to want to physically show retaliation. Naturally, this would be the wrong approach. However, once again, if you have the proper proof, you should contact an attorney and/or the police immediately. One thing for sure is that you would not want this person out there seeking another Nanny position and potentially harming another child. With proper proof, you may want to press charges so that there is a criminal report on file for this action. You may also want to contact *Trustline,* the nationwide child abuse registry. You would not want to take another chance on this particular misconduct. Termination is the proper option.

Chapter Seven

EMPLOYER/EMPLOYEE AGREEMENTS

EMPLOYER/EMPLOYEE AGREEMENTS

This chapter has information that you will hopefully utilize repeatedly throughout the years of hiring help. It contains all the necessary contracts between you as the employer and your domestic employee. There are contracts specifically for you and your Nanny, Housekeeper, and Companion/Caregiver. Many employers insist that their domestics sign a Confidentiality Agreement to preclude them from disclosing any private information. Although one is not included in this book, you can download a form from our web site. The purpose of these contracts is not to show your employee that you are a difficult and potentially litigious employer, but to illustrate to your employee that you are a serious and conscientious employer. These agreements are not provided to scare your employee, but to merely have all the facts agreed to during the interview process clearly stipulated in a contract and signed by all parties. By utilizing these agreements, there should be no confusion whatsoever.

Some of the important points of discussion in the interview process are often overlooked. For example:

- Duties
- Hours and Pay
- Overtime
- Schedule
- Vacation Days
- Sick and Personal Days
- Holidays
- Benefits
- Payment Terms
- Salary Review

- Rest Periods
- Meal Breaks
- Notice
- Severance
- Termination

EMPLOYER/EMPLOYEE AGREEMENTS

Visit **www.domestic-connections.com** *to download a printable pdf version of this form.*

GENERAL HOUSEHOLD EMPLOYER/EMPLOYEE AGREEMENT

Household Employee Agreement ("Agreement") made this day _____, _____, between _____ ("Employer") and _____ ("Employee").

The parties agree as follows:

1. Term of Agreement. The employment relationship is at will between the Employee and Employer and shall commence on _____, _____, and shall continue until terminated as provided in Paragraph 9. There will be a training period during the first _____ of employment. The employee will be compensated $ _____ per day while undergoing the training period. During this training period the duties will be performed as follows:

_____

_____

_____

2. Duties of Employee. Employee shall be employed as a live- _____ (out/in) _____ (Housekeeper, Nanny, Companion, etc.,) Employee's duties shall include such services and duties normally associated with the position of a live-domestic. Such duties shall include all services specifically detailed as an addendum to this Agreement. These particular duties may be changed from time to time by the Employer.

3.   Time and Efforts.   Employee will use her/his full time and efforts to perform her/his duties. The employee will at all times faithfully and industriously and to the best of her/his ability, experience and talents perform all of the duties that may be required to the satisfaction of Employer.

4.   Compensation.

   4.1   Hourly Rate of Pay.   In full payment for employee's services, employer shall pay to Employee compensation in the amount of $_____ for each hour of work performed.

   4.2   Discretionary Bonus   Employer, in its sole discretion, may, at any time, grant a bonus to the Employee which shall be in addition to the compensation provided in paragraph 4.1. The granting of a bonus shall not create a practice or precedent that shall require Employer to grant a bonus at any other time.

   4.3   Salary Review   Employer will give a salary review to Employee after _____ period of employment. It is discretionary whether an Employer chooses to provide Employee with a salary increase. The increase, if any, will be relative to the cost of living increase not less than $ _____ or _____ %.

5. Working Hours and Overtime

   5.1   Hours   Employee's normal work hours are from _____ AM to _____ PM, _____ through _____ not to exceed _____ ( ) hours a day. Hours worked in addition to Employee's normal schedule may be worked only with permission from Employer.

5.2 __Payment Terms__   Employee will be paid $_____ per hour, $ _____ per week, and $_____ per month. The following items will be deducted from the Employee's paycheck:

- State Disability Insurance (SDI)
- California Personal Income Tax (PIT)
- Unemployment Insurance (UI)
- Employment Training Tax (ETT)
- Federal Withholding
- Medicare
- Social Security

5.3 __Overtime__   Employee will be paid at the rate of _____ times her regular hourly rate of pay for all work over _____ ( ) hours in the workday. Employee is not permitted to work overtime unless authorized, in advance, by Employer.

5.4 __Rest Periods__   When employee works a minimum of four (4) hours per day, Employee will receive one paid 10-minute rest period. When Employee works a minimum of six (6) hours per day, Employee will receive two (2) paid (10) minute rest periods, one in the morning and one in the afternoon.

5.5 __Meal Breaks__   When Employee works no more than five (5) hours per day, Employee will receive a _____ ( ) hour or _____ (   ) minute unpaid off-duty meal break. On any scheduled workday, Employer will provide Employee with ( ) Breakfast, ( ) Lunch, ( ) Dinner - during off-duty time.

5.6 __Other Benefits__   The following will be provided to the Employee as follows:

- Meals as indicated _____

- Room and Board _____

- Health Insurance _____

- Dental Insurance _____

- 401(k) Plan _____

- Transportation _____

5.7 __Compensation for Additional Children__   Should another child join the household, the Nanny/Domestic shall be compensated at a rate of $_____ per week. If other children visit the household, the Nanny/Domestic shall be compensated at a rate of $_____ per hour.

6. __Vacation__   Employee will accrue _____ ( ) days of paid vacation after _____ year(s) of employment. _____ (initial) If Employee is due a paid vacation, but is terminated prior to receiving a paid vacation, Employee will be paid for any earned but unused vacation **OR** _____(initial) Employee will be paid vacation time only when a full year of employment is completed.

7. __Sick Leave/ Personal Days__   Employee is allowed _____ (   ) days of paid sick leave per year.   Any other sick leave will be deducted from pay. Employee is allowed _____ (   ) days for personal reasons. Any other personal days taken will be deducted from pay.

8.   __Holidays__   Employee is allowed _____ paid Holidays per year. Specifically: _____

_____

_____

Employer is not obligated to pay Employee for any Holiday not stipulated above as a paid holiday. If employee works on a previously agreed to paid holiday, at the employer's request, the employee will be compensated at a rate of _____ for that day.

9.   __Termination__   This Agreement may be terminated at any time by Employer or Employee, within their sole discretion, with or without cause. If, at any time, Employee breaches this Agreement, or fails or refuses or neglects to perform any of Employer's obligations under this Agreement, or for other good reason, the Employer may terminate the Employee at will.

10.   __Severance__   Employee is entitled to severance pay of _____ only if Employee is terminated by Employer. This severance pay can be omitted by Employer at Employer's sole discretion as a result of but not limited to the Employee's misconduct or gross negligence.

11.   __Notice__   Employee and Employer will make every effort to provide a minimum of two-(2) weeks' notice prior to termination. Notwithstanding the foregoing, Employer can terminate this agreement at will without notice and at Employer's sole discretion as a result of but not limited to the Employee's misconduct or gross negligence.

12.   __Entire Agreement__   This Agreement embodies the entire understanding between the parties and merges all prior discussions or communications between them, and no party shall be bound by any definitions, conditions, warranties, or representations other than as expressly stated in this Agreement or as subsequently set forth in writing signed by the duly authorized representatives of all of the parties hereto or the party whose rights are affected.

13.   __No Oral Change; Amendment__   This Agreement may only be changed or modified and any provisions may only be waived by an addendum signed by the parties.   This includes but is not limited to all agreements between Employer and Employee relating to the work.

14.   __Insurance and Taxes__   The employer will provide Worker's Compensation. Any other insurance provided is stipulated in section 5.6 of this Agreement. The employer is to withhold any mandatory taxes for which they are responsible on the employee's salary. The employee is responsible for paying all state and federal income taxes.

• __Additional Agreements__   Employer and Employee additionally agree to the following comments:

_____

_____

EMPLOYER/EMPLOYEE AGREEMENTS

_____

_____

_____.

    The date indicated and Employee's signature below acknowledges Employee's review, understanding and full knowing and voluntary acceptance of the terms and conditions set forth in this Agreement.

This Agreement is executed by Employer and Employee at: _____ ,

on **(Date)** _____ , _____ .

_____
Employer's Signature

_____
Employer's Signature

_____
Employee's Signature

EMPLOYER/EMPLOYEE AGREEMENTS

DOMESTIC CLEANING DUTIES PER EMPLOYEE/EMPLOYER AGREEMENT

1. **Parties** _____ (Employer) contracts with

_____ (Employee) to provide household

duties per the Employee/Employer Agreement dated _____ attached hereto.

2. **Responsibilities:**

   a. **Interior Rooms** All of the rooms within the household shall be cleaned and maintained unless specified as follows: _____

   _____

   _____

   b. **Exterior Areas/Frequency**

   - Front Porch _____ per week _____ per month
   - Back Porch _____ per week _____ per month
   - Patio Furniture _____ per week _____ per month
   - Garage _____ per week _____ per month
   - Guest House _____ per week _____ per month
   - Cabana _____ per week _____ per month
   - Tennis Court _____ per week _____ per month
   - Other _____

   c. **Other Duties**

   - Laundry _____
   - Towels change _____ per week on _____
   - Sheets change _____ per week on _____
   - Ironing _____
   - Polish Silver _____ per week _____ per month
   - Cooking _____ daily or _____ as requested
   - Marketing _____ per week _____ as requested
   - Errands _____
   - Windows _____ per week _____ as specified

EMPLOYER/EMPLOYEE AGREEMENTS

- Plant Care _____
  _____

- Pet Care _____
  _____

- Other _____
  _____

• **Special Instructions:**

_____

_____

_____

_____

    This Agreement is executed by Employer and Employee at: _____ .

On: (Date) _____ ,_____ .

_____
Employer's Signature

_____
Employer's Signature

_____
Employee's Signature

EMPLOYER/EMPLOYEE AGREEMENTS

Visit **www.domestic-connections.com** *to download a printable pdf version of this form.*

NANNY - EMPLOYEE/EMPLOYER AGREEMENT FOR CHILD CARE AND HOUSEHOLD DUTIES

Child Care Duties

1. Meals - This includes the preparation of a healthy breakfast, lunch and/or dinner for the children. Meals can be discussed prior to preparation until Nanny becomes aware of what the children normally eat for each meal. The Nanny is not expected to prepare meals for the Parents or other adult members of the household, unless otherwise specified.

2. Dressing - The Nanny shall ensure that the child is appropriately dressed for activities in which they are engaged, taking into consideration the weather and nature of the activity. The Nanny must ensure that the clothing is clean and worn properly. The Nanny is responsible for teaching the child all personal hygiene including dressing, potty training, washing their hands after going to the restroom and before eating, cleaning their teeth after each meal and taking a daily bath/shower.

3. Child Development and Nap Time - The Nanny shall engage the child or children in all activities striving to teach them proper speech, basic phonetics and arithmetic, shapes, colors, animals. The Nanny shall also teach the child how to share with other children, etiquette and how to keep their toys and things in an orderly fashion. The Nanny will play with the child to encourage speech and personality development. The Nanny must supervise the child at all times and never leave the child unattended. All activities must be supervised. When it is time for the child to take a nap, the Nanny must do her best to ensure that the nap is taken at the proper time each day. While the child is taking a nap, the Nanny must keep the monitor near and periodically check on the child.

4. Discipline - The Nanny must never hit nor touch the child in an aggressive manner. The Nanny must never use any profane or derogatory language in front of the child. The Nanny must never grab the child harshly or shake the child in any way. There will be activities that the Parents deem dangerous for the child and forbid the child from engaging in these activities. The Nanny must adhere to the Parents' choices for what they deem dangerous and forbidden. Time-outs are used as a method for discipline. All other punishment is the Parents' responsibility. Any child behavioral modification and suggested solutions should be discussed with the Parents and given full approval and authorization prior to implementation.

5. Communication - The Nanny must keep an open line of communication with the Parents at all times. Problems or issues with the child's behavior, routine, attitude or discipline must be discussed immediately. If the Nanny has personal problems that might interfere with the care of the child, this must be discussed immediately. If the Nanny has problems with her childcare or household duties, then the Nanny must inform the Parents immediately. The Nanny promises to be honest with the Parents regarding all aspects of the child's care and in return asks the same of the Parents. All issues will be resolved with good communication and without confrontation. The Nanny will never ask the child (children) to do something that the Parents do not want the child (children) to do and/or keep secrets with the children with respect to this conduct.

6. Transportation - Whenever the Parents direct, the Nanny will take the child to and from activities such as parks, parties and special events in the vehicle provided by the Parents or the vehicle belonging to the Nanny if the Parents have agreed to its use. Whenever the Nanny is taking the child from the house for a walk or drive, the Parents must be made aware of such activities. If the Parents cannot be reached, or are not at home, then a message must be left for their information as to where the Nanny is going and as to how long the activity will take. The Nanny must never veer off the intended activity to do something that the Parents do not know about. The Nanny must never take the child in anyone's vehicle or to any strange location that has not been discussed with, and approved by, the Parents. The Nanny must never, under any circumstances, leave the child alone in the car.

7. Releasing Children - Under NO circumstances will the Nanny release a child to any relative, neighbor, family friend or personal friend without the direct approval and authorization of the Parents. If the Parents give such authorization, then the Nanny must be certain that the child is being released to that specific person by checking identification.

8. Termination - The Nanny agrees to provide the Parents with at least two (2) weeks' notice prior to leaving employment and the Parents agree to provide two (2) weeks' notice before terminating the Nanny unless the personal safety of either the Nanny or the children is involved. In such case, the Nanny can leave employment immediately. Upon notice to terminate this agreement either by the Nanny or Parents, each party will attempt to end the relationship amicably and professionally.

Household Duties

1. General Household Maintenance - The Nanny will be responsible for the general household maintenance as it directly relates to the care of the children. However, at no time will the general household maintenance interfere with the direct care of the child or children. These duties must be done while keeping a close eye on the child or children. The priority is always the care of the children first.

2. Kitchen - Daily cleaning of the kitchen area which includes dishes used by the Nanny and/or children, highchairs, toys in kitchen area, floor underneath the eating area and highchairs and other chairs used by children. All dishes used to cook for the Nanny and/or children must be put into the dishwasher or washed by hand after each meal. Also, the floor in the kitchen area must be swept and mopped daily.

3. Playroom - Nanny must pick up the toys daily after each play period and at the end of each day. Clothes or any other items left in the play area must be returned to their place. Vacuuming or mopping is done daily/or weekly as needed.

4. Garbage - The Nanny will be responsible for emptying the diaper pail and removing any garbage from the child's bedroom and bathroom on a daily basis.

5. Child's Bedroom and Bathroom - The Nanny is responsible for complete maintenance of the child's bedroom and bathroom. This includes changing the sheets, keeping the room vacuumed and organized, wiping down the bathroom counters, removing clothes from the hamper and keeping all mirrors wiped after washing of hands and brushing of teeth.

6. Laundry - The Nanny is only responsible for the bedding of the child's crib/bed and the laundry belonging to any child under her care.

7. Cooking - The Nanny must cook for any child under her care and learn what meals are desired for each child. However, the Nanny does not have to cook gourmet meals or special meals for each child unless it is easy to do and time permits at breakfast and lunch times. Dinners will be a set meal for all children. The Nanny must be aware of any food allergies and be careful NOT to bring such foods into the house or provide such foods to the child.

8. Medicine - The Nanny shall not administer any medication, including over-the-counter drugs, unless specifically directed to do so by the Parents. The Parents also know that the Nanny will need a written request and approval for all medication administered by the Nanny. All medicine administered by the Parents or the Nanny must be logged with exact dosages and the time given so that no overdosing occurs.

9. Emergencies - In the case of an emergency, the Nanny will contact the Parents immediately. If the situation requires immediate attention by a professional Doctor or Paramedic, then the Nanny must dial 911 or the Poison Control Center prior to calling the Parents. If the Parents cannot be reached, then the Nanny must turn to her list of people to call in the event of an emergency and follow the steps previously outlined by the Parents as to who should be called next. This list of phone numbers for emergency use will be posted next to telephone in the kitchen area. The Parents will sign and date two "Authorization to Treat a Minor" cards per child: one to be put on file in their pediatrician's office, and the other held in the Nanny's possession. In the unlikely event of an emergency, if the Parents cannot be reached by the Nanny, the Doctor and/or Hospital, this allows the Doctor to ask permission of the Nanny to administer any medically necessary care to the child or children. If the Nanny is required to treat the child or children, the Parents understand that all medical care administered would be on the advice and at the discretion of medical personnel only, and the Nanny cannot be held liable for any decisions made by said medical personnel. Furthermore, the Nanny cannot be held liable for any medical bills incurred by such medical attention.

This Agreement is executed by the Employer and Employee at _____ .
On (date) _____, _____ .

_____
Employer's Signature (Parent)

_____
Employer's Signature (Parent)

_____
Employee's Signature (Nanny)

EMPLOYER/EMPLOYEE AGREEMENTS

Visit **www.domestic-connections.com** *to download a printable pdf version of this form.*

COMPANION/CAREGIVER - EMPLOYER/EMPLOYEE AGREEMENT

Companion/Caregiver Duties

1. Meals - The Companion/Caregiver is completely responsible for the preparation of healthy meals. Companion/Caregiver must abide by special diet that has been prescribed by Employer's Doctor. Gourmet meals will not be required unless specified by the Employer. If the Companion/Caregiver wishes to make meals that are out of the ordinary from what the Employer normally eats, these meals must be approved and be in accordance with the Employer's diet.

2. Medication - Medication, if any, will be administered as requested by the Employer, if competent to do so, or by the appointed Guardian under Doctor's orders and supervision. Any changes to the medication administered must be approved by the Employer and/or the appointed Guardian as well as the prescribing doctors.

3. Dressing - The Companion/Caregiver will be responsible for assisting the Employer to whatever degree needed to dress and undress on a daily basis. The Employer may pick out the clothes or leave that decision to the Companion/Caregiver depending on the condition of the Employer. The Companion/Caregiver will make sure that the Employer is always dressed in clean and appropriate attire for the weather conditions. Most importantly, the Companion/Caregiver will take special care so that the Employer is never too cold or hot.

4. Bathroom - The Companion/Caregiver will be sure that the Employer is always assisted to the bathroom, and in the bathroom, at all times, as necessary. The Companion/Caregiver will change diapers for the Employer and keep the Employer clean as needed.

5. Bathing - The Companion/Caregiver will assist the Employer in the shower or bath as needed. The Companion/Caregiver will never leave the Employer alone in the shower or bath, unless otherwise specified. If the Employer needs a sponge bath, the Companion/Caregiver will provide such on a daily basis, or as requested by Employer or Employer's Guardian.

6. Recreation - The Companion/Caregiver will walk with the Employer on a daily basis so that the Employer gets exercise as needed. The Companion/Caregiver will take the arm of the Employer or walk close enough to the Employer so as to not let the Employer fall. If the Employer is in a wheelchair, the Companion/Caregiver will be sure to stabilize the Employer properly in the wheelchair and assist accordingly.

7. Physical Therapy - The Companion/Caregiver will perform as instructed any physical therapy and massage as prescribed by Doctor to help improve circulation.

8. Driving - The Companion/Caregiver will take the Employer to the following locations as requested and deemed necessary by the Employer and/or Guardian:

- Grocery Store
- Doctor's Appointments
- Park
- Beauty or Nail Salon
- Friend's or Relative's Home
- Theatre /Museum
- Restaurants

Guardian must clear any place, not listed above, if Employer is not competent to make such decisions.

9. Communication and Behavior - The Companion/Caregiver will at all times be kind, gentle and respectful of the Employer. Dignity and Respect will at all times be given to Employer. At no time, will the Companion/Caregiver utilize force or profanity with the Employer. Any problems that cannot be solved directly with the Employer will be addressed to the Employer's appointed Guardian and/or family members and/or Doctor. Any unusual abnormal behavior noted by the Companion/Caregiver will be communicated immediately to the Employer's appointed Guardian and/or family member and/or appropriate Doctor.

10. Emergency Care - Depending on the state of emergency, Companion/Caregiver will provide CPR if necessary and telephone 911 immediately. The guardian and/or other members of the Employer's family will also be contacted according to "Emergency List" as provided to Companion/Caregiver.

11. Housework - All necessary housework will be performed, unless otherwise specified but always to include the daily making of beds, cleaning of kitchen and general straightening of the house. Garbage must be removed from the house and mail/newspapers brought in daily.

This Agreement is executed by the Employer and Employee at _____ .
On (Date) _____ ,_____ .

_____
Employee's Signature (Companion/Caregiver)

_____
Employer's Signature and/or Appointed Guardian

Chapter Eight

GUIDELINES FOR TRAINING YOUR DOMESTIC

GUIDELINES FOR TRAINING YOUR DOMESTIC

DOMESTIC DUTIES

Before giving your domestic the duties and responsibilities you expect completed on a daily, weekly and monthly basis, please review each duty carefully with the appropriate members of your family so that you tailor the schedule to your exact needs the first time around. It is better to be sure the first time, than to keep making changes when your employee has already learned a routine. Also, if you continue to add duties because you simply forgot to include them from the beginning, the employee may suggest a raise for the increased amount of work.

Certainly as your children grow and their particular needs change, your household requirements may also change. At this time, you can rearrange the duties accordingly. For example, when your baby becomes a toddler, there will be less time for your Nanny/Housekeeper to do heavy housekeeping since she will be busy running after your little one who is now walking throughout the house and touching everything. Conversely, when your toddler is now at a pre-school age and attending school, there will be more time to do the housekeeping chores. It is important to always keep in mind the amount of work a housekeeper and/or nanny is capable of handling when a baby or toddler is present. You never want to put the emphasis on cleaning during the time your children are infants and toddlers. If your domestic is hired to do both functions, be sure to allow time when the children are not around so that the housekeeping can be attended to thoroughly and without concern for the safety of a child. This will clearly avoid any potentially dangerous situations that could arise otherwise. Other changes in your household/childcare duties may come up when you have extra entertaining in your home, such as guests on short- or long-term basis, remodeling, and/or during vacations. As long as your employee is informed of what is expected during those events, there shouldn't be any confusion or problems adjusting.

Certainly as your children grow and their particular needs change, your household requirements may also change.

There are notes where necessary explanations will be helpful. These notes are suggestions that will indicate, in some cases, a standard practice, while others will be more of a personal choice for your particular household. Remember that if you over-work your domestic, she/he will feel it rather quickly and soon begin looking for another job. Duties should be laid out in a reasonable fashion so that a domestic has enough time to do the work thoroughly and without pressure or too much stress.

The Household/Childcare Duties section gives you an overall and specific description of the responsibilities your domestic has in your home while breaking it down to a daily, weekly, biweekly, monthly and even bimonthly timeline. (The bimonthly can be adjusted to every 3 or 6 months if preferred). Also provided is extra space in various locations so that you may give special instruction.

Remember: **The more thorough you are in your instructions, the less likely you will have problems. When you hand over these instructions to your domestic, go over them in detail. Never presume that your domestic understands everything. You must take the time, even if it means one full day to work together so that she is fully aware of just how you like things done. Take the time now to be as descriptive as possible when filling this out so that you don't have your domestic guessing. Review your manual with her daily until she gets the routine down, and periodically to refresh her memory.**

Daily Cleaning Guide

- Be Ready to Work at _____ AM (**1**)

- Turn off house alarm (**2**)

- Take in the newspaper and/or make coffee

- Help the children get dressed (**3**)

- Set table and prepare breakfast (**4**)

- Prepare lunches for children (**5**)

- Be sure children brush their teeth and hair (**6**)

- Drive children to school (**7**)

GUIDELINES FOR TRAINING YOUR DOMESTIC

- Take care of the pet(s) **(8)**
- Clean breakfast dishes and table
- Make the beds **(9)**
- Take away any glasses/newspapers that are left in rooms **(10)**
- Empty all wastepaper baskets **(11)**
- Bring all dirty laundry to laundry room and start a wash **(12)**
- Organize the bathrooms **(13)**
- Open windows or sliding doors for fresh air **(14)**
- Take in mail
- Refer to Weekly Work Schedule **(15)**
- Be ready for children to be picked up from school **(16)**
- Afternoon with children home **(17)**
- Bath time **(18)**
- Dinner time **(19)**
- Bed time **(20)**

Notes:

(1) Your live-in domestic should allow at least one hour from the time she begins her day to the time the children need to be off to school. A live-out domestic should arrive to work on time, ready to start the work day.

(2) Alarms have the ability to program more than one alarm code. You could give your domestic a separate code from yours. This is further discussed in the Emergency Procedures section.

(3) In some instances, the family may want their children to learn to become self-reliant, in which case it would be best to have any child of 5 years of age and up to begin getting dressed, with perhaps only the guidance of a domestic.

(4) Go over carefully the options there are for breakfast. A varied weekly menu is suggested. Keep the options simple on school days since there is little time available for elaborate meals.

(5) Go over carefully what options there are for lunch every day. Give your domestic clear instructions of what your children like to eat. (If there are allergies, keep a list of those foods out in clear view.) Also, keep a list by the refrigerator of those days when lunch might be served at school. If a lunch box is used, be sure that it is labeled with the child's name and remind your domestic that a lunch box must be cleaned every day with soap and water.

(6) No matter what the age of the child, brushing his/her teeth is like pulling teeth. It seems to be easier to get a child to brush his/her own hair; although, frequently, supervision is needed.

(7) If your domestic has the responsibility to drive your child, continually remind her of the rules as they pertain to making sure the children always wear their seat belts and are seated properly in the vehicle (not in front of an air bag as applicable). Go over the route to get to school and drive with your domestic as many days as possible in the beginning to give her pointers regarding the traffic and parking. This will also give you a better insight to her driving capability. A driving record may be clean, but that doesn't always mean she is a good driver. Mr. Magoo never got a ticket either.

(8) Taking care of a pet may include anything from simply letting it out, to feeding, bathing, and picking up after it. Pets may or not be an issue here, but very often it is a source of concern among domestics, especially as it pertains to cleaning after it and giving it a bath. Provide the appropriate pooper-scooper, gloves and/or bag. This might make it easier for the domestic to do it. Be clear as to how many times a day a pet is fed, which food and how much the pet should eat. If a pet should never be fed human food, make that clear. Do not let your domestic assume that any bone is great for a dog. Many types of bones can be harmful to a dog.

If your domestic has the responsibility to drive your child, she should be making sure the children always wear their seat belts and are seated properly in the vehicle.

GUIDELINES FOR TRAINING YOUR DOMESTIC

(9) The way in which you like your bed made should be carefully illustrated to your domestic. Instruct her to air out the bed, then stretch the bottom sheet, tuck in corners properly, fluff up all pillows, arrange them the way you like and straighten the ruffle if applicable. Remind her that after vacuuming, a ruffle should again be straightened.

(10) Anything that you don't want removed from your bedroom or office should be pointed out to your domestic. Start a system so that it is clear which items can or cannot be taken away.

(11) Wastepaper baskets should be disinfected from time to time by cleaning them with soap and water.

(12) Every household needs either one good central hamper or individual hampers. Either way, it is important to let your domestic in on what needs to be washed and/or taken to the cleaners. It is a good idea to train children and adults to hang up their clothes instead of throwing them on the floor whether they are clean or dirty. This helps keep your domestic from guessing. It is suggested that laundry always be done on the first and last day of the employee's workweek. You may also want her to do wash in the middle of the week so that it doesn't pile up. However, this all depends on the size of your family and the regularity that is most suitable for your family needs. It is also suggested that you do the wash with your domestic for the first few weeks. Have her observe carefully how you like your wash handled, with what kinds of detergents, what water temperature, what size of a load, etc. Show her what items must be hand-washed. If you like to do your own hand wash, then keep those items separate. I have seen the worst arguments with domestics over the laundry. Many have been spontaneously fired just because they ruined a favorite item of clothing. So much of this can be avoided if the employer would just find the time to train their employee initially on how to separate and wash their laundry.

It is suggested that you do the wash with your domestic for the first few weeks.

(13) Organizing the towels makes the final statement in a fresh-looking bathroom. There are certain ways to fold towels; decide which way you think is best and show your domestic how you like it done. You may want your towels changed once or

twice a week. Pick the day or days that you prefer. Inform her if you want the same towels replaced or to use a different set each week.

(14) Bedrooms need to be aired out, even in the winter. If you are concerned over the waste in using the air conditioner or heater, instruct your domestic to open just certain doors or windows for up to 20 minutes. After, be sure to remind her to close and lock all doors and windows properly.

(15) Assuming your child/children go a long day to school, there will be plenty of time to follow the Weekly Schedule. If your child/children go to school for only half a day, then the daily work schedule may have to be moved around a bit.

(16) If your domestic is picking up the children from school, give her an exact time when she should leave the house so that she is never late. Give her enough time to allow for any potential problems with traffic. Remind her that she must NEVER be late to pick up the children. If there is an emergency that is causing her to be late, she must call the school and parents immediately.

(17) Have the children put their school belongings away. It is a good practice to have them wash their hands and face after school and before having a snack.

Remind your domestic that she must NEVER be late to pick up the children.

Have your domestic prepare them a snack from the list of allowable snacks. It would be good if no snacks were given 1 to 2 hours before serving dinner so that little appetites are not lost. Be sure she only gives the types of snacks allowed.

If there is homework to be done, have your domestic be firm about the children getting to their homework. It is best to eliminate any potential interruptions during their time to concentrate on homework, including TV and music. A domestic might be able to help with homework, but doing the job for the child is defeating the purpose.

If your household has a limitation on the number of hours TV is allowed, and only on certain days, inform your domestic of this rule. Be sure that she abides by it. Be sure your domestic isn't using the television as a babysitter.

Be sure your domestic is clear that she should ***always keep an eye on the children*** *whether they are doing homework, playing or anything else they might be doing. If they are playing outside, never leave them alone. If they are inside, depending on age, either never leave them alone or always check on them periodically.*

(18) Unless your family prefers bath time after dinner, it may be more convenient to get bath time over first. (However, if you choose to do bath time after dinner, remember that if you want your domestic to help, usually she will be occupied with the dinner dishes at this time.) Either way, be sure that if she is involved with bath time that she knows never to leave any child under 7 alone in the bathtub. She should run the water and check the temperature. If the child requires assistance with bathing, do so with care, especially when the child gets in and out of the bathtub.

(19) At dinner hour, have your domestic set the table. If you want your domestic to cook dinner entirely, be sure that there are no little children running around under her feet while she is cooking dinner. If she is simply instructed to help prepare, then have her begin washing and cutting any vegetables, seasoning the meat and making the salad. If your domestic becomes "one too many cooks in the kitchen," then have her look after the children to make it easier on you.

If you want your domestic to cook dinner entirely, be sure that there are no little children running around under her feet while she is cooking dinner.

If your domestic is going to eat with the family, be sure she helps get all family members served before she sits down. If you do not plan to have her eat with the family and you have an infant, this is a good time for her to care for the baby while the parents have a minute to eat alone together or with other older children. (Remember: Decide early on whether you want your domestic to sit down and eat with you or not. It becomes uncomfortable to make changes later.) After dinner, have your domestic be responsible for cleaning up. Have her clean dishes and put them all away, turning the dishwasher on if necessary. Instruct her to clean the kitchen table and put chairs back in an orderly fashion and to quickly sweep and/or mop the floor. Finally, be sure she takes the kitchen garbage out. This is all standard after-dinner clean-up procedure.

(20) At bed time, if the parents are out and it is the domestic's responsibility to

GUIDELINES FOR TRAINING YOUR DOMESTIC

put the children to bed, if age-appropriate be sure the domestic reads them a bedtime story. She should be firm about the hour they are to go to bed and that they brush their teeth. Remind her that she should not allow the children to break the rules of the house. (If the children think they can get away with not doing what they are supposed to when their parents are away, your domestic will lose their respect and always have problems with them.) Tell your domestic and remind your children of the following: ***When you, the parents, are away, the domestic is in charge.*** It is helpful to also have everyone understand that in the event the children are not mindful, there will be some sort of privilege taken away, such as T.V. or video games. If the child or children are not minding the domestic, this is a serious problem that sometimes requires the parents to get on the phone and let the child or children know that punishment is soon on its way if they don't stop their misbehavior. It is very difficult to expect a domestic to always have the kind of control that a parent naturally holds over a child. A domestic often walks a fine line between being liked and respected by a child. Very often, a domestic will think that if she is too harsh with the child, the child will not like her. Yet, in reality if she isn't firm and consistent in following the rules of the house, a child will easily take advantage. It is your responsibility as a parent and employer to get your children to show respect.

A domestic often walks a fine line between being liked and respected by a child.

If the parents are home and prefer to put the children to bed, then the day for the live-in domestic should be finished after dinner once the kitchen is clean. A live-out domestic may or may not be held responsible for many of the early evening activities if the day ends sooner.

Weekly Cleaning Guide

Laundry

Begin on _____ by removing all sheets from beds and towels from the bathrooms. Sheets are changed _____ times per week on _____. Towels are changed _____ times per week on _____. Empty hampers. Take all necessary wash to laundry room. Separate the white and dark items, and those items that go to the dry cleaners.

GUIDELINES FOR TRAINING YOUR DOMESTIC

- **Wash** sheets, towels, rugs, rags and regular clothes all separately. Wash delicate clothes separately on delicate cycle. Do not mix any of these items, unless instructed to do so. Use the proper cleaning products and check the settings on the washer and dryer accordingly. Be sure to use the right detergent for each wash. Be especially careful not to wash any item that should go to the DRY CLEANERS. Read the instruction manual for any new washer/dryer that is unfamiliar to you.

- **Remove wash** and shake each item separately (this helps take out some of the wrinkles and makes it easier for ironing later). Hang up those items that should not go into the dryer. Some items must be laid flat to dry. Put other items directly into the dryer at the proper setting.

- **Dry** only those items that should go into the dryer. Be sure the lint tray is clean prior to each use of the dryer. Check the setting for permanent, delicate or regular wear. Check the necessary time for each load. Be aware of when the drying cycle is finished so that you can take them out quickly after the drying cycle is completed. (This also helps prevent wrinkling.)

- **Fold and Iron** - It may be better to fold soon after the drying cycle is finished and perhaps iron in the evening if there is little time during the day. Be sure the iron has water in it for the steam use. Use starch only when instructed. Be very careful not to iron when small children are around. Never leave a hot iron unattended. Some of the modern irons will turn off after 5 minutes of non-use for safety purposes. When finished, place iron in safe location for cooling.

Bathrooms
On a daily basis, all bathrooms used frequently must be checked and organized. However, _____ per week on _____ , all bathrooms should be cleaned thoroughly. First take out the rugs (if any) and set them aside for washing, vacuuming or shaking out. Remove any other items like wastepaper basket or scale, hamper, standing towel rack, etc. Take out any wash cloths that need to be laundered. Empty the trash can.

GUIDELINES FOR TRAINING YOUR DOMESTIC

Never use any abrasive cleanser or sponge on any brass/chrome/gold leaf fixture in bathroom or anywhere in house.

- **Shower/Bathtub/Toilet/Bidet** is cleaned with the appropriate cleanser as provided. Wash shower/bathtub. Dry shower doors (wipe them down daily so that they do not get water spots). Clean soap dispenser. Replace soap if needed. Never use any abrasive cleanser or instrument to clean toilet and/or bidet. (You can scratch the bowl easily.) Do not just clean inside of toilet and/or bidet; you must clean it from top to bottom. Wipe down shower and return bath items in their place. Polish the fixtures with the appropriate cleanser. *(Never use any abrasive cleanser or sponge on any brass/chrome/gold leaf fixture in bathroom or anywhere in house.)*

- **Mirrors/Counters/Sinks** are cleaned by removing carefully all accessory items off the counter (tissue container, toothbrush holder, cups, soap dishes, etc.) Do the mirrors from top to bottom first. You may have to clean it more than once to free it from all smudges. Use a ladder if necessary. Dust and/or clean with damp cloth any light fixtures. Then clean counters and sinks with the necessary cleanser. Polish fixtures. Clean each accessory item that goes on the counter carefully and put back as you found it. Wipe down any smudges on cabinets, bathroom doors as needed.

- **Floors** in the bathrooms get dirty rather quickly. It is best to first sweep the floor to remove any excess hair and debris and then proceed to mop. Use a bucket of water diluted with the appropriate floor cleanser. Make sure the water is rather warm. Use gloves so that you can handle the warm water without scalding your hands. In a small area, it is more efficient to clean a floor with your hands on your knees than to use a mop. This way you can reach into the corners and do the baseboards all at once. You want to disinfect the floor, so the hotter the water, the better. Let the floor dry for a few minutes before stepping on it.

- **Accessories** such as towel racks, hamper, scale, telephone, wastepaper basket, etc. should all be wiped down. Check the quality of the item and use the appropriate cleanser or simply a damp cloth.

- **Light fixtures** are cleaned regularly, as needed. Use the proper cleaner and a ladder, if necessary. Check and change bulbs as needed. If you unscrew a fixture to change the bulb, be sure that the electricity is turned off first.

- **Final touches.** Replace rugs, or any other accessory items. Put things back as you found them in an orderly fashion. Put out fresh towels. Be sure to check the tissue and toilet paper holders for any replacements needed. Check if new soap is needed. Wipe down all windowsills and shutters with a damp cloth.

Kitchen

- **Cabinets** should be wiped down with the appropriate cleaner and rag as suggested; otherwise, you can ruin a cabinet that costs way too much to replace. Do not use a sponge with an abrasive side on a wooden cabinet. The soft side to a sponge or a damp cloth is best. Keep the cabinets organized as needed. Occasionally put aside some time to wipe down the interior of a cabinet.

- **Counters** must be wiped down daily with a clean sponge. It is important to use clean rags and/or sponges in a kitchen especially. Bacteria can accumulate easily in a kitchen and spread with a dirty sponge or rag. This is what can cause people to get very sick. Counter tops must be wiped down with a CLEAN rag/sponge so that it is disinfected properly. Also, never use the same rags/sponges on the kitchen countertop that you are using in the bathroom or on the floor. There are specific cleaners for tile, marble and granite; be sure to select the proper cleaner. Weekly, take all items off the counter and clean separately while cleaning the countertop from corner to corner.

- **Stove/Ovens/Microwave**(depending on use) is cleaned either daily or weekly. If a stove and/or microwave is used daily, it is obviously cleaned daily; however, where an oven is concerned, it is usually not necessary to clean it more than one time per week, unless it is a toaster oven that is used daily. When cleaning a stove, be sure to take off the iron holders and clean them separately. Do not use a scratchy scouring pad to clean stove. The key

There are specific cleaners for tile, marble and granite; be sure to select the proper cleaner.

GUIDELINES FOR TRAINING YOUR DOMESTIC

with cleaning an oven is that you know what kind of oven you are cleaning. Read the manual for all appliances. There are many modern day ovens that have a self-cleaning function. Be sure to know exactly how each oven and any other appliance is cleaned, so as not to ruin it. If you are using a product to clean the oven, follow the directions carefully. Take the racks out and clean separately. Wipe the oven clean so that there isn't any residue from the cleaning product.

- **Refrigerator** is cleaned out weekly by taking all items out and throwing away any spoiled items. If you are not sure whether an item is spoiled, ask. (Remember: Food items can spoil rather quickly and create harmful bacteria.) Clean out drawers that hold vegetables, snacks, and meats. Clean the bottles and containers before putting them back in the refrigerator. Every so often, defrost the freezer and clean icemaker out so that the ice is fresh. On a daily basis, check the refrigerator for any spills or food stains. Wipe down outside of the refrigerator. Keep a list handy of any items that need replacing so that the family isn't running out of something at the last minute.

- **Sinks** must be cleaned daily with a good cleanser. Use the garbage disposal daily to clean out any debris. Clean the faucet and any other items attached to sink. (Weekly, it is a good idea to check below the kitchen sink and organize it by changing sponges/rags, and checking on needed products.)

- **Trash Compactor** should be emptied as needed (usually daily) and the inside wiped down weekly. Wipe the exterior daily. Change the bag whenever the trash is removed.

- **Breakfast Room** is usually considered part of the kitchen. Wipe down the breakfast table daily, this includes the legs of table and chairs. If there is a high-chair for a baby, clean it thoroughly after each meal. Weekly, wipe down windowsills, baseboards and any other items present in room.

- **Floor** must absolutely be cleaned daily. Use the appropriate cleaner (disinfectant) that is suggested. Always sweep the floor first and then mop. Shake any rugs outside. Some households would require the floor to be cleaned twice daily (morning and night after meals).

Dining Room (This room is not usually used very often, but nonetheless cannot be neglected. Weekly it can be cleaned thoroughly unless it is utilized more frequently.)

- **Dining Table** will be different in every household. For example, it may be of wood, marble, or glass. Whatever the make, you can be sure that it was expensive and can be ruined easily if you do not use the proper cleaner. A wood table may only require a damp cloth for cleaning and a soft cloth for drying and/or dusting. A marble table will require a marble cleaner. A glass table, a glass cleaner. Remember: A table has legs and chairs. Clean them as well, and be sure not to get the cleanser on the upholstery.

- **Miscellaneous** items may be in a dining room, such as a breakfront or other kind of table. If there is a cabinet with china, crystal or silver in it, be sure to clean inside either every two weeks or monthly as required (see separate section for cleaning crystal and silver). If there are any art items in the dining room, carefully wipe down as instructed. If there is a bay window or any other glass opening, clean it as needed.

- **Light fixture** can be one of many types. If it is a chandelier, it will have many individual crystals. These crystals are delicate and can be broken if not careful. Lay a heavy towel under the chandelier when cleaning in the event a crystal should fall. Use a special cleaner for crystals and do each one carefully either every two weeks or monthly as required. Any other light fixture should be also cleaned carefully with appropriate cleaner. Most brass fixtures only need polishing with a soft cloth; the individual bulbs may need dusting.

- **Floor** can be cleaned weekly or after each use of the dining room. Take chairs out from underneath table to clean floor properly (lift chairs, do not

Lay a heavy towel under the chandelier when cleaning in the event a crystal should fall.

drag them on floor). If there is a rug under the dining table, vacuum it as needed.

Family Room (This room is often the most used room of the house and therefore must be organized and cleaned daily.)

- **Toys** are sometimes maintained in a family room so that the children can play while supervised. If there are toys here, they should be kept very organized. If there is a bookcase with cabinetry underneath, the toys might be put inside carefully at the end of the day. If the toys are brought down from the child's room and left in the family room, then pick them up and put them away. (It is good practice that children after a certain age learn how to put their own toys back after playing.)

- **Cabinetry and Coffee Table** are found in a family room, holding books, television, magazines, newspapers, etc. Dusting of these items is important on a daily basis. When dusting a television, be very careful not to scratch the screen. Do not use an abrasive sponge or cleaner on any part of a television. Use waxing polish on the cabinet as instructed. (Usually, it is best to dust daily with a soft cloth and use polish weekly or biweekly.) Keep magazines and newspapers organized and throw out old newspapers. Clean the coffee table daily with the appropriate cleaner. (Remember: Always remove all items from a surface to clean it properly, then clean each item before putting it back in its place.)

- **Sofas and Chairs** with cushions should be vacuumed weekly or bi-weekly, and fluffed up and organized daily.

- **Floor or carpet** must be vacuumed and cleaned daily. Do not bang into the furniture when vacuuming and/or mopping. When mopping a floor, whether it is of tile, marble or wood, be sure to use the appropriate cleaner.

Living Room (This room, along with the dining room, is seldom used in most households. It usually contains the nicest artifacts and artwork and needs careful attention when cleaning at least one time weekly.)

Always remove all items from a surface to clean it properly, then clean each item before putting it back in its place.

- **Cabinetry and Coffee Table** will often contain crystal, china and/or silver. The interior of the cabinet will need to be cleaned every other week or monthly. In so doing, you will need to take each item out, starting with the top shelf first, and clean each shelf either by dusting, or with glass cleaner, depending on type. Then you must clean each individual item and return it to its place exactly how it was found. Crystal items can be cleaned with warm soapy water and rinsed and dried immediately. Silver items are polished with silver cleaner only and a soft cloth. China items of porcelain can be wiped with damp cloth and dried with soft cloth. Books are dusted. Cabinet is dusted and maybe polished occasionally. The coffee table will need cleaning by also removing all items first and then replacing the items by cleaning them individually before putting them back.

- **Sofas and Chairs** can be vacuumed weekly and organized after each use. If the living room is not used often, you may only need to vacuum the upholstery bi-weekly or monthly.

- **Fireplace** If the fireplace is natural wood burning and used, then you will need to clean it out frequently. Begin by sweeping up the ashes and taking out old used firewood. If it is gas burning, with fake wood, leave the wood in place and sweep around it. Check the type of fireplace and clean accordingly.

- **Piano** must be cleaned by first removing all the items on top and dusting it with a soft cloth.

Master Bedroom (This room is used daily and must be cleaned daily as follows.)
- **Beds** are usually more complicated in the master bedroom in that they may have a more formal look. Begin by laying and tucking the sheets properly, fluffing up the comforter and/or blanket, laying the bed spread or duvet cover neatly, fluffing and arranging all the pillows in a decorative manner, and pulling out the dust ruffle so that it lays nicely. Every time, when changing the sheets, be sure to wipe down the bed frame first with a damp cloth or dry soft cloth. Depending on the type of bed frame, you

may need to vacuum it.

- **Vacuum** the master bedroom at least _____ times per week. Again, always be careful not to damage nightstands or any other furniture while vacuuming. Use the necessary vacuum attachments for underneath the bed, closets and corners. Vacuum any throw rugs.

- **Furniture** in the master bedroom will often consist of nightstands, secretary or desk, and/or bookcases. Dust all these items carefully, including any lamps, using the proper solution. In some cases, there might even be exercise equipment. Dust this only with a damp cloth or as instructed. In most cases, there will be a television in the master bedroom. Do not use any cleaner on the television. A dry cloth is best.

- **Windows/Doors/Baseboards** get very dusty and dirty. Clean any windows as needed weekly. Run a cloth over the door runners so that dirt that is caught in between does not get on the carpet. Run a cloth over the baseboards every week or as needed.

- **Final Touches** Check the bed skirts on the beds to be sure they are evenly tucked and laying properly. Check the hanging curtains that drape on the floor to be sure they are properly hanging.

Other Bedrooms (These bedrooms may be for a child or guest. A child's room must be cleaned daily like the master bedroom, whereas a guest room is cleaned only one time per week or more when used.)

- **Beds** are usually changed in the children's rooms _____ per week on _____ . Beds are changed in the guest room _____ per week, when used, on _____ . Most often in a child's room there may be extra things on a bed such as stuffed animals, blankets tucked behind the pillows and other items of special importance. As described in the guide to making beds in master bedroom, the beds in each room have special individual requirements. Learn to make the bed properly by stretching the bottom sheet, airing out the top sheet and tucking in the top sheet, fluffing and laying flat the comforter, duvet cover or blanket, pulling out the dust ruffle and laying it evenly, puffing and decorating the bed with the shams and other pillows, returning any accessory items neatly (stuffed animals, blankets, throw pillows, etc.) as instructed. Be thorough and make the bed look perfect every time.

- **Vacuum** in a child's room at least _____ per week on _____ . Vacuum the guest room _____ per week, or _____ per week when in use on _____ . When vacuuming, always be careful not to hit the furniture. Move items so that you can vacuum underneath. Vacuum under the bed and in the closets using the necessary attachments for the vacuum.

- **Furniture** in most bedrooms (whether child or guest) will comprise nightstands, desk, bookcases, and/or an armoire. All of these furniture items need to be dusted any time you vacuum the room. Be careful to remove items completely before dusting. Only use polish and/or oils when instructed to do so. Always use a soft cloth for dusting.

- **Windows/Doors/Baseboards** get very dusty and dirty. If a window has shutters, they should be wiped down weekly with a very damp cloth and then with a dry cloth. Open the shutter and clean the windowsill and any smudges on the window that are reachable. If a window only has curtains or any other window dressing, then clean the windowsill and window at least one time per week. Doors (entry to the room and closet) should be checked for smudges, especially in the children's rooms. If the doors are mirrored, clean the mirror doors regularly, as needed. Baseboards should be wiped or vacuumed with the necessary attachment weekly.

- **Organization** is extremely important particularly in a child's room. The amount of time you need to devote to organizing a room will depend on the age of the child. Babies don't make too many messes. Toddlers require the most attention to organization. Older children, by now, will have (or certainly should have) learned to put their own toys and clothes away. Toys

Organization is extremely important particularly in a child's room.

GUIDELINES FOR TRAINING YOUR DOMESTIC

should be carefully put back in their place. Many kinds of toys have separate pieces that if lost can render a toy unusable. Do not haphazardly throw a toy in a place where it does not belong. It will be frustrating for the child when a toy cannot be found. Clothes can be organized in a closet so that each type of clothing is together. Keep closets as well as drawers organized. A good time to keep the clothing items organized is when putting laundry items back in their place. Every room of the house needs constant organization on a daily basis. If you see something out of place, do not wait until you need to clean that particular area of the house. Put it where it belongs as you see it out of place.

Entry Hall (This area of the house is used daily and should be swept or vacuumed daily.)

- **Floor** in the entry hall is utilized frequently and will therefore require sweeping/dust mopping almost daily, cleaning with a wet mop _____ times per week on _____ . An entry floor may be of marble, wood or tile. Learn what cleaning product and cleaning procedure is used and follow the instructions carefully. Floors can be ruined if they are improperly cleaned. If there is an entry rug, remove it when cleaning the floor and vacuum the rug.

- **Furniture** may include an entry table with accessory items. Clean the table when doing the floor. Remove the accessories from the table before cleaning the table. Carefully clean each accessory item separately and put back exactly how you found it. If there is a mirror above the entry table, clean it carefully with the proper cleaning fluid.

- **Light fixture** could be anything from a crystal chandelier to recessed lighting. If it is your responsibility to clean the chandelier, you must step up carefully on a ladder and clean it with care. Put a heavy blanket underneath in the event a crystal should slip from your hands. Each crystal must be hand cleaned. A brass fixture will most likely only need dusting with cleaning of bulbs. The light fixture should be cleaned at least one time per month or as required.

Guest Bathroom(s)

• On a daily basis, the guest bathroom should be organized and checked for clean guest towels, toilet and tissue paper, and removal of trash. However, _____ times per week clean the guest bathroom thoroughly by cleaning the toilet, sink/counter, any mirrors and floor. (Refer to Bathrooms for detailed guidelines).

Gym/Gym Bathroom

• Clean the gym _____ times per week by dusting or wiping down the gym equipment, cleaning any mirrors and sweeping, mopping and/or vacuuming the gym floor. The Gym Bathroom should be cleaned_____ times per week. Clean the toilet/sink/mirrors and floor (refer to Bathroom guidelines for details).

Office

• Empty trash daily as in all rooms of the house. Be very careful not to throw away any papers that are not already in the trash can.

• Organize the room; however, no matter how disorganized the desk may seem, do not attempt to move or organize items that are on the desk.

• Dust any computer equipment with a very damp cloth and then dry with a soft cloth. Do not use any chemicals on any computer or electronic piece of equipment. Dust the bookcases and desk. Only use a polish as instructed.

Laundry Room

• Should be kept up whenever used and cleaned thoroughly at least one time per week.

• Clean the exterior of the washer and dryer. Clean the detergent holder in

GUIDELINES FOR TRAINING YOUR DOMESTIC

washer in the event there are any clumps of soap caught. Clean the lint tray of dryer (always check before each use). Organize and clean the cabinets. Keep the floor clean. Keep a list handy of any items in the laundry room that need to be replaced.

Housekeeper's Room/Bathroom If this room is utilized for a live-in housekeeper, it should be maintained daily like any other bedroom, and left thoroughly clean on the last day of the workweek.

- Change the bed sheets one time per week.

- Vacuum and dust all the furniture. Clean the closet doors and any mirrors.

- The bathroom, like any other bathroom of the house, should be kept clean daily and thoroughly cleaned on the final day of the workweek.

- If eating in your room is permitted, never leave dishes or utensils in the room after a meal. Food left behind attracts all sorts of bugs.

- The domestic's quarters should be kept clean and organized daily.

Patio/Cabana/Pool Area (It is suggested, especially during the good weather months, to clean the patio and/or pool area one time per week.)
- Clean the patio by sweeping or hosing down, whichever is appropriate. Clean the patio furniture _____ times per week on_____ . When cleaning the patio furniture, use a damp cloth. Dust the cushions. If there is a cabana, clean any furniture in it and sweep it clean. If there is an outside barbecue, you may be required to clean it after each use.

Garage
- Sweep the garage floor _____ times per week on _____ . Wipe down the garage cabinets _____ times per month on _____ . If the washer and dryer are kept in the garage and not in a separate laundry room, then wipe them down at this time. If there are any items that can be organized, do so at this time.

- **Plants** may need watering inside and in the front and back patio areas.

GUIDELINES FOR TRAINING YOUR DOMESTIC

Take away any dead leaves and dust those plants that might require cleaning. Some plants need water only one time per week while others require every other day or daily. Be sure not to over-water or under-water any plants. Orchids, in particular, need very special care. If part of your job is to water the plants, you need to follow the schedule below:

Water the plants _____ in the _____ times per week on _____ .

Water the plants _____ in the _____ times per week on _____ .

Water the plants _____ in the _____ times per week on _____ .

Take care of the orchids as follows: _____

_____

_____

- **Flowers -** If there are flowers in vases, carefully change the water in the vase daily. Clean the vase if necessary and take out any flowers that are dead and wilting.

- **Silver -** Any silver items will need to be polished as needed. When polishing always use the appropriate silver cleaner with a soft cloth or soft sponge, drying it immediately with a soft cloth. Follow instructions on cleaner and NEVER use an abrasive cleaner or sponge on the silver so as not to ruin it. If you are cleaning silver picture frames, take out the pictures first and lay on a dry surface. Clean the frame separately and dry very carefully before returning the pictures to their individual frames. If you do not dry the picture frame carefully, you can ruin the picture when you put it back inside the frame.

  If you are cleaning silver picture frames, take out the pictures first and clean the frame separately.

Polish the silverware _____ times per month or as otherwise instructed if needed for special entertaining.

GUIDELINES FOR TRAINING YOUR DOMESTIC

Product Use

- **Kitchen:** Granite _____
  Tile _____
  Wood _____
  Stove Top _____
  Oven _____
  Breakfast Table _____
  Floor _____
  Refrigerator _____
  Cabinets _____

- **Bathrooms:** Granite _____
  Marble _____
  Tile _____
  Toilet _____
  Tub _____
  Sink _____
  Shower _____
  Mirrors _____
  Floor (tile) _____
  Floor (travertine/limestone) _____
  Floor (marble) _____

- **Furniture:** Wood cabinets _____
  Wood furniture _____
  Glass furniture _____
  Kids' furniture _____

- **Floors:** Wooden _____
  Travertine/Limestone _____
  Tile _____
  Marble _____

GUIDELINES FOR TRAINING YOUR DOMESTIC

- **Windows:** _____
- **Silver:**_____
- **Crystal:** _____
- **Bar sink:**_____
- **Walls and Doors:** _____
- **Piano:** _____
- **Patio furniture:** _____
- **Gym equipment:** _____
- **Art work:**_____
- **Brass fixtures:** _____
- **Gold-plated fixtures:** _____
- **Nickel-plated fixtures:** _____
- **Chrome-plated fixtures:** _____

ATTIRE AT WORK

How you would like to see your domestic dress at work in your home is something that needs to be addressed during the hiring process. Wearing a uniform may or may not be something that you want. However, the decision as to whether or not you want a uniform used must be made from the start. You do not want to tell your employee that wearing her/his street clothes is fine only to later discover that you would prefer a uniform. Your employee may be offended that you disapprove of her clothes and may also simply refuse to wear a uniform. Many domestics, whether they are nannies or housekeepers or companions, do NOT want to wear a uniform because they see it as putting them in a "subservient role" or simply unacceptable. Then there are those employees who welcome the use of a uniform so that they do not have to use their own clothing and potentially damage it.

Uniforms, in my opinion, are a great way to go because the attire is always very presentable. You do not have to worry about offending your employee because you do not think his/her clothing is appropriate. When an applicant states that he/she prefers not to wear a uniform because it is degrading, respond as follows: "When a doctor, policeman, paramedic, military officer, airline pilot, fireman and nurse wear a uniform, do you think they too find it degrading? I hardly think so. These are educated people who worked hard to attain their titles. They are proud to wear their uniform, and you should be as well."

If you do choose to have your domestic wear a uniform, then keep in mind that you are responsible for purchasing all uniforms for your employees. Plain white or black tennis shoes are preferable and should also be purchased by the employer. It would be a good idea to have at least two uniforms available. These uniforms can remain at the work place and the employee can have the option to change once they arrive at work or come to work in uniform. Remind your domestic that the uniforms should be cleaned and pressed as needed.

Keep in mind that you are responsible for purchasing all uniforms for your employees.

One of the reasons that uniforms are disliked is because they can be uncomfortable. As an alternative, some domestics prefer wearing black stretch pants with white plain t-shirts. If that is suitable to you, then everyone is happy. If you decide to allow your employee to come to work dressed in her/his own attire, then my suggestion is that you set some parameters with respect to an appropriate choice of clothing that is conducive to perhaps playing with children and/or cleaning the house.

You need to tell your prospective employee that you have certain requirements for personal grooming.

PERSONAL GROOMING

This can be an uncomfortable discussion. Let us assume that you have hired a Nanny who came very nicely put together for the interview. You are very impressed with her résumé and decide she is the one for you. There is one slight problem: She came with heavy perfume, lots of make-up, high heels and plenty of jewelry. (My personal opinion is that she did not come properly dressed to the interview.) However, you love the candidate and now just need to deal with this issue. You need to tell this prospective employee that you have certain requirements for personal grooming. Tell her that perfume cannot be worn at work because it would be too strong if you have a baby and could even possibly give other members of the family a massive headache or an allergic reaction. Next, make-up should be kept simple and not excessive. Finally, you would prefer no jewelry being worn (except for a wedding band and perhaps small earrings that are not long and dangling). You also proceed to tell her that shoes should be flat, rubber soled (preferably tennis shoes). If you are asking yourself right now, "How could I possibly tell anyone all these things without offending the person?" the answer is that you have every prerogative to politely state exactly how you want your employee to arrive at work. If the employee finds this discriminatory and offensive, then you need to find another employee. Basically, you are not out of line in asking your employee to abide by a dress code that is specific to your workplace. The employee has every right to say, "I do not want to comply to your dress code," and simply not take the job. As you can see, all of these discussions must be handled prior to an employment commencing.

What you do not want to do is to hire someone to work for you and then three weeks later decide you do not like her perfume, fishnet stockings, long earrings and excessive make-up. So as part of the interview process, be sure to observe how your applicant is put together and ask, in a nice manner, if he/she would be opposed to your particular dress code. You may also include in your dress code the need to have the domestic's nails kept short and impeccable and that your domestic keeps her long, beautiful hair wrapped up and put back.

Whatever you require as part of your dress code is fine, as long as it is appropriate and customary practice. Most domestics who are professional should already know the personal grooming and attire requirements that come with the territory. Do not hesitate to be very open and direct with your requests.

RESPECT, APPRECIATION AND AN OPEN LINE OF COMMUNICATION

How do you maintain respect and show appreciation and keep an open line of communication between you and your employee? The first rule is to never cross the line. This means that you are the employer at all times. This may be a big responsibility for you because perhaps you have never had an employee in your home before. You think that you should be friendly and in so doing, you decide that what constitutes "friendliness" is being talkative and sometimes even sharing

GUIDELINES FOR TRAINING YOUR DOMESTIC

your personal thoughts and views on subjects that would normally be discussed with close friends and relatives. You may even decide to sit down on occasion and cry your heart out and share some intimate problems that you feel you need to talk about because no one else is there at that particular moment. You may feel lonely and decide you want your domestic to join you for drinks and dinner or to go shopping together. BIG MISTAKE! YOU HAVE NOW CROSSED THE LINE. THERE IS NO TURNING BACK. How do you expect to tell this same person that has now become your "new best friend" that she has to stop coming to work late and isn't doing her job properly?

So here are some tips on how you can be a good employer without crossing the line and losing your position of authority.

Keep your private business to yourself. Your employee does not need to know about your spousal, financial, physical or psychological problems.

- There is no problem with being friendly to your employees. It is actually preferred. However, being too friendly as indicated above could land you with a "new friend" that you didn't exactly want. *Keep your private business to yourself. Your employee does not need to know about your spousal, financial, physical or psychological problems.* Turn to appropriate people to discuss these issues, but not to your domestic. By the same token, you should show your domestic the same respect by not delving into her personal affairs. As long as whatever is going on with your domestic's life is not interfering with her work, then it isn't any of your business. If your domestic, on the other hand, chooses to discuss with you something that she needs assistance with, it is up to you to decide whether to engage in this conversation. However, be careful as to how you advise your domestic to proceed. For example, if she is having domestic issues with her husband, it is generally not a good idea to advise her to "dump him." You would not want that kind of message getting out to the spouse. Keep your opinions, jokes and discussions on a professional basis.

Never use profanity nor raise your voice in their presence.

- Another way of maintaining respect between you and your employee (and anyone else for that matter) *is to never use profanity nor raise your voice in her/his presence.* You may think it is appropriate to scream at the top of your

GUIDELINES FOR TRAINING YOUR DOMESTIC

lungs to your children, your spouse or friends, but you do not want to use this tone with your employees.

- *Use constructive criticism* when telling your employee that you are unhappy with her performance at work. Try to maintain your cool and do not use phrases like you would use when talking to your child, such as:

"How many times do I need to remind you of the same thing?"

"Why can't you remember what I told you this morning?"

"You obviously aren't with it today!"

"What is wrong with you?"

"You are absolutely driving me crazy."

Make every attempt to remain professional when you are reprimanding your domestic. It is terribly frustrating to find yourself repeating instructions or simply being misunderstood. The best way to solve this problem is to write your instructions down and quietly go over them carefully so that the employee is absolutely clear as to what you expect for the day.

- Sit down quietly to discuss issues that are upsetting to you, and/or use the review periods for this purpose. Do not just randomly blurt out your dissatisfaction as your employee is getting ready to leave for the day.

- Be respectful of overtime, adhering to a vacation, review and salary increase schedule as previously agreed to in your employment agreement. Overlooking these important issues for your employee will indicate that you are not an appreciative nor a conscientious employer, resulting in a breakdown in communication. The employee may be too shy or uncomfortable to remind you of these things and may simply quit on you one day for your negligence.

- Show your appreciation with kind remarks by saying "thank you"

Make every attempt to remain professional when you are reprimanding your domestic.

Be respectful of overtime, adhering to a vacation, review and salary increase schedule.

GUIDELINES FOR TRAINING YOUR DOMESTIC

occasionally. You may feel that you are paying top dollar and do not need to say "boo" to your employee. Think how you would feel if your boss stopped during the day to tell you of his/her appreciation for your good hard work. Wouldn't it make you feel great? Everyone occassionally likes and needs a pat on the back.

• Keep an open line of communication by checking in on your employee from time to time to be sure that everything is going well. Make your employee comfortable and at ease to speak openly to you regarding the job. Even if you are completely overwhelmed at home or work, find the time to sit down and ask questions that pertain to the job.

• If your domestic asks you for a loan or advance in pay, it will be your call whether you choose to accommodate the situation. In the past, many employers have done so and regretted it. There is nothing wrong with helping a person in need; however, if you choose to do so, make a promissory note and have it signed and notarized. Work out the terms for payment and when it will be completely paid back. Make it official so that it cannot be forgotten. This loan could be set off against salary with written consent from employee.

• If you want professionalism out of your employee, begin by setting the first example in being professional yourself. Keep in mind that many of these domestic employees may be skilled at cleaning and great with children, but may not know how to be professional. It is up to the employer to train the domestic in all areas to ensure great results.

Chapter Nine

SAFETY AND EMERGENCY PROCEDURES

SAFETY AND EMERGENCY PROCEDURES

P arents do many things in the course of a child's life to keep a child healthy; they keep their children from getting sick, take them to check-ups and provide preventative care. However, in the United States, disease is not necessarily the greatest threat to a child. Each year, about 8,000 children die from injuries, and many of these injuries could have been prevented. One way is to keep your children away from things that might harm them. Another way is always stay near children so that you can act quickly in the event they come close to danger. Finally, children and their child care providers should be made aware of all important safety rules.

Certainly, we all understand the importance of handling an emergency properly. In this day and age, we are all so vulnerable to dangerous situations. There are so many different types of potential emergencies and in order to avoid leaving it to common sense, it is preferable that each potential emergency be discussed. There is a list of these for you, your children (if age appropriate) and your domestic to review. Generally speaking, consider the following rules:

- Think ahead; plan for unexpected dangers.

- Never leave a baby or toddler alone.

- Keep small items away from small children.

- Do not leave children of any age unsupervised.

- Discuss your child's curiosity with your Nanny.

- Always hold a child's hand when crossing the street.

- Buckle up children in motor vehicles in accordance with age and body weight.

- Know how to access all the necessary emergency numbers.

- Never open a door to strangers.

- Keep all gates to pools locked.

There are so many different types of potential emergencies and in order to avoid leaving it to common sense, it is preferable that each potential emergency be discussed.

SAFETY AND EMERGENCY PROCEDURES

- Stay close and never take your eyes off a child near water.

- Check your home for fire and burn dangers.

- Keep a fire extinguisher handy.

- Do not mix water with electricity.

- Know how to administer CPR.

- Always have signed parental consent form with you in case a minor needs medical attention.

- Be prepared for an emergency.

EMERGENCY DOS AND DON'TS

Specifically, here are some emergency and safety measures that you should share with your domestic, your children and other members of the family:

Security in the Home

- ***Never open the front door for anyone unless you are told that a particular person is expected or can enter at any time.*** This is a general rule that everyone needs to know. If there are certain friends, neighbors or relatives that can have free access to your home at any time, then inform your domestic of the these people and have them introduced beforehand. If an ex-husband, ex-wife, or ex-employee is or is not allowed entry, you must inform the domestic as well.

- ***Do not open the door for any utility (gas, electric, telephone, cable, and delivery service) or any other service company that randomly knocks on your door.*** (It has been reported that some criminals will pose as utility workers, even with the appropriate vehicles for these companies, so that they can easily invade your home.) Tell the delivery service to leave the package at the door. If the utility person tells the domestic that the owner of the house scheduled for this person to come and fix the cable, you need to instruct your domestic to verify that this information is correct before opening the door. In addition, the utility person should have identification indicating that he/she indeed is working for that company. Some homeowners go as far as to call the company to verify the name of the employee. If your domestic is at home alone and even more so alone with your child, every precaution must be taken to ensure the safety of your child and home.

- *If a police officer shows up at the front door, have him/her wait outside while you telephone the police department and ask if this person is on the force.* The fact this person has a badge and uniform can be deceiving. Remember, it is very easy for a criminal to get a fake police uniform and badge that may appear real. You may be intimidated when you first see the police at your door and your first impulse may be to open the door; however, real police would understand your trepidation, provide you with the necessary identification and would be patient while you call the station and verify the identification.

- *If and when you leave the house daily to get the mail, newspaper, or to take out the trash, be sure you have not locked yourself out.* Unlock the door temporarily or take the house key with you, if one is available. If you leave the door open, you may find that the wind will shut it closed and leave you outside. This could be a potential disaster, especially if a small child is inside the house. The best way is to leave through a door that has been temporarily unlocked. Remember to re-lock the door after you are back inside the house.

- *Always keep the doors closed and locked.* If you live in a community where there is a guard present, and as a result feel a great sense of security, you may leave your back and side door open, while using your monitoring system on your alarm to indicate when a door is being opened. However, even under these circumstances, it is a good idea to keep all your doors locked. Intruders will come in brazenly through easy entry. It is quite unfortunate that we have to be so concerned; however, it is better to be

If your domestic is at home alone and even more so alone with your child, every precaution must be taken to ensure the safety of your child and home.

informed and safe.

How to Avoid Electrical Incidents

- *Always check that the oven, microwave and stove are turned off.* If you have a fireplace that is gas, be sure to turn it off when leaving the house. (When turning on the fireplace, be sure the flue is open.) It is very easy to use these utilities and forget to turn them off.

- *Do not allow a child access to gas valves near a fireplace.* If the key to the gas valve is left inside the valve, a child could easily turn on the gas.

- *Children should never have access to any electrical appliance items.*

- *Keep child safety covers on electrical outlets and safety locks on cabinets.* They are there for one purpose only. Therefore, if you take them off to run the vacuum or for any other use, remember to replace the child safety covers on the electrical outlets. If you open a cabinet with a child safety lock, replace the lock after you are finished with the cabinet. (Small children especially find it fascinating to stick things in open holes like an electrical outlet. They also love to open drawers and cabinets to see what is inside.)

- *Safety measures when using all electrical items:* If you are using an electrical apparatus and you smell smoke, unplug it and stop using it immediately. Do not attempt to fix something without proper assistance. You could damage it further and start a fire. If a light bulb burns out, unplug the lamp when removing the bulb. Do not leave the lamp plugged without a bulb, especially in the presence of children who might decide to stick their finger in the socket while you are getting the bulb. The best way to change a bulb in a lamp is to first get a new bulb; use a cloth or let the old bulb cool off; unplug the lamp; remove the old bulb and replace it, and then re-plug the lamp.

How to Prevent a Fire

- *Matches, lighters, candles, cigarettes and incense:* Keep all of these items

If you are using an electrical apparatus and you smell smoke, unplug it and stop using it immediately.

out of reach of children. Never leave any candles burning for a long period of time, especially when you are not in the same room. If you leave the house, make sure all candles are extinguished. (Warning: Be extremely careful with birthday candles that re-light themselves. It is a fun novelty, but has caused many a home to burn down to the ground because the candles were thrown away and managed to re-light unbeknownst to the homeowner.) Never leave lit or extinguished cigarettes near a child's reach. It is preferable that you keep smoke away from a child, as secondary smoke may be very damaging to the health of anyone.

Warning: Be extremely careful with birthday candles that re-light themselves.

- **Check all smoke and carbon dioxide detectors periodically to be sure they are working properly.**

- **If there is a fire, call 911 immediately and get the family members out of the house.** If the fire is very small, call the fire department anyway and try to use the fire extinguisher. You may think you have been successful in putting out the fire; however, you should still have a professional fireman come in to check the area and secure it completely. A fire extinguisher should be handy in various parts of the house, particularly the kitchen, near barbecue area and the garage. (Every house should have one handy and adult members should know how to use it.)

Pool Area – Preventing a Drowning

- **Never leave any small child by the pool alone.** Always keep the gate to the pool locked. If the pool does not have a gate, then you must keep all doors leading to the pool locked. If there is a gate, it should be at least 5 feet high with a self-closing latch above the child's reach. However, when there is a gate around the pool, and a gardener or anyone enters the backyard and opens it, always remind this person to keep it closed. Do not assume that your pool man or gardener will remember to do so. You must re-check the gate while they are there and once they leave. Keep your eye on any child that enters the backyard. Never assume anything when it comes to a child's safety. (It would be prudent to install a telephone at poolside with the necessary emergency numbers clearly posted and/or programmed into speed dial.)

- *If drowning does occur, you should immediately pull a child from the water. If the child is not responding to usual stimuli, do the following:*

  - Check for breathing – if none present, immediately open the airway and attempt rescue breathing.

  - If no air enters the lungs, re-tilt the head and try again. If air enters then check for signs of circulation (moving, breathing and coughing).

  - If signs of circulation are present but breathing is questionable, give rescue breaths every 3 seconds.

  - If no signs of circulation are present, begin CPR – 5 chest compressions followed by another breath.

  - Continue rescue breathing or CPR (chest compressions and breathing) until the paramedics have arrived or until child responds. Consider supportive breathing if the child's breathing is weak or very slow. Note that if you are alone with the child or infant – do one minute of CPR rescue breathing before calling paramedics.

Vigilance and Discipline of Children

- *Never leave any small child alone anywhere in or outside of the house.* Keep your eyes on children of all ages at all times. Especially keep a constant eye on small children. We hear constantly about children being abducted in all types of neighborhoods. You can never be too careful anywhere. Once again, these guarded communities seem to be the safest for letting your children at a certain age run out the door and walk down the street. However, all children under 7 years of age should be carefully watched at all times. Keep in mind that many backyards are an easy access for wild animals that could attack a small child.

- *If a child is throwing a temper tantrum and refuses to behave, sit the child down quietly and try to talk it out first.* Do not yell or show any temper. Be firm and serious as you attempt to calm the child down. If the misbehavior continues, give the child a warning that a "time out" is forthcoming. If the child continues not to listen to you, then give the "time out" as instructed in your warning. Finally, if you cannot get a proper response, call the parents. Make the call to the parents ONLY as a last resort. (The Nanny should make every attempt to handle the situation first. The Nanny will gain the child's respect this way. However, if the only way of getting the child to behave is to make the call to the parents, then it must be done so that the child understands at this point that making the call means the situation is serious.) A parent should never leave the house without taking the appropriate phone or beeper to be contacted in case of an emergency.

- *Never - and this means NEVER - physically hit, shake, slap or spank a child or person under your care.* Even if you think the child deserves it, this is not to be implemented by a childcare provider. Most parents today will not engage in any of this behavior because they themselves are fully aware of how dangerous this can be both psychologically and physically. Children in school are taught to call 911 if they are physically abused (sexually or otherwise) by anyone. It is a serious issue and must be discussed openly so that any childcare provider knows clearly to NEVER LAY A HAND ON ANY CHILD UNDER ANY CIRCUMSTANCES.

The appropriate way of handling a misbehaving child is with a "time out" or by taking away a privilege. If this does not work, and you strongly feel that the child is "out of control," then telephone the parents immediately.

Ironing Hazards

- *Never iron in the presence of a small child.* It is best to do the ironing when children are asleep. If you do iron while a child is present, never leave the hot iron in arm's reach enabling a child to be burned. While ironing,

The appropriate way of handling a misbehaving child is with a "time out" or by taking away a privilege.

do not get distracted by a show on TV, the telephone or a screaming child that can result in a burned garment, or worse, a fire. Always leave the iron in an upright position when not ironing. The newer irons have an automatic switch-off device when the iron is not in use for more than a few minutes. When finished with the iron, unplug the iron and leave the hot iron to cool off on a high countertop away from the reach of a child. This may seem like common sense; yet, being reminded of these safety measures when ironing can't hurt.

Water Safety and Bath Time

- **Water safety is mandatory.** Never leave a child alone in the bathtub, wading pool, swimming pool, pond or any other body of water. The National Center of Health Statistics made this information public as it relates to children drowning:

  - 50% of infant drowning deaths occurred in bathtubs

  - Children ages 1-4 drowned most often (56%) in swimming pools

  - 26% of the 1-4 age group drowned in "natural bodies of water" (oceans, lakes, rivers and streams)

  - Buckets of water remain a risk to an infant and small child

It remains imperative that constant and adequate supervision is given for all children while in and around water.

It remains imperative that constant and adequate supervision is given for all children while in and around water.

- **Precautions for bath time:** If and when you run the bath water for a child, be sure to check the temperature before letting a child enter. If a child is submerged in bath water at a temperature of 130° F or higher, 3rd degree burns can occur within 30 seconds. A majority of these burns can be prevented if the homeowners turn down their thermostat temperatures to a maximum of 120° F. Watch that the water does not overflow. Be especially careful if giving a baby a bath. Never leave any small child alone in the bathtub, or near a bath full of water (or any body of water) even for a second. A small child can drown in as little as two inches of water. If the phone rings, let the answering machine get it. If you do not have an answering machine, then take a portable phone with you in the bathroom. If the doorbell rings, and you must get to the door, take the child out of the water, wrap the child in a towel and take the child with you. Be sure to remember to turn the water faucet off. **DO NOT LEAVE A SMALL CHILD ALONE IN THE BATHTUB UNDER ANY CIRCUMSTANCES.**

• *Always keep an eye open for any running faucets or valves where water may be leaking.* A small leak can result in thousands of gallons of wasted water and potential damage to structures. When you see a leaky faucet in the house, inform a parent immediately.

Preventing Falls and Head Injuries

• **Prevent falls:** Always stay with an infant who is on a changing table or a bed. If reaching for something to use while changing an infant, keep one hand on the infant at all times. Put barriers on the top and bottom of stairs and do not forget to re-instate the barriers when using the stairs. Hold the handrail when walking with an infant. Use skid-proof mats in the bathtub. Use a high chair that is stable and wide-based with a seat belt. Never forget to secure the child in a highchair. Be sure all low windows are locked and the screens are secure.

• *Using sports-related items:* When using bicycles, scooters, and other riding toys, first check to see that they are in good order and are size appropriate for the child. Make sure the child is wearing an approved helmet and necessary shin, elbow and knee guards. Teach and review with children safe riding practices such as obeying traffic signs. Stress the significance of safety at all times.

Avoiding Dog Attacks

• *Prevention of dog attacks:* When walking a dog, keep a strong hold on the leash. If you see another dog approaching, cross the street away from the approaching dog. One never knows how the two dogs will actually react together. When a strange dog that is NOT on a leash approaches, stay still until you are able to locate its owner. If there is no owner to be found, you have a few choices. If the dog seems aggressive and wants to attack your dog, you must do everything in your power to get away from this dog. Lift a small dog in your arms and walk away slowly until you are far away enough to run without distracting the dog. If you are alone walking a large dog, you must get away quickly before the fight ensues. If alone and you are being attacked, roll into a ball and lie still. If walking with a child and you are being attacked, secure the child first as you roll into a ball and lie still until the dog walks away.

Children are often bitten on the head or face area due to their size. This can cause a severe injury or infection. Contact the National Center for Injury Prevention and Control for more information on this issue. Do not disturb a dog that is sleeping, eating or caring for its puppies. Do not pet a dog without letting it smell you first and then asking its owner about its disposition. Never look at an unfamiliar dog in the eye. Never let a child pet a strange dog without asking its owner if the dog is friendly. Never let a small child play with any dog unless supervised by an adult.

Preventing Burns

- ***Household burns occur mostly in children under the age of 16.*** Children this age have a greater mortality risk, particularly with burns over 30% of the total body surface area. The most common cause of household burns are scald burns for children 4 and under. Experts in the field of injury prevention have clear guidelines for parents to prevent burns in the home. For example:

- Turn the thermostat on your home water heater down to 120 degrees F° or have a plumber or baby-proofing expert install a device that will not allow the temperature beyond a certain maximum heat.

- Be vigilant in the food preparation area when it comes to allowing infants and children near hot substances. Be sure to keep hot substances and their

Do not disturb a dog that is sleeping, eating or caring for its puppies.

Be vigilant in the food preparation area when it comes to allowing infants and children near hot substances.

containers away from the edge of a cooking surface or counter top. Keep handles on pots and pans turned to the back of the stove when you cook.

- Put barriers around fireplaces, radiators, hot pipes, wood-burning stoves and other hot surfaces to keep infants away.

- If a burn does occur in the home, immediately pour cool water over the area for at least 30 seconds and then remove clothing to examine burn area. Your efforts will reduce skin temperatures and may reduce the depth and size of the burn. You must seek medical treatment if the burn is deep or large, at which point you would need to call the paramedics, particularly if you are alone with the infant or child.

- Another burn that can easily be obtained without proper care is one that comes from the sun. Be sure to always use sun block on each child in all areas exposed. Most skin cancers that are prevalent in adults are as a result of over exposure to the sun beginning in childhood.

Poisoning

- ***Most poisonings occur when parents or caretakers are not paying close attention.*** Children can get very sick if they come in contact with medicines, household products, pesticides, chemicals, cosmetics or plants. This can happen at any age and can cause serious reactions. However, most children who come in contact with these things are not poisoned, and most who are poisoned are not permanently hurt if they are treated right away.

While you are busy cooking dinner, or planning tomorrow's schedule, your child may be exploring what is in the closet or under the kitchen or bathroom sink. Children like to put things into their mouths and taste them. Therefore, all dangerous items should be kept out of their reach. The best way to prevent poisonings is to lock up all dangerous items. The most dangerous potential poisons in the home for young children are the following:

Most children who are poisoned are not permanently hurt if they are treated right away.

SAFETY AND EMERGENCY PROCEDURES

- Medicines

- Vitamins with added iron are one of the most serious and frequent causes of poisonings in children younger than 5 years of age

- Cleaning products (furniture polish in particular)

- Antifreeze

- Windshield washer fluid

- Pesticides

- Gasoline, kerosene, lamp oil

- Alcohol

- Cosmetics, nail polish and hair products

- Garage supplies, such as mothballs, fertilizer and paints (Use nontoxic finishes and lead-free paint when painting and refinishing toys and infants' furniture.)

It is also important to store medicines and household products in their original containers. Many dangerous items look like food or drinks. Your child could mistake powdered dish soap for sugar or lemon liquid cleaner for lemonade.

Remember that when a child is taken to another person's house (relative, neighbor or friend), their house may not be child proofed. In this case, you would have to be especially vigilant, never taking your eye off the child.

Please note that the American Academy of Pediatrics (AAP) recommends that syrup of ipecac no longer be used routinely as a home treatment strategy. Until now, the AAP advised that parents keep a 1-ounce bottle of syrup of ipecac in the home to induce vomiting if it was feared a child had swallowed a poisonous substance. Ipecac is now recommended for use only on the advice of a doctor or poison control center. Speak with your

Please note that the American Academy of Pediatrics (AAP) recommends that syrup of ipecac no longer be used routinely as a home treatment strategy.

pediatrician regarding this issue.

If you have a poison emergency, call the **Poison Help Line at 1-800-222-1222.** A poison expert in your area is available 24 hours a day, seven days a week. This number is a nationwide toll-free number that directs your call to your regional poison center. You may also use this number if you have a question about a poison or about poison prevention.

Choking

- ***The majority of choking deaths among children occur from household toys and items.*** Seventy percent of choking deaths among 3-year-olds and younger children occur due to the swallowing of toys. The most common cause of non-fatal choking incidents is food. These prevention tips for choking are endorsed by the American Academy of Pediatrics, American Red Cross, and the Centers for Disease Control for the reduction of choking in infants and children.

At mealtime: Insist that your children eat at the table, or at least sitting down. Watch young children as they eat, encouraging them to eat slowly and chew food completely. Give infants soft food that does not require chewing. Cut up foods for older infants into small pieces, especially those foods that are firm and round and can get stuck in your child's airway, such as grapes, hot dogs, raw vegetables. Other foods that can cause a choking hazard include hard candy, popcorn, and peanuts.

At playtime: Remember that toys can serve as a choking hazard. Read toy packages for information on choking hazard(s). Any toy that is small enough to fit through a 1 1/4 inch circle or is smaller than 2 inches long is unsafe for children under 4 years of age. If older children are present and playing with toys that the younger children can find, have the older children keep their toys away from smaller children.

Check often under furniture and between cushions for items that can pose a danger of choking, such as coins, marbles, small batteries, pen or marker caps, toys with small easy-to-remove pieces, small balls or foam

If you have a poison emergency, call the **Poison Help Line at 1-800-222-1222.**

balls.

Remember to never let a small child play with or chew on non-inflated or broken balloons. Many choking deaths have been caused as a result of this material.

• *Suffocation and Strangulation:* Keep plastic bags and filmy plastic away from infants. Use a crib with slats that are only 2 3/8 inches apart or less and a snug-fitting mattress. Keep furniture such as cribs, play pens, and high chairs away from drapery cords and electric appliance cords. Never hang rattles, pacifiers or other objects around an infant's neck. If an infant is old enough to sit up, do not hang toys across the crib.

In the Event of an Earthquake or Other Disasters

• *What to do in the event of an earthquake:* First and foremost, be prepared with all the items necessary that have been recommended in the event of an earthquake. Have these items in a safe and easy-to-access area. Grab all children and attempt to step under a doorway or under a desk. Stay away from windows or glass or any large objects that could fall on top of you. Remain still and calm until the earthquake stops. If the earthquake occurs at night, grab a flashlight and shoes before going through a dark house to check on damage. If the earthquake is severe, turn off the gas from outside. Without electricity, you may not be able to get information on the severity of the quake. Have a portable radio that runs on battery power available to hear the news, as well as working flashlights for everyone's use.

• *Hurricanes, tornados or tsunamis have all been of serious concern lately.* The best response to any of these would be to listen carefully to the advice and direction of your local government and immediately evacuate if informed to do so.

Getting CPR and First Aid Training

Every domestic employee, parent and individual should be CPR certified. In particular, it is mandatory that parents of infants, toddlers and school

Have a portable radio that runs on battery power available to hear the news, as well as working flashlights for everyone's use.

age-children and their childcare providers take the course on a yearly basis. Sometimes you will have already hired your Nanny and discussed taking the course together, but find yourself forgetting to schedule it. Be sure to schedule the CPR course as soon as possible.

Even without children present in a household, knowing adult CPR would also be prudent. Just imagine if your own spouse or relative or friend was choking at the dinner table and slowing dying right before your eyes because there was no one available who knew how to perform CPR.

There are several places to get certified. Your local hospital may provide classes. You could also call a local American Red Cross for class and location schedules near you. There are also individuals who teach CPR at their own facility or even in your home privately. In Los Angeles, check out Richard Pass of **www.savealittlelife.com** for in-home courses as well as those provided at A Mother's Haven: **www.amothershaven.com.**

Learning the Use of the House Alarm

While you have a housekeeper in your home, and if you have an alarm system, it would be a good idea to teach her how to use it so that after she leaves, the house is always secure. In this day and age, you would not want to ever leave your house without putting on the alarm. Also there are silent emergency alarm buttons. Every child care provider and housekeeper should know how to use this emergency system. Inform your domestic how to use the alarm system in the event of an emergency.

If your domestic knows your alarm code, then she should also know your security name in the event she triggers the alarm by accident. Most alarm systems today have a silent panic button to alert the alarm company and police in the event there is an intruder while you are at home. You may need to alert the police without the intruder's knowledge. Instruct your domestic how to use this feature of your system. Remember you can give your housekeeper a separate alarm code. Contact your alarm company and they will inform you how to do this. You might even be able to set up a

Remember, you can give your housekeeper a separate alarm code.

SAFETY AND EMERGENCY PROCEDURES

meeting with your alarm company to come out and go through all features with your domestic. Modern alarm systems have the "monitoring" feature to alert you when a door is ajar. This is good to use when you are home with small children. For example, if a door is opened, the monitor system will inform you which door is ajar.

• Teach your domestic how and when to set the alarm.

Set the alarm in the house as follows:

_____

_____

_____

Set the alarm at the following times:

_____

_____

_____

Use the Panic (silent) Alarm button for the following emergencies:

_____

_____

_____

Alarm Company Number _____

Housekeeper's Password _____

Dealing with an Emergency Situation

• *If there is a medical emergency, depending on the severity, call 911.* If someone is choking and not breathing, perform CPR immediately. Continue performing CPR until you are able to get a response from the victim and/or the paramedics arrive. Next, you must call the parents at the numbers listed on the emergency list and follow down the list of people until you can reach the parents or someone on the emergency list.

• *Be prepared to give the following information to an EMS dispatcher:*

- Location (street address)

- Directions (cross streets/landmarks)

- Telephone number

- How many persons injured

- What happened

- Condition of victims

- Type of first aid given

- *Do not hang up:*

  - Stay calm

  - Speak clearly

  - Listen carefully

  - Do as instructed

Emergency Numbers

- *Home address and phone number:* Be sure that your child care provider has the house address and various phone numbers that include the house phone, parents' numbers (cell and work), neighbor's number and close relative's number at all times, and especially when leaving the house. Since cell phones are very common in today's world, it is advisable that every child-care provider carry one when out with a child. This phone could be provided by the family and used only during work hours. Children that are age appropriate should learn their home address and phone numbers in the event of an emergency. Cell phones should be programmed to speed dial 9-1-1.

- *Post a list of emergency numbers* by each telephone in the house. Include the following:

Children that are age appropriate should learn their home address and phone numbers in the event of an emergency.

SAFETY AND EMERGENCY PROCEDURES

- Emergency Medical Services (EMS)
- Fire Department
- Hospital
- Police Department
- Poison Control Center
- Parents' work, cell, pager
- Physician
- Dentist
- Veterinarian
- Close neighbor
- Children's school
- Address from where you are calling

Chapter Ten

REVIEW PERIOD

WHEN DO I REVIEW MY EMPLOYEE?

When is it appropriate to review an employee's work and offer a salary increase, if any? The first important point is that an employer should discuss this during the time the prospective employee is being hired. She/he should be aware of when you plan to review performance and what salary increase, if any, shall be provided at that time, if the employee is doing a good job and you are in a good position financially to do so. It may be 3, 6, or 12 months. The increase may be 2% all the way up to 10%. If you begin your employee at low wages because there was some doubt that she/he could perform the job well, then you would most likely need to provide a review period in a relatively short period of time. You may have hired your employee paying top-dollar. In this case, a review period is not merited until 12 months from the time of hire. Under any circumstances, a yearly review is certainly appropriate with the possibility of an increase as long as it is within the range the market is paying for the position.

You may want to conduct periodic reviews with your employee just to see how things are going from both perspectives. This does not mean that each time you conduct a review, you need to provide a salary increase. The increase is purely discretionary, but should comply with your original agreement. If the employee is doing a poor job and does not merit any increase, you should take the opportunity to discuss all the problems with the employee during the review period and give the employee a chance to make the necessary changes in job performance.

You may want to conduct periodic reviews with your employee just to see how things are going from both perspectives.

HOW IS THE REVIEW HANDLED?

Begin by asking your employee if she/he is happy on the job. If the employee seems nervous and has trouble looking at you in the eyes, question the employee further by asking anything about the job that is not liked. The employee may begin to say something, and then hesitate. This obviously means she/he is somewhat afraid to reveal any unhappiness for fear of losing the job entirely. Take time to reassure your employee that her/his honesty will not jeopardize your relationship nor provoke termination. Be specific in the review and cover the following topics.

- **Hours** - Does the schedule still work for you? Are you getting to work on time consistently? Are the overtime hours a burden to you?

- **Amount of Work and Job Performance** - How is the workload? Let's discuss your job performance. Is there any duty that you are having trouble doing? Are you able to complete all the work in the same time frame as when you first started the job?

- **Treatment by Family and/or Staff Members** - Is there anything that has transpired that was upsetting in any way? Have the kids ever been disrespectful? Are you getting along with everyone?

- **Future Plans** - Are there any plans for upcoming trips, doctor's appointments or time needed off that might interfere with the normal work schedule? Are there any plans for a trip back home in the near future? Any plans over the holidays?

- **Overall Happiness** - Is the job satisfying? Do you feel fulfilled, challenged and eager to continue employment? Is there anything you would like to change or discuss?

- **Salary** - If there is an agreement for an increase in salary, review the offer and when you propose to make that increase.

Remember: You are there to review your employee and assess the working environment for the benefit of a mutually satisfying relationship.

Based on the response to these questions, you will learn so much about your employee's state of mind on the job. Hopefully, your employee will take this opportunity to be honest with you. Assure your employee that discussing these questions openly will help make for a better working environment for all parties and that you intend on resolving any issues at hand. However, be aware that many employees fear that any form of discussion might be construed as a complaint and provoke being fired. It is up to you to set the mood and illicit information in a gentle manner. At the same time, be prepared for the answer you get. It may not please you to hear the unexpected response. Remember: You are there to review your employee and assess the working environment for the benefit of a mutually satisfying relationship. Stay calm and do not over-react as you listen carefully to all the responses.

This is also the time for you to express your concerns. You, too, must be open and ready to discuss in a professional manner all the things that might be upsetting to you. Have a list ready of those issues that need to be addressed. Be prepared to give your employee the list so she/he understands your concerns and knows how you want these issues resolved. Have this list added as an addendum to the household manual. Of course, make sure that your list includes things that can actually be corrected. Try to be circumspect regarding the choices you make when conducting a review. As we do with our children, pick your fights and don't nit-pick at everything unless it is an important issue to raise. Be complimentary as well so that the criticism does not dominate the review. Be open and frank, but professional at all times.

WHAT IF WE CANNOT AFFORD A RAISE?

Let's assume that you come across hard times and cannot provide an increase in salary. The best thing for you to do is to sit down and clearly explain your circumstances to your employee. You may think that it is "none of the employee's business," when in fact, providing an honest, legitimate reason for not increasing your employee's salary is quite important. Perhaps in the near future, your luck will change, at which point you will be happy to show your employee your appreciation for hard work and loyalty. Unless you fall on hard times, you truly should always remember your employee. Of course, this is only relevant if your employee is good and merits a raise.

If you absolutely cannot give any more because your budget just doesn't allow for it, then find another way to compensate your employee.

If you absolutely cannot give any more because your budget just doesn't allow for it, then find another way to compensate your employee. Perhaps a bonus at the end of the year, or a very nice birthday gift (along with extra time off to celebrate, if possible). Explain to your employee that you are currently on a tight budget and every penny counts, but that you plan on providing a raise as soon as things improve. Remember, that means following through. This person is taking care of your most dearest loved ones: your children, your parents, your pets, and/or your home. Oh, and by the way, if you really have financial problems that prevent you from raising your employee, then please don't come home continually with a car full of shopping bags from the mall while explaining that there is NO MONEY to spare for a raise.

WHAT IF THE EMPLOYEE AND POSITION DO NOT MERIT A RAISE?

There isn't any law that makes it imperative to give a raise to an employee. Raises are discretionary, unless you have agreed otherwise in your agreement with your employee. If you use the Employer/Employee Agreement, there is a clause that clearly stipulates that no raise is mandatory if the employer does not feel the employee merits one. If you feel that the salary you are providing is sufficient for the job performed and you do not want to address any changes in the "cost of living" or "market," then SO BE IT. If your employee is satisfied and is happy enough to stay without a raise, then you do not have anything to discuss. Hopefully, the loyalty and devotion your employee feels will never run dry. However, the rule of thumb is that 50% of the people who go out looking for a new job will report the reason for needing a change is due to a low salary and no raise.

The decision is yours. However, please do not be surprised if the person leaves you suddenly for a better paying position. Ultimately, everyone is forced to do what is necessary to survive.

HOW TO HANDLE AN EMPLOYEE'S THREAT TO LEAVE

Nobody likes to be threatened under any circumstances. You are already put on the defensive when someone begins the conversation with "If you don't give me a raise, I will leave." Not a good approach to any negotiation. Certainly, your first impulse is to say, "Well, then, leave." However, it might not be the best decision if this employee is outstanding. Let's backtrack and see if you wrote in your employee contract that you would review this employee within a period of time and consider a raise if you deemed it appropriate. If the answer to this is "yes," then let's discuss why that didn't happen. Were you busy and simply forgot to follow through? If so, then you are in the wrong and what has happened is that your employee feels angry about your neglect. She might have waited and waited for you to discover that the review and raise were due, only to be left building a sense of anger over the fact that so much time has passed and you have never mentioned it. Now she believes you might even have bypassed the discussion intentionally.

If this employee is worth keeping, then don't be stubborn. Yes, there are a million domestics out there looking for jobs every day. Are there many wonderful employees who know how to run your household how you like it and understand your job requirements? Do you want to revisit the process of hiring and risk the chance of needing to go through several employees to find a good one? Perhaps the employee could have used better tact in approaching you. However, take into consideration the fact that you could have been a more professional employer by not overlooking a well-deserved raise. Don't make any foolish decisions because you don't like the way in which the issue was presented. You might have reacted in the same way if it had happened to you.

On the other hand, if the employee is not worth giving a raise, you don't have to think too hard. Perhaps this is a great time for you to make that change that you kept thinking about so many times but did not have the energy to pursue. This could be your chance to get out of this relationship without hurting the employee's feelings. Simply state that you are sorry, but you cannot afford to provide a raise at this time, and that it perhaps would be a good idea to begin looking for a better paying job while you look for another employee.

Chapter Eleven

PROBLEMS - WARNINGS - NOTICE - TERMINATION

PROBLEMS - WARNINGS - NOTICE - TERMINATION

HOW TO HANDLE ON-THE-JOB PROBLEMS

When a family has contracted the employee through an agency, the employer will usually call the agency to help solve any problem. The agency can advise the employer how to handle it and even intervene and discuss the issue at hand with the employee. Some problems may be such that the employer prefers not discussing them directly with the employee due to the sensitivity of the issue. It may be related to personal grooming or something else that could offend the employee. There are a number of things that can be discussed by a third party who can serve as a buffer without causing the employer/employee relationship any damage or embarrassment.

Keep in mind, however, that if the issue is something that you can handle on your own directly with the employee, it is recommended that you do so first. Employees sometimes get alarmed when the agency is contacted. They interpret that action as though the issue must be very significant if the agency had to be notified. It may cause a rift in the relationship and the direct line of communication. If you can, try to keep your discussions open and direct in order to help maintain a good line of communication between you and your employee.

You may or may not be very comfortable confronting your domestic with certain issues. You may feel that the employee has done something so wrong that it is completely unacceptable and requires immediate termination. For example, let's say that it has been reported that your employee has hurt or severely neglected the safety of your child. Before taking corrective action, be confident about the facts and accusations. Take the necessary time to discuss the issue carefully and analyze the events as they happened. If you have all the facts and are sure that the employee was completely in the wrong, then you will probably want to terminate this employee on the spot. Living in an "at-will employment state" and having an "at-will" employment agreement further protects you when terminating an employee. Keep in mind, however, that you would never want to terminate someone for discriminatory reasons such as gender, race, age, use of tobacco, ethnicity, religion and sexual orientation.

Before taking corrective action, be confident about the facts and accusations.

Remember that the employer must pay an employee upon discharge all wages owed to the employee. Failure to do so could subject the employer to penalties. Handle the termination in a professional manner. Document the entire termination and keep a record of this. Avoid belittling conduct or threats. If you are sure that your child has been hurt or endangered, you may want to report this to the authorities. However, before doing so, please contact an attorney. Don't make any defamatory or unsupportable allegations.

If the problem is less severe, and one that can be rectified, then try discussing this first before becoming an emotional basket case and over-reacting. Calm yourself down and be prepared to act as a professional employer when you are ready to approach the employee. Discussion means just that. Sit down and talk it out. Ask the employee why it happened. Let the employee explain the situation. Listen to all sides of the story and then explain clearly what it is that you do not want this employee doing. Even though you will have the ultimate say in the matter, it is important that you listen carefully and that the employee has participated in this discussion and provided an explanation. She/He may appear remorseful and apologetic. Find a solution to make sure the incident isn't repeated. Write out instructions about what was discussed and keep a record of it in the "household manual." If you like this employee, then try to work things out. A working relationship is like a marriage. It requires understanding, discussions, hard work and sometimes your ability to compromise.

Relationships fall apart easily because people are impatient and expect perfection. If you have not noticed already, there is no perfection in anything. You certainly are not going to begin finding it in a domestic employee. Most of these people are not professionally trained. They may come with years of work experience, but that is about it. A previous work environment may have been quite different than yours. You will need to train this person. There may be some things that truly bother you about this employee, but other qualities that are stellar. Weigh the differences and decide if you can accept the weaknesses. If you find yourself compromising more than you would like, then you may be left with no recourse but to let the employee go.

PROBLEMS · WARNINGS · NOTICE · TERMINATION

PROVIDING WARNINGS FOR MISCONDUCT

By law, you do not need to give warnings in an at-will employment state, unless you have otherwise promised to do so. However, you may choose to give warnings in hope of improving your employee's work performance. This way, you gave it your all, and if it doesn't work out, termination will not come as a complete surprise. By following through with the periodic reviews, you will have every opportunity to give these necessary warnings. Document your discussions to protect yourself. Remember that warnings do not have to be construed as threats. They are simply methods by which you can express your unhappiness with the employee and in so doing, give your employee an opportunity to make the necessary changes. It is not always what you say to someone that causes an ill feeling; it is most often the manner and tone used to say it.

HOW MUCH NOTICE AND SEVERANCE IS APPROPRIATE?

Unless you promised in your employer/employee agreement that you will provide notice, then notice is discretionary. However, if you choose to give notice, then how much you give depends on the reasons for termination.

As mentioned earlier, if your employee is being terminated for misconduct such as stealing, neglecting your child, or doing something that puts your home and family at risk, then no notice needs to be given because you have this clearly stated in your agreement. This would be acceptable and understandable to anyone, including the employee. Certainly "notice" in this case would not be warranted. In spite of your rage, be sure to handle the termination in a professional manner.

However, let us assume that the reason you need to let the employee go is because you yourself have lost your job or are experiencing financial burden and cannot afford to pay her any further. Perhaps your child or children are now in school, and you do not need this person on a full-time basis. Or, perhaps, you simply want to stay home with your child. Under these circumstances, the proper manner of handling the issue of notice would be to provide as much lead-time as possible so that this employee can find another job; one to two weeks would be

By law, you do not need to give warnings in an at-will employment state, unless you have otherwise promised to do so. However, you may choose to give warnings in hope of improving your employee's work performance.

helpful. If this same employee has been with you several years, you would want to provide even more lead-time, perhaps even one month to show this employee your appreciation and concern.

Depending on the amount of time the employee has been with you, your financial position and just how much you really care about the well being of your soon-to-be terminated employee, you may want to provide notice along with severance pay. Once again, severance pay is measured by the amount of years under your employ and your generosity. People have been known to give from one week up to one month of severance pay. A good rule of thumb would be one week's pay for one to three years of work; two weeks' pay for more than three years of work; and three to four weeks' pay for more than five years of work.

Depending on the amount of time the employee has been with you, you may want to provide notice along with severance pay.

WHAT IS THE BEST WAY TO TERMINATE MY EMPLOYEE?

Unfortunately, this is the most difficult task that you will ever perform with respect to an employee. The likelihood is that the employee will be devastated. The employee's livelihood depends on your job and losing it will affect economic circumstances instantly. Most of the domestics, as mentioned earlier, are on very small and tight budgets. They are not usually at a high income level, so every paycheck counts. Be prepared for the employee to be upset. If you have given your employee various warnings, the termination may not be a complete surprise. Nonetheless, the employee may not take it well. So, here are some tips:

Terminate your employee in person.

- Terminate your employee *in person.* Do not take the easy way out by calling on the phone and leaving a message. It is important for all parties that this relationship be terminated properly. (It is no different than any "break-up"; nobody wants to know in a letter or a phone call.) If there are children in the house, it is good for them to have closure as well.

- Sit the person down quietly at the end of the workday and workweek. Do not do it when she is walking out the door or in passing. It may be difficult to sit face to face and converse about the reasons why you are terminating the employee; however, it is the proper and respectful way to handle the termination.

- If you are terminating due to poor performance, then begin your discussion with the problems that have previously been mentioned in review periods. Explain that you were hoping these problems would correct themselves, but they have not, and consequently you have no other recourse but to terminate.

- There is always the chance that the employee will begin to cry and become emotional and ask to be given another chance. You may decide that the employee deserves another chance. Although it is always appropriate to be understanding under these kinds of circumstances, be sure that you are not making an unwise decision. If you gave this employee the proper review periods and warnings in writing, then it won't come as a surprise if you suddenly terminate due to non-compliance. However, if you never warned the employee, the termination may come as a complete shock. The employee may sincerely want to make every effort to change and correct the mistakes. If you think there is a possibility of change, then giving the employee a chance may be the right thing to do. Often, at the moment of termination the employee realizes how close she/he came to being fired and consequently makes a complete turnaround.

In spite of your emotional state, treat the terminated employee in a civilized and professional manner to the end.

- Treat the employee with dignity. Have the employee collect his/her belongings that might remain in your home. Even if you are angry and are terminating under difficult circumstances, do not gather the employee's personal items and place them outside the door for pick-up. In spite of your emotional state, treat the terminated employee in a civilized and professional manner to the end. Do not keep any of the employee's property.

- If you are terminating due to a personal problem that has nothing to do with the employee's performance, such as finances, divorce, moving to another state, etc., then begin the discussion with describing how fond you are of the employee and how appreciative you are for her good hard work.

PROBLEMS - WARNINGS - NOTICE - TERMINATION

It may be difficult to be honest with the employee if your reasons are sensitive and private. Some employers disclose the true facts to the employee, and request that the matter be kept confidential and not divulged to a prospective employer or stated on the reference letter. If you prefer to keep it private, simply tell the employee that you are terminating for personal reasons that have nothing to do with the employee's performance and leave it at that. As long as you state this in your reference letter and emphasize the employee's strengths, a prospective employer will understand.

Have a letter of reference available for the employee. Make sure the letter states the dates when the employee worked, the duties and level of performance.

• Have a letter of reference available for the employee. Make sure the letter states the dates when the employee worked, the duties and level of performance. Certainly, if you were very happy with your employee, this would merit a lengthy, positive letter of reference. Short letters of reference are often misconstrued as a "bad reference" simply because the former employer did not elaborate. The same goes for a verbal reference. If you are quick and short on the time you take when providing a verbal reference, the prospective employer will be circumspect and suspicious. If you are adamantly opposed to writing a letter of reference, then tell the employee that any prospective employers can telephone you for a reference. Be specific as to when you would like to be called. It may be easier for you to provide a reference after hours, during the day, evening, or perhaps on the weekend only. Note when you prefer to be called on the reference letter. A busy family may find it very annoying to get calls at all hours. Another idea is to ask your former employee to have someone call only if they are very interested in hiring the employee. You may choose to write this in the reference letter as well. This way, you do not get inundated with unnecessary time spent providing a detailed reference to someone who was only marginally interested in the employee.

• If you have other staff members who supervise this employee, then the House Manager, Butler or Personal Assistant can handle the termination. You may be the type of employer who hardly ever spoke to the employee because you have other staff members who handle all employees. If this is the case, have the senior staff member handle the termination properly as though the employer directly were conducting the termination.

- If the employee has been living on the premises and using a private telephone in her/his room and/or a cell phone under your name, check with the telephone company for any outstanding bills prior to dismissing the employee. You have the right to demand payment for this, or you can deduct it from final pay, if in your employer/employee agreement you have specific authorization for deducting these charges against salary.

- There may be some personal items that have been given to the employee for personal use on the premises. If you choose to let the employee take these items upon termination, then make a list of what can be taken and what must be left behind. Remember to retrieve any house keys, door openers, credit cards or any other belongings given to the employee for use on the job. It is your decision as to whether or not the employee takes or leaves the uniforms purchased by the employer. Most likely, they will not be re-useable and can be taken by the employee.

The employee must be paid immediately upon termination for all wages earned.

- Have the final check and/or severance check ready to give to the employee. The employee must be paid immediately upon termination for all wages earned.

- Inform the fact that your employee no longer works for you to the appropriate people at schools, cleaners, grocery stores, security gate or any other places where the employee frequented.

WHY EMPLOYERS MUST TERMINATE A DOMESTIC

We have heard it all when it comes to the various reasons for an employee's termination. Some of these concepts will sound ridiculous to you; others are truly legitimate reasons. Here are just a few:

- ***The employer no longer will be returning to work.*** Usually it is the wife who has either lost her job or simply prefers staying home with her child (children). It may be more economical to live on one income than two while paying an employee. This is a very legitimate reason for termination. Many new mothers like the idea of going back to work after they have their first child. They enjoy the idea of having it all, but sometimes after working less than a year, find that they are missing out on their child's growth. Mothers who are on their second child often feel that they cannot see leaving both children with a Nanny. It is too stressful for them to work and come home as a part-time mother. They will opt to stay home and find a way of working from home or simply taking an indefinite leave of absence.

• ***The employer is tired of the fact that the employee is not cleaning the house properly.*** The employee started out beautifully, but slowly became lazy and has ultimately proven to be a lousy housekeeper. A way of perhaps avoiding this termination would have been to maintain those "review periods" so that the employee is being continually informed of his/her performance. Keeping a household manual handy for guidance can help the employee to remember the duties on a daily, weekly and monthly basis. Sometimes, an employee may be at a particular job just a bit too long. If the employee is simply "burned out" and has no more initiative, then it is time to move on. This employee may be thrilled at the opportunity to make a change.

If the employee is simply "burned out" and has no more initiative, then it is time to move on.

• ***The children have outgrown the Nanny.*** A Nanny that cares for infants may be superb at her job because she is very skilled at infant care and very nurturing and stimulating toward babies; however, this same Nanny may not be very good with school-age children. She may lack the language skills, training and energy to interact with older kids who need entirely different stimuli. This is particularly sad for the employee who has raised the child from infancy and then suddenly has little interaction with the same child who simply has outgrown her. The Nanny may be very understanding about the situation and welcome the day when she can return to what she does best, which is to work with a newborn. On the other hand, the Nanny may be very hurt and feel a tremendous resentment that she is suddenly being let go after so many years of hard work and loyalty to the family. Although it may be painful, you basically need to do what is best for your family. You may be a working mother who cannot be home all the time to oversee what is happening with the children. The children are now at that age where they are seriously testing the parents and particularly their child-care provider. It may require a Nanny with stronger child development skills and possibly better English to ensure that the children are instructed properly. If the Nanny cannot make the transition from the infant stage forward, you have no recourse but to find a new Nanny.

- ***The employee has developed an attitude.*** The employer finds it difficult to express what needs to be done for fear that it will provoke an argument. There is a negative feeling at the house, causing the employer to feel rather uncomfortable. This is a common occurrence. The question is, how did this attitude develop? Was it as a result of the employer's lack of sensitivity and professionalism? Did the employer keep adding responsibilities and forget to increase the salary or pay for overtime? Did the employee take advantage of the employer by slacking off in her duties? Each situation will have two sides of the story. Like any break-up, a series of problems slowly cause the destruction of the marriage that began so blissfully. A change in an attitude very often cannot be rectified. Feelings have been hurt and the person has taken offense. The employee may no longer feel appreciated or respected. You may be so stressed that you don't even realize you are taking it out on your employee, your kids, your spouse and anyone else in your life. You may be so stressed out that you don't even recognize your own terrible behavior and the effect it has on your household. My only advice to any employer is to be very aware of the fact that a domestic employee is not like a member of the family when it comes to abuse. It may well be that the change in attitude in your employee was brought upon by your

Each situation will have two sides of the story.

actions.

- ***The employee is not able to drive and you now need someone to help you drive the children.*** Many live-in domestics do not drive. This is one of the reasons why they work as live-ins. It is easier for them to live in the house than to attempt public transportation on a daily basis. Unfortunately, these same live-ins find themselves out of a job as the needs change within a family. There is a way of keeping this employee, but it would mean hiring a second person to do the driving. Many students are perfect for this. They can pick up the children and even do some tutoring, if necessary. This would depend on your budget. A way to avoid the problem at hand is to hire a driver in the first place.

- ***The employee has become too familiar; she no longer acts like an employee but more like a friend.*** When it comes to this issue, you walk a very fine line. Many employers begin by telling their employees that they want someone who will be like "part of the family." This may mean someone who eats at the same table with the family, goes on outings together and shares in all activities. However, you risk the chance of having your employee get so close with the family members that you may find it very difficult telling her/him what to do. Just as other members of your family forget to do their chores and pitch in when necessary, "this new member of your family" may do the same; only now you have become so close that you find it hard to return to the days when you played the "employer" role. Suddenly, the line has been crossed. If you want to avoid this from happening, remember your role as an employer and your employee will be forced not to forget her/his role as an employee. It is no different when a parent wants to be a best friend to a child, but as a result loses the ability to be a parent. My view is that you must always be a friend to your child, but you are first and foremost the child's parent. The same applies in an employer/employee relationship.

- ***The children are now older and will begin school.*** This is the most common reason for needing to let a domestic go after the first few years of your child's life. Today, unlike years ago, almost every child will begin an education in pre-school. Some schools take children as early as 3 years of age, as long as they are potty trained. These various schools can cost a fortune but will guarantee that your child will not only learn to be social, but also begin formal academic learning. According to educators, pre-schools will better prepare your child for the big step of kindergarten. Pre-schools are quite the trend, expensive as they are, and most families find the necessary funds to get their children matriculated. However, they sometimes can no longer afford to keep a Nanny employed simultaneously.

Now what do you do with that Nanny of yours who has been there from newborn stage to now? If your child is attending a half-day program at a pre-school, then you may still need someone to drive your child to and from school. You may ask your Nanny to work a part-time schedule. She may or may not be able to afford a part-time salary. If she can find another job that is part-time, it may be feasible. Another option for providing more hours would be to see if she would be flexible enough to change the hours so that she starts later in the day (at the time when your child is collected from school) to later in the evening to help you with dinner, a bath, and bedtime. Finally, another option would be to see if your Nanny wishes to do more housekeeping during the hours that your child is in school so that it would make sense financially to keep her on board full-time. If none of these options work for the Nanny, then you must let her go and move on.

- *Your children are now at an age where they need someone whose English skills are better so as to help with homework, etc.* Very often to lower costs, a family will begin with a domestic who does not speak a lot of English. It is felt that while the children are young, minimal English is fine. Then the children begin school and need more assistance with school and someone who can communicate on a higher level. The Nanny cannot do this because her educational and language skills may be limited. Now the family needs to move to a higher level and hire someone who speaks fairly good English and has tutorial skills.

If you have a large home and can afford two people, you might want to consider keeping the first employee to do the housekeeping and hire a separate, more skilled Nanny to work afternoons with the children. It may cost more, but the reality is you may need two separate employees to handle the changes in your household.

You might want to consider keeping the first employee to do the housekeeping and hire a separate, more skilled Nanny.

- **The neighbor's domestic or another domestic in your household has reported gossip.** Gossip is a serious problem in all work environments. It can be regarding an employee being disgruntled and secretly looking for another job or a myriad of other issues. Gossip can cause great dissension among staff members and become a major distraction and cause for termination. Sometimes the gossip has some validity to it, and other times it is merely all fiction created by a malicious counterpart that simply wants to make trouble for an employee. When the gossip gets reported to the "boss," it can cause enough concern and doubt that the employee usually gets fired. When staffing a home, one of the greatest challenges is having everyone like each other and remain on a professional level. Since it is often human nature to be catty, critical and jealous of others, it is common to have other domestics tell stories or give false information just to get another employee in trouble.

Be sure to speak to all individuals involved, get both stories and carefully weigh the facts.

The key is to get to the truth and be sure that one domestic is not simply trying to sabotage the other domestic. Having a house manager is an excellent buffer for all this potential nonsense and annoyance, but at an economic cost. Whether it is the employer or another higher staff member who ultimately needs to sort it all out, somebody has to seek the truth and decide whether termination is eminent. Be sure to speak to all individuals involved, get both stories and carefully weigh the facts. Sadly, you may find that you can cannot figure out who is being honest and end up firing both staff members.

- ***The employer thinks the employee is "too cute" to have in the house around her husband.*** This happens more often than you might think. Many au pairs and other young nannies may be attractive. Employers are sometimes jealous. Interestingly enough, statistics show that the most attractive people are the *first* to get the job. However, they may also be the *first* to get terminated.

- ***The employer is jealous of the bonding that has taken place between their child and the Nanny.*** This often occurs with new mothers who are experiencing postpartum depression and separation anxiety. They may not want to leave their babies but must return to the work force. They have made a choice to quickly go back to work full-time, and it means that their baby is spending less time with the parent and more time with the Nanny. There is a natural bonding that takes place with every child and its caretaker. Sometimes the bonding is simply stronger with the one who spends the most time with the baby. There is no way to change this unless the mother stays home. There are mothers who work a 50-hour week and get home in time to see their child a few hours before putting the child to sleep for the evening. What in heaven's name do they expect? Be sensible and understanding during this stage of infancy as you learn to share bonding with your baby.

WHY DOMESTICS CHOOSE TO TERMINATE EMPLOYMENT

It may be easy for you to understand the various reasons why you, as an employer, might terminate your employee. However, why is it that employers are always dumbfounded and very angry when their employees terminate of their own volition? The reason for this is because many employers never expect the employees to leave them. The employees also have lives outside of work and personal problems that may conflict with their jobs. Some of these personal problems are unique to immigrant workers, such as loss of legal work permits. Others are due to normal dissatisfaction with the job itself. For example: salary, schedule, workload and a deteriorating employee /employer relationship. The

Why is it that employers are always dumbfounded and very angry when their employees terminate on their own volition?

employee may be shy and afraid to speak out about any problems on the job for fear of losing the job. This lack of communication on the employee's behalf is often the result of some very acute cultural differences. Therefore, lack of communication and awareness on behalf of both the employer and employee may result in a surprise termination. You may take the attitude that domestic employees are easy to replace, however, their very dispensability may not be what you want. Periodically having those review sessions to be sure that all matters are good at the work place might prevent an unexpected termination.

Now let's look at the other side of the coin. There are definitely domestic employees terminating of their own accord even when their employers have acted in a very professional manner, doing everything possible to keep their employee happy. They have provided review periods, vacation time, holidays, incremental raises, showered them with gifts, time off, and even have gone so far as to treat them like a member of the family. Yet, the employee still wants to leave. These terminations are the ones employers find most difficult to accept. The employers are usually very upset and feel somewhat taken advantage of by their employee. Let me review some of these potential scenarios from the employee's perspective, so that you are not shocked if and when it happens to you.

- ***My mother is dying in my country, and I must go to her for fear that I might never see her again before she passes.*** Under normal circumstances, if anyone ever told this to you, you would be completely sympathetic and accept this as a legitimate reason for leaving. You may ask your employee if and when she plans to return to work. The response will either be, "I do not know because I do not know the severity of my mother's condition." OR "Yes, but I cannot not tell you when." OR, flat out "No" and "Oh, by the way, I must leave immediately tomorrow morning." So now, as a result of this emergency, you are left "high and dry." You may work and be truly up a creek without a paddle since you have no one to care for the children. You are panic-stricken as you look for someone to replace this employee. If, in fact, the employee's relative is dying, you must understand the situation. You have no choice but to let your employee go to the dying relative.

The question is: "Is the employee's relative really dying, or is this an excuse to leave the job abruptly without notice?"

Owning an agency for so many years makes one rather skeptical and suspicious. Many of these applicants' relatives must have 9 lives because they seem to be dying over and over again. So you ask yourself: "Why can't they be honest?" The answer is partly due to a cultural difference and possibly the concern over what the employer could do to them. Some people prefer telling white lies, no matter how large the white lie, to avoid confrontation. This is most disturbing for anyone who prefers honesty. You would sincerely hope that your employee would be candid enough to tell you the honest reason for leaving. There is not much you can do about this problem. The point here is that the employee is leaving for a supposed emergency that may or may not be real, and you, my friend, must find another employee, rather quickly.

- *I do not have anyone to watch my children; therefore, I can no longer work for you.* This is a very legitimate reason for leaving a place of employment. Very often, employers will request that the applicants they see do not have small children so as to avoid this problem. However, it would be wrong to discriminate against anyone because they have a child. You would be missing out on some very qualified applicants with that sort of restriction. The hope is that when you hire any help, the question of childcare for the domestic is solved by perhaps a babysitter, daycare or relative. The situation may change, however, during the course of employment. They may have no other recourse but to stay home with their child until they can rectify the problem.

- *I am not making enough money and need to find a job that is better paying.* This reason for termination will not sit well with you. Your first reaction would be "but I am paying you a good salary, and I have been so good to you, how could you let a thing like money get in the way?"

If you do decide to pay more, please don't hold a grudge against the domestic, who needs to make a living just as you do.

Domestics, too, have budgets to meet. They may simply need more money and must try to get a better-paying job, even if it means earning $1.00 more per hour. The employer/employee agreement may not call for an increase in salary at this time and you may not feel that the increase is warranted. However, if you are able to accommodate the employee with an increase, then perhaps the employee will be satisfied and stay indefinitely. This is a choice you have to make without getting too emotional. Money matters tend to upset relationships the most. However, think carefully if it is worth it to you to pay more and save yourself the headache of looking for another employee.

- *You are not arriving from work on time every day and never paying for any extra hours worked.* As mentioned earlier, keeping to an original schedule is very important for any employee. Unless you have an agreement that the employee is to work with some flexibility, without any further pay, then you MUST compensate the employee for any extra time worked. If the employee arrives late in the morning, you may think it is fine for you to arrive late at night. It is best not do this because it can be confusing. Make sure that your employee understands that the job begins at 8:00 AM, NOT 8:15 AM every morning. Clear the issue of being late with her so that she makes every effort to be on time daily, unless, of course, there is an unexpected emergency. In this manner, you should also try to be home each day as discussed, or you should count the overtime and pay accordingly. If it appears that you are taking advantage of your employee, you will be left without one.

- *You have completely overlooked my vacation time and the holidays you agreed you would give me.* Once again, these are very important issues for any employee. Adhere to your original agreement as it pertains to vacation and holidays and note your calendar so that you don't forget these important points. You may choose to provide only certain holidays and no vacation, or all the major holidays as specified in your agreement along with one week's paid vacation at the end of one year of employment. If the employee is aware of this prior to beginning employment, then all is in the open and should be clearly understood. However, if you decide to change your mind or forget what was promised, you should not be surprised at the employee's decision to quit. Keep in mind that, if you have given the employee time off because you have left town for vacation yourself, and you decide that all that time off should make up for any obligation to give holidays off, you are not thinking straight. The vacation and holidays that were agreed upon are separate, no matter how much "extra" time off you have provided.

- ***I have worked for you at least one year, and when I was sick only for 2 days, you have docked my pay.*** Sick days are purely discretionary. You may never choose to provide any sick days. A way of providing a good, long-term employee a certain perk might be to provide 1-5 sick days per year. A sick day might be used as a personal day needed to handle private business. Discuss sick or personal days during the hiring process and document what you want to provide so that the employee does not bring this up in a disgruntled manner.

- ***Your attitude has changed with me and I no longer feel comfortable working for you.*** If your attitude is changing, it might be because you are no longer happy with the employee. Perhaps you did not address issues that have come up in the past; hence, resentment has set in and your attitude toward her is now different. Perhaps you took the time to discuss the issues in review periods and find that no improvement has taken place. You may now wish to terminate the relationship, but simply hope that she notices your disdain and "quits" on her own accord. Your plan has worked.

- ***My husband, boyfriend or other members of the family no longer want me to work such late hours and/or on the weekends.*** Circumstances change in all families. Do not be surprised when your domestic comes to you with such changes. It may be very disappointing and upsetting; but, do not take it personally. You may someday need to give the same excuse to your own employer. Once again, let me remind you that we are dealing with people with ever-changing lives, not widgets.

- *You accused me of stealing something from you and made me feel terrible, when shortly after you found the item you lost.* If and when you misplace something, be very careful NOT to accuse anyone unless you are 100% sure of the facts. You might instantly believe "it had to be the domestic," but the truth is that, unless you have proof, it would not be fair of you to point fingers. Once you speak of the theft in such terms to your domestic, she/he will never feel comfortable around you again. If you are certain that the employee was at fault, then you will welcome the employee's termination. However, if you are unsure, then be careful of your approach to the discussion. You may end up losing a fine employee while later finding that diamond bracelet in a hidden spot you forgot existed.

- *You have added many more responsibilities to my list of duties and have never offered to pay me more.* When you go over the specific duties and responsibilities, be very clear from the beginning of all the items you want and expect to be completed by the employee. If you veer off this list and add numerous other items that require extra time and effort, you should consider whether this merits an increase in salary and discuss it immediately or promise the raise at an upcoming review period.

There are numerous other reasons why an employee spontaneously quits. Some may be excuses to leave for a better job, while others might be legitimate reasons that were caused by changes in the terms and conditions of employment and the overall relationship.

If and when you misplace something, be very careful NOT to accuse anyone unless you are 100% sure of the facts.

Chapter Twelve

STARTING OVER

SHOULD THE OLD EMPLOYEE TRAIN THE NEW EMPLOYEE?

There are two possibilities to consider when you answer the question of whether or not the old employee should train the new one. First, you must establish whether or not the former employee quit for reasons that pertain to unhappiness with the job and the employer. If this isn't the case, then you might have her do the job of training since she knows the house and the way you like things done. However, before you say "yes" to this consideration, also think about whether or not you were completely thrilled with the manner in which the previous employee managed your house. Perhaps there are some methods you would like to change. Perhaps now would be an excellent time to start fresh with a schedule and new approach to getting your house in order. If so, then it might be better for you to take on the laborious effort of showing the new employee how to do the job exactly the way you want it done.

The opposite scenario is when a previous employee is terminated and is not leaving on good terms. It would be a very bad idea to have her train the next employee. You may be saying right about now, "Well, of course, that would not be a smart move." You can be sure, however, that many people will ask their former employee to train the next one just because they are too busy to do it themselves. In the meantime, consider what this "disgruntled" employee might be saying to your new employee. Before the training session is over, you might see her running for the hills. This may be an excellent time for you to re-work the duties and responsibilities for your home and implement them with the new domestic.

This may be an excellent time for you to re-work he duties and responsibilities for your home and implement them with the new domestic.

POTENTIAL SITUATIONS, CONSEQUENCES AND RESOLUTIONS

There have been many incidents between employers and domestic employees that have caused me to pause and truly wonder about people's sense of humanity and consideration for others. People can be completely unaware of their behavior and suddenly find that they are treating their employees as though the employer was the master and the employee is damn lucky to simply have a job. As an employer, it is your responsibility to be professional and to abide by the Labor Code, laws against discrimination, and your obligations under the tax authorities, while providing the same benefits that the industry is offering. The following situations are accounts of true incidents. As you read through the resolutions you will see how to avoid termination and preserve the employer/employee relationship.

Situation

The employer hires a live-in to work a 5-day week. She does not have a separate room and must share the bathroom with the children. Her room is in effect a den that all the members of the household are free to use until she is finally allowed to retire for the day. Or perhaps you have a room for the live-in; however, it used to be the laundry room and is about the size of a small bathroom. There isn't a window, nor an air conditioning or heating system, but you promise to provide a small electric fan in the summer months and a heater in the winter.

Consequence

Your employee is completely uncomfortable. She has no privacy and feels like an unwanted guest. She never seems to get any down time until everyone leaves the room. She will ultimately find another job with better living conditions.

Resolution

If your house has this kind of configuration for a live-in domestic where you do not have separate quarters available, please do not hire a live-in because you clearly do not have proper accommodations. A live-in domestic must have private quarters that meet building standards: a normal-size room with a window and closet with proper ventilation. A private bath may not always be available, but the family must respect the fact that the employee must use the bathroom as well. If you want your Nanny to get up with the baby, she can do so with the aid of a monitor that is placed in her room. Be sure to make your live-in comfortable. Clearly, there might be an employee who is desperate to work and will take a situation as mentioned above no matter the circumstances; however, this same employee will most likely leave as soon as a better situation

A live-in domestic must have private quarters that meet building standards.

materializes.

Situation

You hire a person to work a 40-hour week with a set salary of $480/week. This translates to a $12/hour wage. You ask your employee to be flexible and work overtime whenever needed. Your employee agrees, assuming this also means that you are going to pay accordingly. Time goes by and you find yourself coming home from work late every day. Your employee smiles each time and does not complain about 15 minutes here and 20 minutes there. However, if you were to add up all the time that you were late, it would eventually accumulate to several hours' worth of pay. You do not pay overtime and simply expect your employee to accept the circumstances. After all, she never complained about it, so why do anything about it?

Consequence

No one likes to be taken advantage of in any situation. The adage, "you give them an inch, they will take a mile" was created because it is human nature to do just that. What ultimately happens when someone feels that you are not being sensitive to one's time and wages is that this person will find another job where the next boss might think differently.

Resolution

If you do not like being taken advantage of in life by people, then don't take advantage of others yourself. Count up all the minutes that you were late and compensate your employee accordingly. This is legally required. Just ask the Labor Commissioner.

Situation

You have plans to go for vacation to Tahiti for two weeks. A few months ago, you hired an employee to work as your housekeeper. You decide to tell her that she will not be working during the two weeks that you are gone, and because you just hired her and she is so new to your position, you do not feel that you need to pay her.

Consequence

Your domestic cannot survive without pay for two weeks. She lives week-to-week and has a tight budget. She is upset that you would not consider her financial circumstances and decides to find another job while you are away. She may or may not be lucky enough to get employed so quickly. However, she is upset enough over this issue that she will continue looking for work even after you return. She may or may not tell you the real reason why she is leaving. Most likely, she will make up a lie and simply not show up one day.

Resolution

When in doubt, put yourself in the shoes of your employee and ask the question "How would I feel about the fact that my employer is going out of town and does not need me, so therefore I will not be compensated for that time?" You will most likely not be happy. In fact, you will probably be outraged. So the resolution to this situation is to do the right thing and pay your employee for the time you are gone. You could also ask if she would consider this time off (or one week of it) as her paid vacation for the year while paying the second week in full. Or, you may have projects in the house that could be handled so that there is plenty to do while you are away. For example, getting to those cupboards that need organization or cleaning those closets out and doing some thorough deep cleaning that time does not allow under a normal work week, as well as picking up the mail, newspaper and checking on the house. Although you have not saved money, you have now found a way to keep your employee gainfully employed and happy.

Situation

You have a child who has a propensity to hit your Nanny. This child also likes to bite and kick and use profanity. The child has been told repeatedly to stop this behavior but does not take the request or any discipline seriously. In addition, this child calls the Nanny names and often refers to her as being "stupid." When the Nanny tries to reprimand the child, he

When in doubt, put yourself in the shoes of your employee

laughs in her face and continues the same conduct. The Nanny decides to tell you, the parent, that your child is doing these things continuously. You walk over to your child and say, "Now, Tommy, you know that isn't nice what you are doing to Maria. It isn't nice to hurt her or call her stupid. Please do not do that again." Your somewhat lax attitude has gotten you nowhere. Your child is not in the least bit concerned about your reprimand and continues the bad behavior.

Consequence

The Nanny continues to be offended and upset by Tommy's behavior. She cannot seem to get him to stop, and the little talk by his parent was of no use. He is now in complete control and knows that he can get away with anything. Since the punishment was minimal and the mother did not really make a big deal of it, it must be O.K. The Nanny is frustrated and eventually simply quits.

Resolution

If your child has unfortunately learned to be physically violent toward others, you must address this behavior immediately. This behavior begins with siblings and friends, the Nanny and then transcends to parents or any other person of authority. Perhaps you are unable to stop the child from hitting his/her sister or brother. However, if you do not stop your child from hitting the Nanny, your child will never learn to respect her or any other Nanny who is hired. This Nanny will NOT hang around excusing your child each time because after all, "it's only a child." Teach your children respect at the earliest age possible. Be firm about this point and make sure that your child knows that you mean business. Your Nanny needs your strong support and will appreciate your being proactive in resolving a situation that is very offensive and demoralizing.

Situation

You have been fortunate enough to afford domestic help for your family since the time you started a family. Now your children are of school age

If you do not stop your child from hitting the nanny, your child will never learn to respect her or any other nanny that is hired.

and you continue to have help in the house to do everything. You may have a Nanny for the children and a Housekeeper to maintain your home, or one person that completes both functions. As a result of having so much help in the house, your children have consequently become somewhat spoiled in that they never clean up their rooms, hang up their clothes, do laundry, put dishes away or even make their beds in the morning. After all, why should they? ... "The help is there to do it."

Consequence

Your Nanny and Housekeeper are running around constantly like maniacs picking up everything around the children. They are organizing and cleaning up mess after mess because the children have not been taught to do anything for themselves. Your children have now become dreadfully spoiled and will ultimately never know how to do household chores on their own, to the point that they almost purposely throw their clothes on the floor and leave toys and things in a disarray because they are trained to have someone else clean it up for them. Your help will become weary of the constant extra work involved in such an environment. They will seek employment elsewhere in a home where everyone does at least their share in keeping things orderly.

Children should learn to take responsibility for their own clothes and belongings and to clean up after themselves.

Resolution

You are doing your children a total disservice if you allow them to grow up to become little spoiled slobs. (Their future wives and husbands may not be so thrilled either). Children should learn to take responsibility for their own clothes and belongings and to clean up after themselves so that they become organized, neat and responsible young adults. Your help will be relieved of this laborious duty and in the end, everyone will benefit.

Situation

Your housekeeper lives with you and your family. You decide to have your housekeeper eat alone after you and your family have shared a meal. This is fine; however, you insist that the housekeeper must eat a separate meal.

You essentially have asked her to eat less costly foods. You make it very clear to her that she is to eat only the food items you have selected for her, such as cheese, rice, beans, and tortillas. You have gone so far as to leave notes on food in the refrigerator to tell her what she can and definitely cannot eat. Sometimes when you order take-out, you simply ravage the food with your family and offer the housekeeper whatever is left over.

Consequence
Your housekeeper feels slighted and offended by you, since this behavior on your part is not protocol for most families. She will never get past this act of discrimination on your behalf and will eventually leave you.

Resolution
This situation appears appalling. Yet, it has happened time and time again. Now this does not mean to say that you cannot ask your employee to eat separately from the family so that you have your privacy. This is a very common request and is every family's prerogative. If you set this up from the beginning, no one should be offended. The problem does not lie in the separate private dining but with the idea of eating separate foods, unless, of course, the employee strictly requests these items.

Let us assume that you run a very sophisticated home where you have a staff of domestics. You may have a private chef who makes you gourmet meals at your request. In this case, you are not obligated to provide the same gourmet foods such as caviar, fois gras, duck á l'orange and other exotic delicacies to the other staff members. You do, however, need to provide well-balanced meals.

You should treat a domestic with dignity and respect. One of the ways of illustrating this would be to ask your domestic if there is anything special that she/he prefers to eat. Otherwise, you should allow her/him to eat the same food that you are eating or, at minimum, what the children are eating. If the employee has special dietary needs that are cost-prohibitive to you, then perhaps you need to find another employee. Otherwise, the best approach is to account for an extra person when feeding the family.

REVIEWING THE STEPS FOR HIRING AND TRAINING

Let's review some of the important points that you will need to address each time you approach the hiring process.

- Know your needs and be clear about your job description. Write out exactly what you want accomplished by your employee. Consider whether or not you need a live-in or a live-out, full-time or part-time, driving or non-driving. Choose a schedule that suits your needs and is attractive to a prospective employee.

- Figure out your budget and what would be an appropriate and reasonable salary for such an employee. Consider the issues of overtime and what hourly wage you will pay. Consider whether the salary offer is gross or net of taxes. Think about what other perks you plan to offer, such as holidays, vacation time, sick days, yearly bonus, etc. as part of your employment package.

- Choose the resources that you will utilize to search for the employee and carefully investigate all resources: word of mouth, schools, newspaper ads, religious institutions and agencies.

- If using an agency, go over the "due diligence" list of requirements, such as reference, criminal and driving check, medical tests, fingerprinting and *Trustline* registration. Cover fees, replacement guarantees, and trial periods for each agency. Carefully choose a professional agency that you can trust.

- Prepare an employment application for your prospective candidate to fill out in your presence. Have a list of interview questions to cover during the private interview. Be sure you handle the interview first without children present and then bring in the children to interact with the candidate. After you have interviewed enough people and have narrowed your choices down to a few, have them return for a second, longer interview to interact with the children more directly.

- Once you have chosen a candidate that you would like to try out, be sure that you obtain all the paperwork on this individual: identification, background check, driving record, reference letters, diploma from specialty schools, copies of CPR card and other certifications.

- Present to the candidate a written list of all the requirements and duties for the job so that the candidate can begin to follow them during the trial week with you. Be prepared to do some training to help with this aspect of getting your candidate acclimated. The more time you spend on this, the sooner you will see the candidate's level of performance.

- If the trial week goes well and you decide that this is the right person for you, sit down and complete the Employer/Employee Contract stipulating all the points that were discussed during the interview process. This is essentially the job offer. Go over it carefully with the employee and have it signed by all parties. Be sure to cover hours, schedule, overtime, holidays, vacation, sick days, review periods, salary increases and a complete list of duties.

- Address the issues concerning the labor code, IRS requirements, and immigration laws to be sure that you are not violating the law.

- Begin your relationship on the right foot in a professional manner. Be direct about your needs and do not hesitate to correct bad habits before they turn into permanent problems. Never yell nor let out your stress and anxiety onto your employee. If you are unhappy with her conduct or work habits and performance, then sit down and have a formal discussion about it. Do not let your disappointment linger and fester. Stay on top of your managerial skills with your employee so that everything is learned properly and quickly.

- Remember diligently to have your review sessions as indicated in your agreement, so that you and your employee have an opportunity to cover

Be prepared to do some training to help with this aspect of getting your candidate acclimated.

any issues that either of you wants to discuss, such as problems that might be happening with the children, amount of workload, schedule, salary, etc. Try to solve all the problems before resorting to termination.

- If termination is inevitable, then do it in a professional manner. Preferably provide notice, severance pay and/or a reference letter to the terminated employee. Handle the termination so that no one walks away angry or disgruntled. Have the employee say "good-bye" to the children so that they too have closure.

- Plunge into the process with a positive outlook, knowing that you will find another qualified candidate and that soon your house will be back in order. Try not to generalize nor carry a grudge for the next candidate to endure. Perhaps you have learned from a mistake or two that you made, but do not be hard on yourself or the next candidate. Remember that we are dealing with people, not widgets, and perfection does not exist.

APPROACHING NEW EMPLOYEES WITH A POSITIVE OUTLOOK

Just as it is difficult to forget when a good friend has hurt you after years of what appeared to be a good relationship, it is equally difficult to forget the pain caused by an employee. As with a friend, you will feel anger and resentment that has a tendency to transfer to the next relationship. You now feel that you must be guarded and careful not to get too close to the next employee so that you are not deceived again. You may pledge to "never again do anything nice for another domestic employee." You vow to refrain from giving gifts, bonuses, time off with pay, etc. You may even decide to go one step further and be outright difficult, cold and distant the next time around.

Your feelings may be warranted. However, by dealing with your emotions in this manner, you are not going to make the next situation any better. You may have been treated unfairly, but remember you are dealing with people, not widgets. Every new employee will be different. These are people who have their own struggles and problems that (lucky for you) you may never experience. This is not to excuse the former employee's actions and dismiss the wrongdoing that was unfortunately inflicted upon you, especially after you were so generous. This plea is to ask you to simply learn to FORGIVE. If you can find it in your heart to forgive people for their shortcomings, it will be easier for you to approach others with a positive attitude.

- Do not take their actions personally.

- Carrying grudges will not allow you the necessary freedom to deal properly with the next employee.

- It isn't fair to start the new relationship as an extension of the last.

- Give the new employee a chance to earn your respect and confidence.

- Try desperately NOT to make generalizations.

- Be professional at all times.

There are wonderful domestic employees out there. Do not lose hope. You just have to continue the search until you find the right one for you.

Hiring help is a journey that requires many tools to make it successful. It is a relationship like no other that you will have in your life. Your high level of patience, due diligence, proper training, and good sense of professionalism at all times will assist you in finding a good domestic employee and maintaining a mutually-satisfying relationship.

If you can find it in your heart to forgive people for their shortcomings, it will be easier for you to approach others with a positive attitude.

A Mother's Haven
15928 Ventura Blvd. Suite 116
Encino, CA 91436
Tel: 818-380-3111
Web: **www.amothershaven.com**

Richard Pass, R.N.
Save A Little Life, Inc.
CPR and First Aid Training
5336 Amigo Avenue
Tarzana, CA 91356
Tel: 818-344-1442
Web: **www.savealittlelife.com**

Legally Nanny
37 Trailwood
Irvine, CA 992620-1216
Tel: 714-336-8864
Web: **www.legallynanny.com**

Trustline – California's Background Check
for In-Home Child Care
Department of Social Services
Attn: Trustline Registry Program
744 P. Street, M.S. 19-57
Sacramento, CA 95814
Tel: 800-822-8490
Web: **www.trustline.org**

Public Records Research
Background Investigation
5217 Marina Pacifica Drive South
Long Beach, CA 90803
Tel: 800-616-2900
Web: **www.proeaccess.com**

Dan E. Korenberg
Immigration Attorney
Korenberg, Abramowitz & Feldun
13949 Ventura Blvd., Suite 300
Sherman Oaks, CA 91423
Tel: 818-788-1914
Web: **www.kaflaw.com**

INDEX